NOTABLE WOMEN

IN

WORLD GOVERNMENT

NOTABLE WOMEN

IN

WORLD GOVERNMENT

Volume 1
Abzug, Bella–Joséphine
1–306

edited by
The Editors of Salem Press

SALEM PRESS, INC.
Pasadena, California   Hackensack, New Jersey

Most of these essays originally appeared in the following volumes of *Great Lives from History* (all edited by Frank N. Magill): *British and Commonwealth Series*, 1987, *Ancient and Medieval Series*, 1988, *Renaissance to 1900 Series*, 1989, *Twentieth Century Series*, 1990, and *American Women Series*, 1995. The remainder were first published in *Dictionary of World Biography: The Ancient World*, 1998, *The Middle Ages*, 1998, *The Renaissance*, 1998, *The 17th and 18th Centuries*, 1998, *The 19th Century*, 1999, *The 20th Century*, 1999, and in *Magill's Choice: U.S. Government Leaders*, 1997. Bibliographies and some essays have been updated. New material has also been added.

Library of Congress Cataloging-in-Publication Data
Notable women in world government / edited by the editors of Salem Press.
   p.   cm. — (Magill's choice)
   Includes bibliographical references and index.
   ISBN 0-89356-201-7 (set : alk. paper) — ISBN 0-89356-202-5 (v. 1 : alk. paper) — ISBN 0-89356-203-3 (v. 2 : alk. paper)
   1. Women in politics—Biography. 2. Women politicians—Biography. 3. Women heads of state—Biography. 4. Women legislators—Biography. 5. Women diplomats—Biography.   I. Salem Press. II. Series.
   HQ1236 .N68   2000
   320'.082'0922—dc21
   [B]   99-088983

First Printing

Table of Contents

Volume 1

Publisher's Note

This two-volume set in the *Magill's Choice* series profiles eighty-eight of the world's most-influential women, past and present. Consorts and queens, First Ladies and candidates, world leaders and diplomats, legislators and cabinet members—these women made their marks in the political arena. History has seen women evolve from behind-the-scenes players in royal courts to powerful monarchs to trusted political advisers to elected leaders of nations on the center stage of world affairs. The fascinating portraits in *Notable Women in World Government* examine the strength, talent, and determination needed by women in order to gain power in a man's world.

Notable Women in World Government gathers together material from many different titles in the Salem Press catalog. Most of these essays originally appeared in volumes of *Great Lives from History*: in the *British and Commonwealth Series* (1987), *Ancient and Medieval Series* (1988), *Renaissance to 1900 Series* (1989), *Twentieth Century Series* (1990), and *American Women Series* (1995). Another article had been commissioned for the *Magill's Choice* set *U.S. Government Leaders* (1997). The rest were first published in various volumes of the *Dictionary of World Biography*: in *The Ancient World* (1998), *The Middle Ages* (1998), *The Renaissance* (1998), *The 17th and 18th Centuries* (1998), *The 19th Century* (1999), and *The 20th Century* (1999). These essays have been updated to reflect more recent events, as necessary. In addition, three entirely new entries—on Pakistan's Benazir Bhutto, the Philippines's Imelda Marcos, and Ireland's Mary Robinson—have been added.

Essays range in length from 2,000 to 2,500 words. Each begins with ready-reference information, including dates and places of birth and death and a short statement on the individual's overall contribution to politics and the world. The remainder of the article is divided into four sections. "Early Life" provides facts about the subject's upbringing and covers her life up to the point at which her major work began. "Life's Work" provides a straightforward chronological account of that period during which the subject's most significant achievements were made. "Summary" offers an evaluation of the subject's contributions to or impact on history, providing an analysis of her life and achievements in the larger context of history. The final section is an annotated "Bibliography," which serves as a starting point for further research. These works were chosen for their accessibility and have been updated with the latest biographies and historical studies for this publication. The text is accompanied by many photographs and drawings.

The women are profiled in alphabetical order, but two appendices offer alternative ways to organize the subjects. The Time Line lists the subjects by birth date, spanning the fifteenth century B.C. (Egypt's Queen Hatshepsut) and 1961 (England's Princess Diana). The Geographical List categorizes these figures into twenty-six countries, regions, or empires: Argentina, Australia, Austria, Britain, Canada, Constantinople, Denmark, Egypt, England, France, Germany, Greece, Hungary, India, Ireland, Israel, Norway, Pakistan, the Philippines, Poland, Rome, Russia, Scotland, Spain, Sweden, and the United States, the last of which is also broken down into African Americans, American Indians, Asian Americans, and Latinas.

Special thanks are extended to the many academicians and scholars who wrote these historical essays. Their names appear at the ends of the articles and in a list of contributors and affiliations in the front matter to Volume 1.

Contributors

Wayne Ackerson
Salisbury State University

C. D. Akerley
United States Naval Academy

Amy Allison
Independent Scholar

Eleanor B. Amico
Independent Scholar

Nancy Fix Anderson
Loyola University

Kathy Saranpa Anstine
Yale University

Deborah Elwell Arfken
University of Tennessee, Chattanooga

Mary Welek Atwell
Radford University

Bryan Aubrey
Maharishi International University

Tom L. Auffenberg
Ouachita Baptist University

Cynthia Breslin Beres
Independent Scholar

Margaret Boe Birns
New York University

Nicholas Birns
The New School for Social Research

Fran E. Chalfont
State University of West Georgia

Robert P. Ellis
Worcester State College

Penelope J. Engelbrecht
DePaul University

Stephen C. Feinstein
University of Wisconsin—River Falls

Carol Fox
East Tennessee State University

Richard G. Frederick
University of Pittsburgh, Bradford

Gloria Fulton
Humboldt State University

Lynne M. Getz
Appalachian State University

Lewis L. Gould
University of Texas, Austin

Larry Gragg
University of Missouri, Rolla

Lloyd J. Graybar
Eastern Kentucky University

Michael Haas
California State University, Fullerton

David B. Haley
University of Minnesota

Paul B. Harvey, Jr.
Pennsylvania State University

Peter B. Heller
Manhattan College

Tonya Huber
Wichita State University

Willoughby G. Jarrell
Kennesaw State College

Loretta Turner Johnson
Mankato State University

Margaret Foegen Karsten
University of Wisconsin—Platteville

Z. J. Kosztolnyik
Texas A&M University

Eugene Larson
Pierce College, Los Angeles

Virginia W. Leonard
Western Illinois University

Thomas T. Lewis
Mount Senario College

Margaret McFadden
Appalachian State University

Susan MacFarland
Wesleyan College

E. Deanne Malpass
Stephen F. Austin State University

Annette Marks-Ellis
Antelope Valley College

Toni Marzotto
Towson State University

Donna Mungen
Los Angeles Times

B. Keith Murphy
Fort Valley State University

Frances Stickney Newman
University of Illinois, Urbana-Champaign

Charles H. O'Brien
Western Illinois University

William A. Paquette
Tidewater Community College

Judith A. Parsons
Sul Ross State University

John R. Phillips
Purdue University, Calumet

Julio César Pino
Kent State University

Clifton W. Potter, Jr.
Lynchburg College

Dorothy T. Potter
Lynchburg College

Annette Potts
Monash University, Victoria, Australia

E. Daniel Potts
Monash University, Victoria, Australia

Verbie Lovorn Prevost
University of Tennessee, Chattanooga

Colin Ramsey
University of Arkansas, Little Rock

Betty Richardson
Southern Illinois University, Edwardsville

Joseph R. Rudolph, Jr.
Towson State University

Elizabeth A. Segal
Ohio State University

R. Baird Shuman
University of Illinois, Urbana-Champaign

Andrew C. Skinner
Brigham Young University

Katherine Snipes
Eastern Washington University

A. J. Sobczak
Independent Scholar

Norbert C. Soldon
West Chester University of Pennsylvania

James E. Southerland
Brenau Professional College

Diane Prenatt Stevens
Indiana University, Bloomington

Paul Stewart
Southern Connecticut State University

Glenn L. Swygart
Tennessee Temple University

Alice F. Taylor
Shorter College

Sarah Thomas
Independent Scholar

Kenneth W. Townsend
Coastal Carolina University

Mary E. Virginia
Independent Scholar

Sharon B. Watkins
Western Illinois University

Thomas H. Watkins
Western Illinois University

Robert P. Watson
University of Hawaii, Hilo

Ann Weikel
Portland State University

Abiodun Williams
Georgetown University

NOTABLE WOMEN IN WORLD GOVERNMENT

BELLA ABZUG

Born: July 24, 1920; New York, New York
Died: March 31, 1998; New York, New York

One of the most colorful and best-known members of Congress in the 1970's, Abzug was an aggressive spokesperson for women's rights throughout her life.

Early Life

Born in New York City on July 24, 1920, the second daughter of Emanuel and Esther Savitzky, Bella Savitzky experienced neither great deprivation nor great prosperity in her childhood. Her father, an unsuccessful businessman whose shop failed in the 1920's and who had to turn to bookkeeping and selling insurance to support his family, died in the 1930's when Bella was just entering an all-girls high school in the west Bronx; her mother supported the family on the combination of his insurance money and her earnings as a cashier and saleswoman in local department stores.

What Bella's upbringing lacked in material wealth was, by all accounts, offset by her family's closeness and spiritual wealth. Yiddish and Russian folk songs were often sung at the Savitzky home, an apartment Bella shared with her sister, parents, and maternal grandmother, and one of her mother's bachelor brothers. From her family came her ethnic heritage in the Jewish faith. As a child, Bella regularly attended the solemn services of the church; as a preteen, she joined a Zionist pioneer youth group and collected money for the Zionist cause and dreamed of going to Palestine to help build and establish a Jewish homeland there during the 1930's.

Bella excelled in school. Elected as president of her high school class and later as student body president while at Hunter College, she also found time to teach Hebrew and Jewish history to the young on weekends and to march in protest against the spread of Nazism in Europe and against British and American neutrality in the Spanish Civil War.

Ironically, it was her faith that led somewhat inadvertently to the development of Bella Savitzky's commitment to feminism. As she later wrote in her 1972 autobiography, when she attended synagogue with

1

A campaign poster for Bella Abzug. *(Library of Congress)*

her grandfather, she was offended "that women were consigned to the back rows of the balcony."

A dedicated activist by the time she received her B.A. degree from Hunter College in 1942, Bella entered Columbia University Law School already oriented toward a career in litigation work. In 1945, she received her LL.B. degree and joined a firm specializing in labor law, one of the most confrontational of all areas of the law and one whose practitioners were viewed with suspicion during the Red Scare days following World War II.

It was during her transition from college into the study and practice of law that Bella also embarked on other dimensions of her life important to her: her roles as wife and mother. In 1944, she married Maurice M. Abzug, a man she had met on a bus in Miami on the way to a concert performance by violinist Yehudi Menuhin. Together, the couple had two daughters: Eve Gail in 1949 and Isobel Jo in 1952.

Life's Work

Perhaps the term that best describes Bella Abzug's life is "activist." Tongue in cheek, she noted in her autobiography that her "family used to say, prophetically" that she was born "yelling." She yelled the rest of her life for the causes to which she was drawn.

In the early 1950's, while she was still a young attorney, Abzug became deeply involved in the Civil Rights movement. Indeed, while carrying her second child in 1952, she undertook to defend a black man in Mississippi accused of raping the white woman with whom he had been having an affair. Although she ultimately lost the case, Bella Abzug later noted that she was able to delay the man's execution for two years by appealing the conviction twice to the Supreme Court. These appeals were based on her arguments that her client had been unconstitutionally convicted by a jury from which African Americans were systematically excluded and that in being sentenced to death for a rape conviction—a sentence virtually never given to a white man for the same crime—he had unconstitutionally received a "cruel and unusual punishment." The arguments were nearly two decades ahead of their time; the Warren and Burger Courts would eventually accept both arguments in applying at the state level those provisions of the Bill of Rights guaranteeing a fair trial and prohibiting cruel and unusual punishment.

3

During the 1960's, Bella Abzug juggled the demands of her Manhattan legal practice with her growing interest in banning nuclear testing. She joined with women across the country to protest the resumption of nuclear tests, helped to found the Women's Strike for Peace organization, and often led that organization in its lobbying efforts before Congress and in its demonstrations in Washington, D.C., and New York between 1961 and 1970. After the signing of the Test Ban Treaty, she also helped to refocus the antinuclear movement into an antiwar movement as the United States became involved in the conflict in Vietnam.

By the late 1960's, Abzug's concerns about the war in Vietnam and the continuing decay of American cities drew her even further into the American political arena. She struggled to forge a broad, progressive coalition across party lines to address the concerns of the poor, ethnic minorities, and women's groups in shaping a new national agenda. The 1968 Democratic Party convention in Chicago, however, frustrated Abzug's efforts. Hubert Humphrey's nomination in Mayor Richard Daley's city seemingly signaled that insider politics and the old order were still in control of the national Democratic Party. Two years later, however, political opportunity beckoned in her own backyard.

During the 1960's, New York's Twentieth Congressional District, located along Manhattan's West Side, became a political haven for reformist Democrats, typified by William F. Ryan. First elected in 1960, Ryan was reelected to Congress throughout the decade despite his early opposition to the Vietnam War, his efforts to abolish the House Committee on Un-American Activities, and his embrace of many causes out-of-step with Washington's leadership at the time. Ryan's success, in turn, encouraged progressives in neighboring districts to challenge old-line politicians backed by the Tammany Hall machine, including Leonard Farbstein in the adjacent Nineteenth District of lower Manhattan. Throughout the decade, however, these challengers failed. Then, in 1970, Farbstein confronted a new challenger: Abzug.

Running on her ties with labor to win union support and campaigning with glamorous celebrities such as Barbra Streisand to win over the Jewish vote from her opponent, Bella Abzug won the Democratic primary and comfortably won the 1970 general election. Moreover, once in Congress she rapidly championed progressive causes even more aggressively than Ryan. Unlike Ryan, she also challenged many of the conventions of the House—wearing her wide, trademark hats inside Congress in spite of requests made by the House Doorkeeper to remove them and addressing committee chairs brusquely when disagreeing with them.

Abzug's career could have ended with that one term. Following the 1970 census, which cost New York one of its seats in the U.S. House of Representatives, the New York legislature reapportioned its congressional seats by essentially merging Abzug's district into Ryan's. Instead of accepting the outcome, Abzug took the offensive and challenged Ryan for the Democratic nomination for Congress in 1972. She lost the acrimoniously fought primary by a two-to-one margin, largely because of Ryan's longer years of service in Congress. Three months later, however, Ryan died, and Abzug was chosen by the party's district committee to represent the Democrats in a general election to replace him. During this election, she had to run against a Republican opponent and against Ryan's widow, who campaigned as a Liberal. Abzug won with an outright majority of 56 percent and two years later was reelected with a 79 percent majority.

Having achieved national celebrity and winning praise from mainstream Democrats for her tireless work on the Government Operations and Public Works committees on which she served, Abzug had perhaps as safe a seat as any in Congress. Nevertheless, she announced her decision to run for the Senate in 1976. Her subsequent career in politics was nearly as flamboyant and swift as her rise to national attention. She lost the 1976 Democratic primary for the Senate seat to Daniel Patrick Moynihan, failed the following year to win the New York mayoral primary against challenger Ed Koch, and ended her electoral career in 1978 by losing to her Republican opponent in the race to fill Koch's vacated seat representing New York's Eighteenth Congressional District, a district with a liberal but youthful, trendy, and Waspish constituency quite different from that of Abzug's former district and Bella Abzug herself.

Although they were the centerpiece of her life in public affairs, Bella Abzug's six years in Congress formed only a short period of that life. In Congress, she was a symbol for her time—an outspoken champion of feminism and a variety of other progressive causes. After leaving Congress, she continued her activism, serving in such posts as presiding officer of the National Commission on the Observance of International Women's Year and the National Women's Conference in 1977, acting as cochair of the President's National Advisory Council for Women in 1978, and serving subsequently as a cable television commentator, a Fellow at Harvard University's Kennedy School, and a popular speaker throughout the country for more than a decade. The early 1990's likewise found her active on behalf of numerous causes, cochairing the Women's Environmental Development Organization in 1991, serving as a senior adviser to the United Nations Conference on the Environment and Development in 1992, and actively campaigning on behalf of David Dinkins's 1993 attempt for a second term as mayor of New York. In her work with the Women's Environmental Development Organization, Abzug joined Greenpeace in supporting a worldwide ban of chlorine-based chemicals because of their suspected link to breast cancer. Abzug died in New York City on March 31, 1998, at the age of seventy-seven.

Summary

As a lawyer, a politician, and a leading civil rights and women's rights advocate, Bella Abzug distinguished herself as one of the foremost female activists of her time. As the chair and cofounder of the bipartisan National Women's Political Caucus (NWPC), Abzug joined leading activists such as Betty Friedan and Gloria Steinem in encouraging more women to run for elective office and in generating funding to help these candidates achieve victories. As a regular columnist for *Ms.* magazine beginning in 1979, Abzug shaped public opinion on a variety of issues pertaining to the role of women in society. As a highly visible member of the National Organization for Women (NOW) and a staunch crusader for the passage of the Equal Rights Amendment (ERA), Abzug marched with other supporters in a variety of rallies and parades in order to generate greater attention and support for the amendment.

Finally, at a time in her life when many of her contemporaries chose to relax in retirement, Abzug continued to work on behalf of a number of social causes near to her heart, many of which focused on women's roles in preserving and protecting the environment. As she wrote in *Gender Gap: Bella Abzug's Guide to Political Power for American Women* (1984), women can either "learn to become political leaders and activists, or [they] can sit back and let a minority of men in government, backed by powerful money and military interests . . . try to run the whole world." Certainly the career of Bella Abzug amply demonstrated her unwillingness to sit back and watch the world go by.

Bibliography

Abzug, Bella. *Bella!: Ms. Abzug Goes to Washington*. New York: Saturday Review Press, 1972. With an acknowledgement to her staff, Abzug's autobiography is built around a diary chronicling her first year in Washington, D.C. She combines a warm portrait of her family life with a vivid picture of the challenges she faced in Washington's male-dominated political arena and the in-your-face manner with which she responded to these challenges.

Abzug, Bella, with Mim Kelber. *Gender Gap: Bella Abzug's Guide to Political Power for American Women*. Boston: Houghton Mifflin, 1984. Much more than a "how to" book for mobilizing American women to fight for true equality in American parties and politics, this book provides a clear exposition of citizen Abzug's lifelong political philosophy and fighter's disposition to translate that philosophy into practice.

Barone, Michael, Grant Ujifusa, and Douglas Matthews. *The Almanac of American Politics, 1974: The Senators, the Representatives—Their Records, States, and Districts*. Boston: Gambit Press, 1973. The best source for background reading on the members of Congress, placed in the context of their political lives and the constituents who sent them there. This volume chronicles the career of Congresswoman Abzug at the beginning of her second term.

Barone, Michael, and Grant Ujifusa. *The Almanac of American Politics, 1982: The President, the Senators, the Representatives, the Governors—Their Records, States, and Districts*. Washington, D.C.: Barone, 1982. A later version of this key reference work. The entries on Abzug are chiefly interesting for their account of her failed races for the Senate in 1976 and mayor of New York City the following year.

Howe, Florence. "A Tribute to Two International Feminist Leaders." *Women's Studies Quarterly* 26, no. 3-4 (Fall, 1998): 271-278. Obituaries for Abzug and Alice H. Cook.

Ruben, Barbara. "Bella Abzug: Giving Women a Voice." *Environmental Action Magazine* 24 (Summer, 1992): 12-14. An interview with Abzug that provides insights into her activities on behalf of the environment and in the area of world affairs following her departure from Congress after being defeated for election to the Senate in 1976.

Steinem, Gloria. "Bella Abzug." *Ms.* 6, no. 4 (January, 1996): 62. Noted feminist Steinem discusses Abzug's life, career, and mind-set.

Witt, Linda, Karen M. Paget, and Glenna Matthews. *Running as a Woman: Gender and Power in American Politics.* New York: Free Press, 1993. A journalist, a political scientist, and a historian collaborated on this narrative overview of the experiences of female candidates in American politics. Although this work includes many references relating to Abzug's career, perhaps the most intriguing anecdote is the story of how Mayor John Lindsay of New York City told Abzug that she would be less critical of politicians if she tried being one herself. Lindsay's exasperated comment inspired Abzug to launch her own political career instead of remaining on the sidelines in supporting male candidates.

Joseph R. Rudolph, Jr.

ABIGAIL ADAMS

Born: November 22, 1744; Weymouth, Massachusetts
Died: October 28, 1818; Quincy, Massachusetts

An early proponent of humane treatment and equal education for women, Adams wrote eloquent, insightful letters which provide a detailed social history of her era and her life with John Adams.

Early Life

Abigail Smith was one of four children born to William Smith, minister of North Parish Congregational Church of Weymouth, and Elizabeth Quincy from nearby Braintree, Massachusetts. Both parents were members of prominent New England families of merchants, statesmen, and ministers. From her parents, Abigail learned a conservative, rational Puritanism. She retained throughout her life a solid Christian faith and shared with her Puritan forebears a belief in the fundamental depravity of humankind. These religious convictions influenced her political opinions.

Observing her mother's example, Abigail learned her future duties as wife and mother. Within her role as minister's wife, Elizabeth Smith provided relief for the town's poor, nursed the town's sick, and presented herself as a model of wifely behavior. She was nurturing and kind to her children.

In eighteenth century Massachusetts, education was prized. In government-supported schools, boys studied Latin, Greek, French, mathematics, and literary arts in preparation for higher education either at Harvard or abroad. Girls, however, were educated almost exclusively at home, receiving only rudimentary training in reading and writing; some remained illiterate. Instead, they learned domestic skills such as sewing, fine needlework, and cooking, which were considered vital preparation for marriage. Abigail received only informal home instruction yet shared with her sisters the advantage of a keen intellect and unlimited access to her father's extensive library.

In her early adolescence, Abigail was encouraged in her studies by a young watchmaker and scholar, Richard Cranch. Although self-educated, Cranch conveyed his passion for scholarship to Abigail and to her sisters Mary and Elizabeth. It was through Cranch, who wedded Mary, that Abigail met her future husband.

Abigail Smith proved a shrewd judge of character when at the age of nineteen she married Harvard-educated lawyer John Adams. Although they were not social equals—he was from a markedly less prominent family and practiced a profession that was poorly regarded—the match proved exceedingly profitable and satisfying for both parties. In John, Abigail found a man who appreciated and even encouraged her forthrightness and her intellectual ability, while John in turn received emotional, financial, and intellectual support from Abigail.

Life's Work

Abigail Adams is best known for her remarkably detailed, eloquent letters. Although many creative outlets were considered unsuitable for women to pursue, letter writing was a socially sanctioned literary art for women in the eighteenth century. Abigail, who felt compelled to write, naturally selected that medium.

During her first ten years of marriage, however, Abigail's letter writing was not prolific as she was kept extraordinarily busy with domestic affairs. Enduring five pregnancies in seven years, she also suffered the death of an infant daughter. In addition, she was plagued by several physical afflictions including frequent colds, rheumatism which caused acute swelling of joints, and insomnia.

During these early years, she moved her household several times to remain with John in his work. The turmoil of their lives as they uprooted their family paralleled the contemporary political events in which John played a leading role. This was a pattern they would repeat throughout his working life and would include residence in Boston, Philadelphia, New York, Paris, and London. Abigail demonstrated repeatedly that she was extraordinarily adaptable and found pleasure in observing foreign customs. She always, however, longed for the idealized pastoral life in Braintree that she had shared with John during their first few years of marriage.

In 1775, John embarked for Congress on the first of frequent extended absences from Abigail. With her husband away, Abigail weathered several personal tragedies, including a difficult pregnancy in 1777, during which she apparently suffered from toxemia and finally eclampsia, a condition that is usually fatal to the infant and often to the mother. A remarkable series of letters were written between John and Abigail during this period; in them, Abigail expressed loneliness and fear for her unborn child. The child, a girl, was indeed stillborn. John and Abigail's letters provide invaluable information on the social history of parent-and-child relationships.

The pattern of intimate and frequent letters between husband and wife continued over the next twenty-five years as John, an extraordinarily ambitious man, accepted political positions that removed him

Abigail Adams *(Library of Congress)*

from home for periods often extending to years. While Abigail considered their separation as a patriotic sacrifice, she nevertheless frequently expressed her loneliness to John, imploring him to return home.

Because she was a married woman, Abigail was legally prevented from owning property in her own name. Notwithstanding, she repeatedly demonstrated her ingenuity and self-sufficiency. During their first ten years together, John's legal fees and the income from their farm supported the family. As events took him farther from home, his legal practice was largely abandoned and Abigail assumed most financial duties. She never welcomed the addition to her already burdensome domestic responsibilities, yet she consistently proved herself a competent manager. Abigail deplored debt and worked to ensure that her family avoided it. She successfully ran the farm for four years during which she was responsible for the odious chore of collecting rents from several tenants as well as supervising agricultural production. Scarcity of labor and acute inflation made the task a difficult one. After four years, she lessened her burden by renting the farm.

In 1778, Abigail began requesting luxury goods from John, who was then serving as a diplomat in France. She then profitably sold these items, which, because of war shortages and inflation, were scarce in Massachusetts. At the same time, Abigail also purchased land and speculated in currency. Through these endeavors, she kept her family solvent.

During the ten years in which she saw her husband only sporadically, Abigail expanded her literary interests, exploring, through John's guidance, political theory, biography, and history. She also wrote voluminously, to John and to other family members as well as to friends. It was during this period that Abigail wrote to John of her political views regarding women's roles in the new nation. Her famous letter of March 31, 1776, in which she requested John to "Remember the Ladies," has established Abigail's reputation as an early proponent of women's rights. In context, however, it is clear that Abigail wrote not of political rights but of women's legal rights, specifically those which guaranteed them protection from physical abuse. At the time, divorce, although allowed in a few extreme instances, was generally unavailable. In addition, women abrogated all rights to property ownership upon marriage, which in turn made them ineligible to vote because property ownership was a key qualification for voting.

Abigail also advocated equal education for women. She argued for equal education within the context of her perception of women's traditional domestic roles. The concept of Republican Motherhood held that because women taught the sons who were destined to become leaders, women had an important role in maintaining the existence of an informed citizenry capable of supporting a republican government. To teach their sons successfully, these women required equal education, which Abigail hoped would be supported by law.

Although she is now viewed as an early advocate for women's rights, Abigail Adams saw her own life as highly traditional. An adept manager of her family's resources, she nevertheless viewed her role as currency speculator, land purchaser, and farmer as aberrant and a patriotic sacrifice. She was comfortable only in her domestic role, and in that, as in all else, she excelled. Abigail was an affectionate mother and grandmother who lived to see her son John Quincy establish a successful diplomatic and political career. Several personal tragedies marred her happiness, including the death of her son Charles from alcoholism when he was thirty years old and her daughter Nabby's brutally painful mastectomy and subsequent death from breast cancer.

Until 1800, when John retired from government office, Abigail functioned at times as hostess during his several years as a diplomat, first in England, then in France. She also served two terms as the vice president's wife during the Washington administration and finally as First Lady during her husband's presidency.

During the last eighteen years of her life she retired with her husband to Braintree, already renamed Quincy, and lived in relative domestic peace surrounded by children, grandchildren, sisters, nieces, and nephews. At the family's Quincy farm, Abigail pursued her lifelong hobby of gardening. Dying of typhoid fever in 1818, she was mourned by John, who, lamenting the loss of his "dearest friend," survived his wife by eight years.

Summary

Abigail Adams always functioned within the prescribed social roles for women of her time. She was an affectionate, protective mother who cared for her children physically and emotionally her entire life. She provided intellectual and emotional companionship as well as financial support for her brilliant but irascible husband John. Although

Abigail for a time functioned as merchant, farmer, and speculator, she viewed these roles as a patriotic sacrifice on her part to support the political career of her husband.

While her own marriage provided her intellectual and emotional satisfaction, she condemned the tyranny of men over women and longed for legal protection for women. Women's education she hoped would one day rival that of men. She also yearned for the day when women could limit their number of children. Nevertheless, her life must be viewed within the context of her eighteenth century world, where she functioned primarily within the domestic sphere. She was not a public advocate for women's rights; the term "women's rights" was not even used in her time. Neither did she view her role within her marriage as less valuable than that of her husband. To Abigail and to John, marriage was a true partnership. She was a supremely shrewd, able woman who took every advantage available to her to expand her intellectual horizons and enjoyed a wide correspondence through her letters. In addition to insights which they provide into this remarkable woman's psyche, Abigail Adams's copious letters provide a detailed social history of her era as well as invaluable insights into the character of her husband John Adams and into those of several other political leaders, including her close friend Thomas Jefferson.

Bibliography

Adams, Abigail. *The Book of Abigail and John: Selected Letters of the Adams Family, 1762-1784.* Edited by L. H. Butterfield, Marc Friedlaender, and Mary-Jo Kline. Cambridge, Mass.: Harvard University Press, 1975. Because Abigail Adams's literary achievements were her eloquent, informative letters, particularly to her husband John, the letters in this volume are illuminating and interesting.

Akers, Charles W. *Abigail Adams, an American Woman.* New York: Longman, 2000. Written specifically for the college undergraduate and high school student, Akers's work is admirably detailed yet readable. Abigail's life is well grounded in historical context, and the 220 pages of text are not formidable.

Gelles, Edith B. *First Thoughts: Life and Letters of Abigail Adams.* New York: Twayne, 1998. Gelles tells Adams's story through her letters with her husband, Mercy Otis Warren, and others.

_____. *Portia: The World of Abigail Adams.* Bloomington: Indiana

University Press, 1992. This is the most insightful biography of Adams, viewing her not only as John's wife and John Quincy's mother but also within the context of her domestic and predominantly female world. Because it requires a knowledge of fundamental historical events, it should be read in conjunction with a broader history, such as Charles W. Akers's (above). Includes an instructive introductory historiographic chapter, footnotes, bibliography, and chronology.

Keller, Rosemary. *Patriotism and the Female Sex: Abigail Adams and the American Revolution*. Brooklyn, N.Y.: Carlson, 1994.

Levin, Phyllis Lee. *Abigail Adams: A Biography*. New York: St. Martin's Press, 1987. By far the most detailed biography of Adams; makes extensive use of the sources. Unlike other Adams biographers, Levin provides ample discussion of Abigail's life during the years after John Adams's retirement, although she does so against the backdrop of John Quincy's career. Similarly Abigail's earlier life is viewed against John's career. Just shy of 500 pages, the work is footnoted, contains a bibliography, and provides a family tree.

Nagel, Paul C. *The Adams Women: Abigail and Louisa Adams, Their Sisters and Daughters*. New York: Oxford University Press, 1987. While not exclusively about Abigail Adams, Nagel's work is useful for placing her life within the context of her close female relations, including her sisters Mary and Elizabeth. Despite his admiration of her intellect, Nagel provides a portrait of Adams that is largely unsympathetic; she appears domineering and shrewish.

Withey, Lynne. *Dearest Friend: A Life of Abigail Adams*. New York: Free Press, 1981. Withey's biography is one of the less satisfying works on Adams because the author judges Abigail by twentieth century standards rather than understanding her within her historical context. Withey focuses extensively on Abigail's political views while paying scant attention to her more notable successes in her domestic roles, viewing Abigail as a "prisoner" in her world.

Mary E. Virginia

MADELEINE ALBRIGHT

Born: May 15, 1937; Prague, Czechoslovakia

As ambassador to the United Nations and as the first woman to hold the office of secretary of state, Albright helped to shape a foreign policy emphasizing an activist role for the United States.

Early Life

Madeleine Korbel was born in Prague, Czechoslovakia, in 1937, shortly before Nazi Germany took control of the country. Her father, Josef Korbel, was an intellectual and a member of the Czech diplomatic corps. Her mother, Anna Speeglova Korbel, was the daughter of a prosperous family who gave birth to two other children, Katherine Korbel Silva and John Joseph Korbel. Madeleine's grandparents were Jewish, and three of them died in the Holocaust—facts that Albright discovered only after her appointment as secretary of state. Her parents converted to Catholicism, apparently to escape persecution, and Madeleine grew up celebrating Christian rituals such as Christmas and Easter.

Madeleine's earliest experiences were shaped by World War II. When German agents took power in Czechoslovakia in 1938, her father, an outspoken opponent of the Nazis, was targeted for execution. While Josef Korbel tried to get false diplomatic papers that would get his family out of the country, he and his wife walked the streets of Prague with the infant Madeleine, making sure they stayed in public places where the Nazis would not assault him. They were able to escape to England; Madeleine later recalled staying in London air-raid shelters and sleeping under a steel table during bombing raids. During her stay, she became fluent in English. After the war, the Korbel family returned briefly to Prague. Josef, though, soon resumed his diplomatic career, which took him to Belgrade, Yugoslavia, and then to New York when he was assigned a position at the United Nations.

While the Korbels were in New York, Czechoslovakia experienced another coup; the communists had taken charge, and Josef Korbel was once again a wanted man. The family was granted political asylum in the United States, and in 1949 they moved to Colorado, where Josef became a professor of international relations at the University of Denver. A respected scholar and the author of many books on diplomacy, Josef Korbel was Madeleine's first major intellectual authority; she has attributed many of her views to her father's influence.

In Colorado, Madeleine attended a small private high school. She won a scholarship to Wellesley College in Massachusetts, where she majored in political science, edited the college newspaper for a year, and campaigned for Democratic presidential candidate Adlai Stevenson. In 1959, she was graduated with honors.

Only three days after her graduation, Madeleine married Joseph Medill Patterson Albright, the heir of a prominent newspaper family. They moved to Chicago, where he was employed with the *Chicago Sun-Times*; Madeleine, however, was told that as a journalist's spouse, she would never be hired by a newspaper. Instead, she worked briefly in public relations for the *Encyclopedia Britannica* before the family moved to New York City in 1961. During the next six years, Madeleine gave birth to three daughters: twins, named Alice and Anne, and Katherine. She also enrolled in the graduate program in public law and government at Columbia University.

Life's Work

Madeleine Albright credited her success to her willingness to work hard. While she pursued graduate study and reared a family, she typically awoke at 4:30 A.M. and worked late into the night. She earned a master's degree, a certificate in Russian studies, and, in 1976, a doctorate; her dissertation concerned the role of the press in the 1968 crisis in Czechoslovakia, during which dissidents had tried to end Soviet control of the country. Her dissertation, like much of her later career, would combine her fascinations with journalism and foreign policy. At Columbia, Albright studied with Professor Zbigniew Brzezinski, who directed the Institute on Communist Affairs. Along with her father, Brzezinski would be one of Albright's most important intellectual mentors.

In 1968, Madeleine's husband was transferred to Washington, D.C., where he became the bureau chief of *Newsday*. She became involved with her daughters' private school, for which she organized several successful fund-raising projects. As a result, a friend recommended her as a fund-raiser for Senator Edmund Muskie's campaign for the 1972

Democratic presidential nomination. Although Muskie did not win the nomination, he hired Albright to serve as the chief legislative assistant in his Senate office. She was especially involved in assisting Muskie with his duties as a member of the Senate Foreign Relations Committee.

When Jimmy Carter was elected president in 1976, he appointed Zbigniew Brzezinski to be his national security adviser. Brzezinski brought Albright onto the staff of the National Security Council, where she worked as congressional liaison. When Ronald Reagan became president in 1981, Albright moved from governmental service to a position as senior fellow in Soviet and Eastern European affairs at the Center for Strategic and International Studies.

In 1982, Albright and her husband separated, and she began to devote herself wholeheartedly to her career as a foreign-policy analyst and advocate. With the support of a fellowship from the Smithsonian Institution's Woodrow Wilson Center for Scholars, she published *Poland: The Role of the Press in Political Change* in 1983.

Also in 1982, Albright joined the faculty of Georgetown University, where she remained until 1993. Her experience as a university faculty member was a decided success. She served as a professor of international affairs and directed the school's Women in Foreign Service Program, and she was named the university's teacher of the year on four occasions. While on the Georgetown faculty, Albright began inviting a variety of guests from academia, the diplomatic service, journalism, and politics to her home for discussions of international issues. Among those who attended Albright's "salons" was the governor of Arkansas, Bill Clinton; among the topics was the shape that U.S. foreign policy might take if the Democrats regained the White House.

Albright coordinated foreign policy for Democratic presidential nominee Walter Mondale and vice presidential nominee Geraldine Ferraro during the 1984 campaign. Four years later, she was senior foreign-policy adviser and a major speechwriter for Democratic nominee Michael Dukakis. During the next four years, Albright served as president of the Center for National Policy, a Democratic think tank and a resource for members of Congress, where she dealt principally with Eastern European affairs. She was also involved with the Georgetown Leadership Seminar, an annual session for government officials, bankers, journalists, and military officers. Albright was a frequent guest on the public television program *Great Decisions*, which provided her with the chance to reach a larger audience with her views on international affairs.

When Bill Clinton ran for president in 1992, Albright helped to write the foreign-policy sections of the Democratic Party platform as well as position papers for the nominee. She was, therefore, an obvious choice for a diplomatic post in the Clinton administration, and in December, 1992, the president-elect named her U.S. ambassador to the United Nations and made her a member of his cabinet.

Albright brought great energy to her role at the United Nations. She traveled to the capital of every member nation of the Security Council, visited Somalia when U.S. troops were stationed there, and went to Bosnia, where she strongly advocated greater American involvement in the conflict with Serbia. In 1995, she attended the U.N. Conference on Women, held in China, where she spent a day escorting First Lady Hillary Rodham Clinton. She also led Mrs. Clinton on a tour of Prague in 1996.

Albright increased the visibility of the seven female ambassadors to the United Nations by organizing lunches for them, and she led the effort to oust Secretary General Boutros Boutros-Ghali from his leadership post. Boutros-Ghali was intensely unpopular with conservatives in the U.S. Congress, and her opposition to him later helped to win Senate approval of her appointment as secretary of state. While serving in the United Nations, moreover, Albright remained closely tied to the decision-making process in Washington, D.C., where she attended cabinet meetings and sessions of the National Security Council's principals group.

After Clinton was reelected in 1996, it soon became apparent that Secretary of State Warren Christopher would step down from his post. The president considered several former senators and career diplomats to fill the position, but he eventually chose to nominate Madeleine Albright. She was easily confirmed by the Senate, which supported her nomination by a vote of 99 to 0.

As secretary of state, Albright faced instability in many areas of the world, financial crises that had diplomatic repercussions, and a reconsideration of relations with some of the United States' friends and adversaries. For example, in the Middle East, hostile relations with Iran continued as Saddam Hussein apparently persisted in threatening his neighbors and in resisting United Nations' inspections of its weapons capabilities. The United States maintained a hard line against the Iraqi leader while trying to ease the hardships endured by the people of that country. On the other hand, a dialogue emerged between the United States and Iran, with Secretary Albright suggesting the two former adversaries might look for common ground. She encouraged the Israelis and Palestinians to continue their peace process and negotiate the future of disputed territories.

With respect to Europe, Secretary Albright was an enthusiastic supporter of an expansion of the North Atlantic Treaty Organization (NATO) to include Poland and the Czech Republic and of the "Good Friday" agreement to resolve the political and religious conflicts in Northern Ireland. She advocated a strong multilateral response to the crisis in Bosnia, including a U.S. "police" presence, economic assistance, and punishment of war criminals. Albright also encouraged economic assistance to Russia to avert a political and economic emergency there.

The secretary of state visited a number of African nations, including South Africa, as well as important Asian countries such as Korea, Japan, and China. In addition to reaffirming support for the United States' traditional allies, she explicated President Clinton's policy that promoted expanded trade with China while keeping the issue of human rights on the diplomatic agenda.

In the light of nuclear tests conducted by India and Pakistan, Albright called for both countries to sign the Comprehensive Test Ban Treaty and reaffirmed the administration's desire that the U.S. Senate ratify the treaty. She also urged Congress to provide assistance to Indonesia and other nations experiencing economic crises through the International Monetary Fund, and to appropriate funds to pay the United States' obligations to the United Nations.

Unlike some of her predecessors who saw foreign policy as a highly personal achievement, Albright believed in developing a competent team to carry out the U.S. diplomatic agenda. For example, during Albright's term in the Department of State, Richard Holbrooke, who had negotiated the Dayton Agreement to resolve the Bosnian crisis, became ambassador to the United Nations. Albright described Holbrooke's appointment as part of her program to surround the secretary of state with strong people. Albright was also involved in promoting the human element in international development efforts, focusing on the connections between economic investments and everyday family life in less developed countries.

Albright was particularly aware of the connection between the status of women around the world and its implications for U.S. foreign policy. She pressed for Senate ratification of the Convention on the Elimination of All Forms of Discrimination Against Women (CEDAW) and emphasized the need to stabilize birthrates, educate women, and involve them in international development efforts. She used her office to promote the empowerment of women as an integral element in achieving peace and prosperity and to attempt to increase the representation of women in diplomatic service. Albright saw herself as part of a network of women foreign ministers, many of whom became acquainted through their service in the United Nations. In response to questions about how she was viewed by leaders of countries whose cultures did not recognize the equality of women, Albright stated that she was always viewed with the highest respect. She noted that having a woman represent the most powerful country in the world was a message in itself.

Summary

Prior to Albright's appointment as secretary of state, no woman had held so high a position in the U.S. diplomatic service; moreover, only one woman, Jeane Kirkpatrick, had preceded her as ambassador to the United Nations. Albright assumed the secretary of state's post with a reputation for being candid, and she was also outspoken about affirming her identity as a woman. For example, she noted immediately that the secretary of state's office had been designed with a male occupant in mind. It was equipped with conveniences such as racks for men's suits and drawers for socks. Albright's occupancy of the office clearly defied the traditional image of a secretary of state.

With respect to foreign policy, Albright was an enthusiastic advocate of the assertive use of American power and influence. She stated that her "mind-set is Munich"; in other words, her view was formed by the experience of Czechoslovakia: At Munich in 1938, diplomats from Great Britain and France effectively handed control of her native country over to Adolf Hitler in return for his promise to cease aggression. Hitler promptly took Czechoslovakia, continued his conquests, and provoked World War II. The lesson of Munich that Albright described, therefore, was that one should not compromise with aggression.

As secretary of state, Albright was a severe critic of nations charged with violations of human rights, including Cuba, Iraq, and Iran. On the other hand, she had to find a way to balance disapproval of China's internal repression with efforts to promote trade with the world's most populous country. During her tenure, the Department of State also faced instability in Russia, conflicts in the Middle East, and tensions caused by expansion of NATO. Madeleine Albright thus had an important influence in two areas of public life: both as a model of a woman's achievement in a nontraditional role and as a major architect of American foreign policy.

Bibliography

"Altered State." *The New Republic* 215 (December 30, 1996): 17. This editorial concerning Albright's nomination as secretary of state describes her excellent qualifications for the position.

Blackman, Ann. *Seasons of Her Life: A Biography of Madeleine Korbel Albright*. New York: Charles Scribner's Sons, 1998.

Blood, Thomas. *Madam Secretary: A Biography of Madeleine Albright*. New York: St. Martin's Press, 1997.

Cooper, Matthew, and Melinda Liu. "Bright Light." *Newsweek*, February 10, 1997, 22-29. Cooper presents a brief biography and portrait of Albright. The article includes related profiles of Clinton's foreign policy team.

Dobbs, Michael. *Madeleine Albright: A Twentieth-Century Odyssey*. New York: Henry Holt, 1999.

Gibbs, Nancy. "The Many Lives of Madeleine." *Time*, February 17, 1997, 52-61. Gibbs argues that Albright's rise to the highest government position of any woman in U.S. history resulted from her political strategy, determination, diplomatic prowess, and perfectionism.

_____. "Voice of America." *Time*, December, 16, 1996, 32-33. Provides a brief overview of Albright's rise.

"Madeleine Albright." *Current Biography* 56 (May, 1995): 8-12. A brief biography that highlights Albright's role as a U.S. representative to the United Nations.

Sciolino, Elaine. "Madeleine Albright's Audition." *The New York Times*

Magazine, September 22, 1996, 63. Sciolino evaluates Albright's career as a key member of Clinton's foreign policy team and discusses her chances of becoming secretary of state.

Weymouth, Lally. "As I Find out More, I'm Very Proud." *Newsweek*, February 24, 1997, 30-32. In this interview, Albright discusses her reaction to finding out that her grandparents had been killed during the Holocaust in concentration camps.

Mary Welek Atwell

QUEEN ANNE

Born: February 6, 1665; London, England
Died: August 1, 1714; London, England

Through her devotion to the Church of England, Anne maintained the provisions of the Act of Settlement of 1701, thereby fostering the cause of constitutional government while preventing another civil war.

Early Life

Of the seven children born to James, Duke of York, and his first wife, Anne Hyde, only two survived infancy: Anne, who was born on February 6, 1665, at St. James's Palace, London, and Mary, who was three years her senior. Concerned by his younger daughter's poor eyesight, James sent her to Paris to be treated by a noted oculist. While in France, Anne lived first with her paternal grandmother, the Dowager Queen Henrietta Maria, who died in 1669, and then with her father's youngest sister, Henrietta Annie, duchess of Orleans. At the age of five, Anne returned to England, but she continued to be troubled by poor eyesight all of her life.

When Anne was six her mother died of cancer, and rather than leave his nieces under the sole supervision of their father, Charles II sent them to live with Colonel Edward Villiers, a devout Protestant. Both the duke and the duchess of York had made the politically unwise decision to accept the Roman Catholic faith, but the king would not allow Mary and Anne, who stood next in line for the throne, to make the same choice. While under the care of Colonel Villiers, Anne met and fell under the spell of Sarah Jennings, who, as the duchess of Marlborough, would dominate the early years of Anne's reign. In 1673 the duke of York married an Italian princess, Mary of Modena, and Sarah Jennings entered her service as a maid of honor.

Neither pretty like her sister Mary nor clever like her friend Sarah, Anne was soon forgotten amid the glitter of the Restoration court. Then Charles II discovered that his shy niece possessed one gift worth developing, her voice. Under the supervision of Elizabeth Barry, a leading actress of the day, Anne mastered elocution, a skill which would later earn for her the reputation of being perhaps the finest public speaker to occupy the British throne.

In November, 1677, Anne's life was changed by the marriage of her sister to their first cousin, William of Orange. Ill with smallpox, Anne was unable to attend the wedding, and Mary, on the eve of her departure for her new home in the Netherlands, was forbidden to visit her sister lest she risk infection. A year later Sarah Jennings married John Churchill, leaving thirteen-year-old Anne alone. During the next five years she grew into an unassuming young woman who longed to imitate the private bliss of her sister and her best friend. In 1683, she married Prince George of Denmark, a man twelve years her senior. Dull-witted and troubled by chronic asthma, he was nevertheless a loving and under-standing husband who sus-

Queen Anne *(Library of Congress)*

tained his wife through her various illnesses and the loss of their seventeen children. On her twentieth birthday, February 6, 1685, Charles II died, and Anne was thrust into the midst of national affairs by the accession of her father as James II.

Life's Work

During his brief reign of almost four years, James II managed to forfeit the goodwill of his subjects by offending most of them, including his younger daughter; but these affronts still lay in the future. Anne was now permitted to choose the members of her own household, and predictably Sarah Jennings Churchill was appointed first lady of the bedchamber. "Mrs. Freeman," Sarah's pet name, provided "Mrs. Morley," Anne's pet name, with the intellectual companionship not found in her marriage, as well as sage advice in times of trouble. Although James II treated his daughter with love and deference, he would not permit her to visit her sister in June, 1687, fueling speculation that pressure would soon be put upon her to change her religion. Mary was the wife of the champion of the Protestant cause, but Anne, always so eager to please, might prove a better choice as sovereign if she were to become a Roman Catholic. With Sarah's support, Anne prepared to defend her devotion to the Church of England, but this crisis of conscience never materialized.

Rumors began to circulate during November, 1687, that the queen was with child. Princess Anne had her doubts, about both the pregnancy, because of her stepmother's age, and the legitimacy of the healthy prince, born the following June, which was a month ahead of schedule. Anne was not alone in her doubts, and the prospect of an unending dynasty of Roman Catholic monarchs rallied opposition to James II and his policies. By November, 1688, when William of Orange landed at Torbay at the invitation of a group of prominent noblemen, England was on the verge of another civil war. Luckily the crisis passed with the flight of James II, his queen, and their son to France the following month. Through the tense weeks, Anne supported her sister and brother-in-law, despite her deep love for her father.

The years of separation had changed the sisters, and Anne soon learned to her dismay that Queen Mary did not approve of Sarah Churchill. Anne refused to dismiss her dearest friend, and so a breach developed between the royal sisters which was widened when John Churchill was arrested for treason in 1691. Although he was acquitted, relations between Mary and Anne never really improved before the queen's death from smallpox in December, 1694. King William and his sister-in-law were never friends, and after the death of Mary they became almost open enemies. William would reign alone until his death, then Anne, and after her the duke of Gloucester, her only surviving child. The boy was delicate, but he was England's hope of a continuing Protestant line.

In July, 1700, the eleven-year-old duke of Gloucester died of scarlet fever; Anne acquiesced with reluctance, the following year, to the Act of Settlement. After William's death she would become queen, and if she died without issue the Crown would pass to her cousin, the

Protestant Electress Sophia of Hanover and her heirs. James II died in France on September 6, 1701, and Louis XIV publicly recognized his son as James III. Anne's father had forgiven her for her rebellion before his death, and with his blessing she calmly waited for the inevitable. Six months later William III was dead, and Anne was queen.

Anne's coronation on April 23, 1702, was a triumph for her and the Churchills. Sarah was made mistress of the robes, and John was created duke of Marlborough. The power to reward was pleasant, but the reality of governing an imperial state was almost overwhelming. Queen Anne, who had received no training for the task she had to perform, wisely relied on her ministers for advice, and in the first eight years of her reign, that meant Marlborough and the Whigs. In May, 1702, England was drawn into the War of the Spanish Succession, and although the government was supposedly bipartisan, the Whig policy of total commitment to a land war prevailed over the Tory preference for a purely naval war with economic sanctions. Anne might have been inclined to the Tory position, but she was too dependent on Marlborough and his close friend Sidney Godolphin to oppose their policies. Hoping to dislodge the queen, the Tories appealed to her special interest, the Church of England, with the Occasional Conformity Bill which would restrict the activities of the dissenters (non-Anglican Protestants) who were active supporters of the Whigs. The measure passed the Tory-dominated House of Commons only to be defeated in the Whig-controlled House of Lords.

The Tories then concentrated their attack on Marlborough, but he countered their criticism with the brilliant victory at Blenheim in August, 1704. Once again the Tories tried to punish the dissenters, only to fail. The nation and the queen supported the ministry, a fact that was demonstrated by a resounding Whig victory in the election of 1705. As more Tories left the government, Queen Anne began to lose confidence in her advisers. The key to this change was the duchess of Marlborough. Always a woman of strong opinions, Sarah now became tyrannical and overbearing. While her husband was winning the war, Sarah was losing the affection and support of the queen with her constant badgering.

The duchess of Marlborough introduced a poor relation, Mrs. Abigail Masham, into the queen's service in 1707, an event that went unnoticed by most. One person who saw Mrs. Masham's potential was

Robert Harley, a moderate Tory who had held various positions in the ministry. Quietly he began to work through her to undermine Sarah's influence. Even his removal from office at Marlborough's insistence in 1708 did not retard the erosion of the power once enjoyed by "Mrs. Freeman." The election of 1708 proved another Whig victory, and the war-weary queen was forced to replace more Tories with politicians who now arrogantly refused to make peace with King Louis XIV on any terms but their own.

Dr. Henry Sacheverell delivered his famous sermon at St. Paul's Cathedral on November 5, 1709, the anniversary of William III's landing at Torbay in 1688. Queen Anne, who was in mourning for her husband, seemed cheered by the Tory divine's attack on the government and the Glorious Revolution, but she, like many others, was shocked when the Whig leaders dragged Sacheverell into court. The move to impeach him proved a fatal mistake. The trial was a sensation, and every day the courtroom was packed. Even the queen attended incognito. Sacheverell was found guilty, but his punishment was minor, and when his three years' suspension from preaching was done, Queen Anne rewarded him with a handsome living. It was really the Whigs who were convicted in March, 1710, and at the polls they were sentenced by the voters to defeat.

As her Whig ministers began to depart, Queen Anne turned on the duchess of Marlborough, whom she dismissed in April, 1710. By September only the duke of Marlborough remained; his public dismissal and humiliation were postponed until December 31, 1711. Queen Anne was served for the last four years of her reign by politicians who fully shared her views on church and state. At the head of the Tory ministry was Robert Harley, who was raised to the peerage as earl of Oxford in 1711. His most able colleague, indeed his chief rival, was Henry St. John, to whom fell the task of making a secret peace with the French. For his masterful negotiating of the Treaty of Utrecht, St. John was made Viscount Bolingbroke, a reward which he resented because it placed him below Oxford in the peerage.

The signing of the treaty in 1713 did little to enhance Great Britain's prestige abroad; her allies felt betrayed and not inclined to trust her again. Among those former friends was the elector of Hanover, who, after his mother Sophia, was heir to the throne of Great Britain. Firmly in league with the Whigs, he was determined to punish Oxford, Bolingbroke, and their political friends for their perfidy. For their part, the Tories now feverishly began to work for a restoration of the son of James II and Mary of Modena, and at first they had the halfhearted support of the queen.

As the war came to a close, Anne's health seemed to deteriorate. Everyone she had loved was gone, and her only consolation was alcohol, which relieved both pain and loneliness. Few were completely aware of the queen's condition until July 24, 1714, when she collapsed during a cabinet meeting. All during her reign she had faithfully attended those weekly sessions, but the bitter altercation between Oxford and Bolingbroke on that occasion was too much for her nerves. Two days later she dismissed the earl of Oxford from her government, but it was the moderate Whigs and not Bolingbroke to whom she turned in her last hours. The queen who had refused to discuss the succession during her lifetime, now, on her deathbed, chose her cousin, the elector of Hanover, to follow her. Sophia was dead, but George I would preserve the church which Anne had loved and served. On Sunday, August 1, 1714, she died, with only her personal physician in attendance.

Summary

Queen Anne was a woman of average intelligence who governed an exceptional generation. Her education was at best superficial, but she recognized her inadequacies and relied on her ministers for their advice. Her personal life was tragic, but she was sustained by the Church of England in every adversity. At the end of her reign she accepted a distant cousin as her heir because he would preserve that church. Anne was a monarch who saw her duty and did it.

Bibliography

Butler, Iris. *Rule of Three*. London: Hodder and Stoughton, 1967. This work provides valuable psychological insight into the characters of Queen Anne, Sarah Churchill, and Abigail Masham. It is rich with many previously unpublished items.

Feiling, Sir Keith. *A History of the Tory Party, 1640-1714*. Oxford: Oxford University Press, 1924. Although somewhat dated in its analysis of events, this is nevertheless a work of remarkable scholarship, providing a very valuable overview of the period.

Green, David. *Queen Anne*. New York: Charles Scribner's Sons, 1970. A well-written and easily read biography, but lacking the sympathy and understanding which must be part of any study of Queen Anne.

Gregg, Edward. *Queen Anne*. London: Routledge and Kegan Paul, 1980. More scholarly than earlier biographies, this work presents a sympathetic portrait of Anne in a forthright and lively way. Until a complete revisionist study appears, this is the best work available.

Hamilton, Elizabeth. *The Backstairs Dragon: A Life of Robert Harley, Earl of Oxford*. London: Hamish Hamilton, 1969. The character of Harley is restored by this study, and the reader's understanding of the politics of the early eighteenth century is enhanced.

Holmes, Geoffrey. *British Politics in the Age of Anne*. London: Macmillan, 1967. This work contains a wealth of information, and it carefully unravels the tangled knot of politics in the early eighteenth century. It is perhaps the best book on the subject.

Jones, David Martin. *Conscience and Allegiance in Seventeenth Century England: The Political Significance of Oaths and Engagements*. Rochester, N.Y.: University of Rochester Press, 1999. An examination of British constitutional history and the divine right of sovereigns that focuses on the Stuarts.

Rowse, A. L. *The Early Churchills*. New York: Harper and Brothers, 1956. Although some knowledge of English history is assumed, this work provides a thorough exploration of the rise of an exceptional family. The style and the author's command of the subject are without peer.

Trevelyan, George Macaulay. *England Under Queen Anne*. 3 vols. London: Longmans, Green, 1930-1934. Long the standard work on the period, its conclusions may find detractors, but none can fault it on style or scholarship.

Clifton W. Potter, Jr.

CORAZON AQUINO

Born: January 25, 1933; Tarlac Province, the Philippines

Aquino became the first woman president of the Philippines. She led the revolution that ended twenty years of dictatorial rule and restored democratic government.

Early Life

Maria Corazon Cojuangco was born on January 25, 1933, in Tarlac Province, about fifty miles north of Manila. The sixth of eight children, "Cory," as she became known, was born with a silver spoon in her mouth. She belonged to a wealthy and politically influential landowning family in the Philippines. Her father, Jose Cojuangco, was a sugar baron who also managed the family bank and later served in the national assembly. Both her grandfathers were senators. She was educated at exclusive girls' schools in Manila, run by Roman Catholic nuns. In 1946, when her father moved to the United States, she continued her education at Raven Hill Academy in Philadelphia and Notre Dame School in New York, both Catholic high schools. As a young girl, she showed deep religious conviction that would continue to be a major influence in her life. While a student in the United States, she had a brief foray into American politics as a member of the Junior Republicans and supported Governor Thomas Dewey in the 1948 presidential campaign.

In 1953, Cory was graduated from Mount St. Vincent College in the Riverdale section of the Bronx, with a degree in French and mathematics. She returned to Manila to study law at Far Eastern University, not because she was contemplating a career in law but out of an interest in the discipline of law. Soon after her return to the Philippines, she began a courtship with Benigno "Ninoy" Aquino, Jr., a dynamic and intelligent journalist from a well-known family in Tarlac Province. They were married in 1954, and Cory Aquino ended her legal studies.

Life's Work

For the next thirty years, Aquino played the traditional roles of a dutiful and loyal wife and mother. She reared four daughters and a son and supported her husband unobtrusively but effectively in his mete-oric political career. Shortly after their marriage, Ninoy was elected the youngest mayor in the Philippines. When he became governor of Tarlac Province in 1959, he was also the youngest in the country. He performed a similar feat in 1967 by winning a seat in the senate and at thirty-five became the youngest senator. As Benigno Aquino's career advanced, he became a formidable opponent of Philippine president Ferdinand E. Marcos.

Cory Aquino's life received a major jolt in 1972 when President Marcos suspended the constitution, imposed martial law, and arrested her husband on charges of murder, subversion, and illegal possession of firearms. Marcos was seeking an unprecedented third term in the presidential elections scheduled for 1973, and it was widely believed in the Philippines that his redoubtable foe, Benigno Aquino, would defeat him. Ninoy's imprisonment was the first in a series of acts of repression by Marcos that included incarcerating hundreds of other opponents, abolishing the congress, ending the independence of the judiciary, and muzzling the press.

Corazon Aquino *(AP Wirephoto)*

During her husband's seven and a half years in prison, Cory Aquino became the only link between him and the world beyond the prison gates. When Benigno Aquino went on a hunger strike in 1975, she not only solicited the help of her family to persuade him to end his fast but also tried to raise international public opinion against the conditions that had prompted his hunger strike. She regularly smuggled out messages from him to his supporters and reporters. In 1980, Benigno Aquino suffered a heart attack, and Marcos allowed him to go to the United States for a bypass operation. He subsequently became a fellow at Harvard University's Center for International Affairs. The Aquino family lived in Newton, Massachusetts, where Cory later said they spent the three happiest years of their lives.

While in the United States, Benigno Aquino further developed and refined his political philosophy. He also felt an obligation to return to the Philippines and resume the struggle against Marcos. Although aware of the risks involved, he was undeterred. On August 21, 1983, Benigno Aquino was assassinated while disembarking from a plane at Manila International Airport. Initially, the Marcos government asserted that Benigno Aquino had been murdered by Rolando Galman, who they alleged was a Communist agent and who was shot at the scene by security guards. Although the evidence pointed to a military conspiracy, the Marcos-appointed court eventually acquitted General Fabian Ver, the armed forces chief of staff, and twenty-five others who had been charged with murder.

The Philippine economy, which had been in decline since the mid-1970's, worsened dramatically after the assassination of Benigno Aquino. The gross national product declined, inflation increased, and the government was unable to make interest payments on its foreign debts. The national economic and fiscal crisis, which in part had been caused by mismanagement and corruption, had severe social costs. Unemployment rose, the standard of living of the majority of Filipinos fell, and the gap between the rich and poor widened even further. These economic and social problems fueled the communist insurgency mounted by the New People's Army (NPA), as large numbers of people, particularly in the rural areas, became disaffected with the existing order.

The assassination of Benigno Aquino galvanized the Filipino people into action. It resulted in widespread anger and frustration, and sparked demonstrations against the Marcos regime. Benigno Aquino became a national martyr, and his widow rapidly acquired the stature of a national saint. The scale and intensity of the attacks by the Communist guerrillas also increased. The Roman Catholic Church, led by the archbishop of Manila, Jaime Cardinal Sin, became more vociferous in its criticisms of Marcos, a significant development in a country where 85 percent of the people are Catholic.

Cory Aquino, the symbol of the newly energized opposition, used her growing popularity and prestige to compaign against Marcos in the May, 1984, National Assembly elections. The opposition won a third of the seats, and although Marcos retained control of the assembly, the national consensus was that the opposition would have won a majority in a completely free and fair election. Faced with continuing calls domestically and internationally for a return to democratic government, Marcos announced on an American television program in November, 1985, that elections would be held the following February. From then on, Aquino was encouraged to run for the presidency, for many were convinced that only she commanded the support necessary to defeat Marcos and had the stature to unify a split opposition. A self-effacing and private woman who had never considered going into politics, Aquino was a reluctant presidential candidate. After receiving a petition with a million signatures and having spent a day of fasting and meditation at a convent near Manila, Aquino took up the challenge and agreed to run for president. Cardinal Sin was instrumental in persuading Salvador Laurel, who had presidential aspirations of his own, to become her running mate under the banner of Laurel's United Nationalist Democratic Organization (UNIDO).

A political neophyte, Aquino was thus pitchforked into the political arena. What she lacked in political experience she compensated for with her sincerity, forthrightness, and moral courage. Her image as a modern-day Joan of Arc bolstered her popularity. In speeches across the country, she challenged Marcos directly, holding him responsible for the political decay, social dislocation, and economic malaise that had plagued the Philippines during his long and autocratic rule. Yellow—her husband's favorite color—could be seen in the cities, towns, and rural hamlets and came to symbolize the desire for change and the aspirations of a restive populace. As her campaign progressed, Aquino became not only a symbol of opposition but also a dynamic leader who inspired a populist movement that came to be known as "People Power."

The election, which was held on February 7, 1986, was marked by fraud and intimidation of voters by supporters of Marcos. After both candidates claimed victory, there was a stalemate that lasted for more than two weeks. On February 25, 1986, Marcos and Aquino held rival inaugurations. Faced with intense domestic and international pressures to concede defeat, and after key military officers defected to the Aquino camp, Marcos fled into exile in the United States.

Aquino inherited many daunting political, economic, and social problems from the Marcos era: promulgation of a new constitution, a foreign debt of more than twenty-seven billion dollars, land reform, endemic corruption, and a communist insurgency. Shortly after her inauguration, she ordered the release of more than five hundred political prisoners, thus fulfilling one of her campaign pledges. She ruled by decree until a new constitution was overwhelmingly endorsed in a referendum in early 1987. The economy would show modest improvements, although many structural economic problems would remain to be corrected, in order to ensure sustained growth. The newly elected congress, dominated by landowners, passed a compromise Land Reform Bill in June, 1988, that was riddled with loopholes and fell far short of a radical redistribution of agricultural land. Caught between the powerful landed aristocracy (to which she belonged) and nationalist, communist, and military factions that rose to challenge the new government, Aquino's popular support waned. An interim agreement was reached in October, 1988, with the United States, which guaranteed the operation of the United States' military bases in the Philippines until 1991. Under the agreement, the Philippines would receive $481 million annually. She declined to run for reelection in 1992.

Summary

Since her childhood, Corazon Aquino has possessed a strong religious faith, high ethical principles, and moral integrity. Her strength of character sustained her during the trying years of her husband's imprisonment and the arduous period following his assassination. She demonstrated the same moral and religious conviction as she mobilized the Filipino people against the Marcos regime. This essentially peaceful democratic revolution enhanced the stature of the Philippines in the Southeast Asian region and in the wider international community. She set a new standard of ethical conduct for leaders throughout the world and demonstrated that politics can be shrewd but humane.

Although naturally shy and unassuming, Corazon Aquino grew in confidence and self-assurance as a leader. Following her speech to a joint session of the United States Congress in September, 1986, House Speaker Thomas P. O'Neill, Jr., said that hers was the "finest speech" he had heard in his long congressional career. After surviving several coup attempts and domestic upheaval, she restored greater political stability to the Philippines. The tourist industry was invigorated, and there was an increase in new local and foreign investment in the economy. Aquino has showed tact, compassion, and fairness in dealing with the practical problems of politics. Under her leadership, the Filipino people gained a new faith and pride in themselves and in their nation.

Bibliography

Burton, Sandra. *Impossible Dream: The Marcoses, the Aquinos, and the Unfinished Revolution.* New York: Warner Books, 1989. A lucid account of the Philippine revolution. It contains interesting anecdotes that throw light on the relationship between Aquino and her husband.

Haskins, James. *Corazon Aquino: Leader of the Philippines.* Hillside, N.J.: Enslow, 1988. A sympathetic biography of Aquino. Her early life is treated more briefly than her role as a political leader and public figure, which is the real focus of the study. Intended for young readers.

Johnson, Bryan. *The Four Days of Courage: The Untold Story of the People Who Brought Marcos Down.* New York: Free Press, 1987. A journalistic but thorough account of the Aquino-Marcos election campaign. Good use is made of interviews with government, military, and civilian participants in the revolution.

Karnow, Stanley. *In Our Image: America's Empire in the Philippines.* New York: Random House, 1989. One of the best historical accounts of the United States' special relationship with the Philippines. It provides penetrating insights into the circumstances that led to Aquino's rise to power. The book includes information gained from exclusive interviews with Aquino before and after she became president.

Komisar, Lucy. *Corazon Aquino: The Story of a Revolution.* New York: George Braziller, 1987. Although written without the cooperation of Aquino or members of her family, this "unauthorized biography" gives a well-rounded account of her personality. It also contains a useful background chapter on the history of the Philippines. A detailed account is given of Aquino's first year as president.

Mercado, Monina Allarey, ed. *People Power: An Eyewitness History of the Philippine Revolution of 1986.* Manila: James B. Reuter Foundation, 1986. A collection of personal accounts of events leading to the fall of Marcos, as seen from the perspectives of people from various segments of Philippine society.

Reid, Robert H., and Eileen Guerrero. *Corazon Aquino and the Brushfire Revolution.* Baton Rouge: Louisiana State University Press, 1995.

Abiodun Williams

ASPASIA

Born: c. 475 B.C.; Miletus, Asia Minor (modern Turkey)
Died: After 428 B.C.; probably Athens, Greece

Aspasia's role as companion to the Athenian statesman Pericles made her the target of contemporary abuse and criticism; that same status and her reputation for skill in rhetoric made her a philosophic and historical ideal of the independent, educated, and influential woman.

Early Life

Aspasia was born in the ancient Greek city of Miletus. Her father was named Axiochus; her mother's name is unknown. Located on the southwest coast of Asia Minor (modern Turkey), Miletus enjoyed a reputation for wealth based on extensive seaborne trade and for philosophic inquiry into the nature of the universe.

The city suffered severely in a Persian attack of 494 B.C. It is therefore not surprising that Miletus in 479 B.C. joined the Athenian-led league against Persia. The political and military relationship of Miletus with Athens was, however, problematic. For some years after 450 B.C., an Athenian garrison occupied the city, and toward the end (after 411 B.C.) of the long-term war of Athens with Sparta, Miletus was suspected of collusion with the enemies of Athens. Nevertheless, during this same period, several Milesians left their home city to achieve prominence in Athens. Those emigrants included the city planner Hippodamus, the poet and musician Timotheus, and the most famous woman of fifth century Athens, Aspasia.

Life's Work

The surviving ancient sources for fifth century Athenian history do not permit a connected biography of Aspasia. The most reliable sources are a few notices in contemporary Athenian comic literature and several references to Aspasia by Socrates' pupils (including Plato). Many details are offered by the Greek biographer Plutarch in his *Life of Pericles*, but that brief account was written about A.D. 100, more than five hundred years after Aspasia's lifetime.

Aspasia must have come from Miletus to Athens before c. 450 B.C.

Aspasia *(Library of Congress)*

She first appears in the historical record about 445 B.C., when the prominent Athenian politician and military leader Pericles (c. 495-429 B.C.) divorced—under, it was asserted, amicable circumstances—the mother of his two sons. Soon thereafter, Pericles began living and appearing in public with Aspasia. Ancient sources consistently identify her as a *hetaera*, a Greek term literally meaning "female companion" and used of women (often of slave or freedwoman status and usually of foreign origin) who were sexual, social, and occasionally intellectual nonmarital companions of prominent Athenian men.

Because of her status as a foreign-born, intelligent, articulate companion of Pericles, Aspasia was, throughout Pericles' later political career, consistently attacked as a malign influence on his public policies and his political and military leadership. She was, for example, viewed by Pericles' enemies as responsible for his leadership in a war Athens fought with the island of Samos, a traditional rival of Miletus. The Athenian comic poet Aristophanes, in his play *Acharnians* (425 B.C.), which amusingly, but quite seriously, expressed the Athenian longing for a peaceful resolution to military conflicts, represented Aspasia as partially responsible for provoking the Peloponnesian War between Athens and Sparta. Another Athenian comic poet, Aristophanes' peer Cratinus, referred to Aspasia on the stage as nothing but a shameless prostitute who influenced Pericles with her sex. A third Athenian comedian, Hermippus, also abused Aspasia publicly and was said to have prosecuted her for impiety in an Athenian court; Pericles, in turn, reportedly offered in court an emotional, tearful defense of his mistress. These legal episodes, however, are almost certainly apocryphal, prompted by later generations' overly literal readings of Hermippus's comedies.

All these accusations simply reflect the perceived influence of a woman of independent judgment, education, intelligence, and resourcefulness. She may well have been, as were other *hetaerae*, the owner and operator of a brothel. She was certainly Pericles' mistress, but other prominent Athenian men of the time also enjoyed relationships with similar "companions." For example, Pericles' political opponent, the great Cimon—whose own sister, Elpinice, had once been the object of Pericles' attention—reportedly had liaisons with two *hetaerae*. In a later generation, the Athenian rhetorician Isocrates was reported to have had a similar female "companion."

More significant than the political abuse she attracted as Pericles' partner is the strong tradition that Aspasia was skilled at oratorical composition, instruction, and philosophic conversation. Pericles himself is recorded as praising her wisdom and sense of politics. Thus, several ancient authorities imply or allege that Aspasia advised Pericles on his own acclaimed public speeches (including the famous funeral oration of 430 B.C., reported in the works of Thucydides), and several sources state that she participated actively in philosophic argument with Socrates.

Aspasia had a child by Pericles. The son's irregular status had been defined by Pericles' own law denying Athenian citizenship to anyone who did not have two Athenian citizens as parents. Pericles' eldest son by his wife, Xanthippus (with whom his relationship was said to be tense), died in the great plague that struck Athens in 429 B.C. Before Pericles' own death later that year, therefore, the Athenian democracy bestowed a special exemption so that his son born of Aspasia could become an Athenian citizen. Pericles the Younger, as he was called, grew to maturity and served the Athenian democracy as a general at the naval victory of Arginusae in 406 B.C. Soon thereafter, however, he was among the generals executed by the Athenians for having failed to rescue naval crews after the battle.

After Pericles' death, Aspasia virtually disappears from the historical record. A single reference mentions that she became the companion of another rising politician, a man named Lysicles, who died in 428 B.C.

Summary

In his philosophic dialogue *Menexenos*, written after 387 B.C. and therefore after the life and prominence of its characters, Plato portrayed Socrates as praising Aspasia's literary and oratorical skills. Indeed, Plato presented Socrates as reciting a brief funeral oration claimed as Aspasia's own composition. Plato's depiction of Aspasia in this dialogue is sarcastic—Aspasia is said to have composed speeches well, for a woman—and typical. For Plato manifestly enjoyed pretending that some aspects of his master Socrates' knowledge were derived from sources other Athenians would have thought unlikely. Thus, in his dialogue *Symposium*, composed before 378 B.C., Plato asserted that Socrates learned the philosophic basis for and logical consequences of love from Diotima, a probably fictitious woman identified as coming from a rural Greek setting. Plato's mention of Aspasia, and the rhetorical exercise he attributed to her—along with the tradition about Aspasia maintained by other contemporaries in the circle of Socrates—turned her memory into a rhetorical commonplace: She became the ideal philosophic woman, one who could influence statesmen and converse on equal terms with philosophers.

This process of idealization began with Socrates' students Antisthenes and Aeschines, both of whom wrote philosophic dialogues entitled "Aspasia." The process continued in Greek philosophic and rhetorical schools down through the fourth century A.D. Aspasia's likeness adorned Roman gardens; much later, in the nineteenth century, she became the idealized figure of an educated ancient Greek woman and was represented in numerous academic paintings and historical novels. More recently, she has become a symbol of independence for the North American feminist movement; for example, Aspasia is prominently depicted in artist Judy Chicago's multimedia work *The Dinner Party* (1979).

Bibliography

Bertoch, Marvin J., and Julia Brixen Bertoch. *Modern Echoes from Ancient Hills: Our Greek Heritage.* Edited by Stan Larson. Salt Lake City, Utah: Blue Ribbon, 1998. A discussion of Greek statesmen, including Pericles and Aspasia.

De Ste. Croix, G. E. M. *The Origins of the Peloponnesian War.* Ithaca, N.Y.: Cornell University Press, 1972. A scholarly, detailed, and convincing discussion of the issues that led to the Peloponnesian War. The policies and personality of Pericles are treated prominently throughout. The accusations made against Aspasia regarding her influence on Pericles are discussed in pages 235-243.

Dover, K. J. "The Freedom of the Intellectual in Greek Society." In *Greeks and Their Legacy.* Oxford, England: Blackwell, 1988. A critical examination of the tradition of Aspasia's trial for impiety. Pays full attention to social context and to the ancient evidence.

Ehrenberg, Victor. *The People of Aristophanes.* New York: Schocken, 1962. A classic introduction to Athenian society and social history in the age of Aspasia and Pericles. Ehrenberg provides (especially in pages 177 to 181) a reliable, lively treatment of what is known of the *hetaera* in Athenian society, and he discusses throughout what the Greek comic dramatists of fifth century Athens can—and cannot—tell modern readers about the realities of Greek life.

Henry, Madeleine M. *Prisoner of History: Aspasia of Miletus and Her Biographical Tradition.* New York: Oxford University Press, 1995. A rare attempt at writing the biography of an ancient woman for whom the sources are far from satisfactory. The first several chapters provide a scholarly account of Aspasia, with a critical review of the evidence for reconstructing her biography. The remainder of the book is an entertaining introduction to how Aspasia has been represented by primarily male interpreters in the literary, philosophic, and pictorial traditions of Western European society.

Kebric, Robert B. *Greek People*. Mountain View, Calif.: Mayfield, 1989. A reliable account of classical Greek history presented in terms of biographical portraits. Chapter 6 offers a highly readable, nuanced, but very traditional perception of Aspasia as a participant in fifth century aristocratic Athenian society.

Richter, G. M. A. *The Portraits of the Greeks*. Revised by R. R. R. Smith. Ithaca, N.Y.: Cornell University Press, 1984. Pages 99 to 100 show a Roman portrait of Aspasia. The accompanying discussion is an important supplement to Henry's work.

Stadter, Philip A. *Commentary on Plutarch's Pericles*. Chapel Hill: University of North Carolina Press, 1989. Stadter's commentary is the best available introduction to the historical and historiographic issues surrounding Plutarch's presentation of Pericles and Aspasia.

Paul B. Harvey, Jr.

NANCY ASTOR

Born: May 19, 1879; Danville, Virginia
Died: May 2, 1964; Grimsthorpe Castle, Lincolnshire, England

Born a Virginian, Astor was the first woman to sit in Britain's House of Commons. Always a controversial figure because of her outspoken views on almost every subject from temperance to race relations, she was a zealous campaigner for the rights of women and children.

Early Life
Nancy Witcher Langhorne was born on May 19, 1879, in Danville, Virginia. Her mother, Nannie Witcher Keene, was of Irish descent; her father, Chiswell "Chillie" Dabney Langhorne, had been a soldier in the Confederate army. Ten of their eleven children were born in Danville, a moderate-sized Southern city notable for its tobacco markets and cotton mills. Nancy was the third of five surviving daughters.

Although various members of the Langhorne family had distinguished themselves in Virginia politics since the eighteenth century, the Civil War and Reconstruction had devastated the Southern aristocracy. Chillie (pronounced Shillie) Langhorne was forced to take a number of menial jobs and eventually decided, when Nancy was six years old, to move to Richmond, the state capital, to better his situation.

It was several years before his luck turned, but Chillie was eventually able to make a fortune contracting laborers for the railroad. In 1892, he bought a country house, Mirador, and settled down to lead the life of a Virginia gentleman. Hunting, riding, and gracious hospitality were considered more important than a formal education, especially for a young girl. Nancy attended several schools and loved to read, and though she was no scholar, she was no mere social butterfly. She had strong religious feelings and briefly considered becoming a missionary. A searching for spiritual values and concern for the poor were to be important aspects of her personality throughout her life.

All the Langhorne women were attractive. Irene, Nancy's elder sister, received more than sixty proposals of marriage before she accepted that of Charles Dana Gibson and became the model for the Gibson girl. Nancy was not as conventionally beautiful as her sister, but she was a striking woman, small and athletic, with sparkling blue eyes.

In 1897, Nancy married Robert Gould Shaw II of Boston. The marriage was not a success. Shaw was a heavy drinker, and Nancy, only eighteen and homesick for Mirador, refused to play the role of a submissive wife. Soon they were separated, and they were divorced in 1903 so that Shaw could marry another woman. From this unpleasant experience, Nancy bore her first son and also conceived a lifelong aversion to drunkenness.

After the divorce, Nancy, her mother, and a friend visited Europe to lift her spirits. A few months later, Nannie Langhorne died unexpectedly, and Nancy stayed at Mirador to keep house for her father. Chillie soon saw that this arrangement was not satisfactory; his daughter was miserable, and he and Nancy were temperamentally too alike. In 1904, he sent her and her sister Phyllis to England, where they visited friends and moved freely in society. The following year, accompanied by her father, Nancy met Waldorf Astor, son of William Waldorf Astor, one of the world's wealthiest men. The attraction was mutual, and they were married in May, 1906. The senior Mr. Astor gave the young couple his magnificent country house Cliveden as a wedding present.

Like many wealthy and well-educated men of his day, Waldorf decided to enter politics. In 1910, he was elected Conservative member for Plymouth, beginning an association with that city which would be a part of his and Nancy's political lives for thirty-five years.

In 1914, Nancy reached a spiritual crisis. She had had an extended period of illnesses and found no comfort in either conventional medicine or conventional religion. Her sister Phyllis introduced her to Christian Science. Nancy embraced its tenets with enthusiasm and attempted to convert her family and friends. Her missionary efforts were not entirely successful, but they, along with a military hospital set up at Cliveden during World War I, provided an outlet for her boundless energies.

Life's Work

In the general election of 1918, women in Great Britain were allowed for the first time to vote and to be elected to Parliament. A number of women stood for election, but all were defeated except a Sinn Féin candidate who refused to take the oath of allegiance.

Death, not the rising feminist movement, decided who would be the first woman in Parliament. In 1916, William Waldorf Astor had been given a peerage, which meant that the younger Waldorf could stay in the House of Commons only as long as his father lived. In October, 1919, the first Viscount Astor died. Shortly thereafter, the Plymouth Conservatives approached Nancy, who agreed to stand. She won her first election against two men, with a majority of more than five thousand votes.

Nancy Astor's resounding success was not based solely on her husband's reputation and support, although both were important. She was a natural politician, full of confidence. She knew the people of Plymouth, especially the poor among whom she had worked as the wife of a member of Parliament, and they supported her. She had a lively wit and loved to confront hecklers. She was never shy.

On December 1, 1919, Nancy Astor was officially introduced to the House of Commons by David Lloyd George and Arthur Balfour.

Nancy Astor *(Library of Congress)*

Most of Astor's new colleagues were polite, although some, like Winston Churchill, disapproved of female politicians on principle and of Astor herself in particular. Her bold, direct manners did not change; she was always ready to interrupt or even make personal remarks about another member. Those who took themselves seriously found this disconcerting.

For two years, Astor was the only female member, and so it was natural that she pursued women's issues, though not to the exclusion of others. Her first speech was on controlling the sale of drink. In 1923, she was able to put through an act which limited the sale of drink to minors. Particularly prior to the 1930's, she concerned herself with such social issues as widows' pensions, equal guardianship of children, nursery schools, the raising of the school age, naval and dockyard conditions—an interest particularly important to Plymouth—and slum clearances. Nor was her influence limited to Parliament and the various women's groups of which she was a member. As mistress of Cliveden, where she held court not unlike a modern Elizabeth I, Astor was the center of an ever-changing galaxy of European, English, and American politicians; literary figures such as Henry James, T. E. Lawrence, and George Bernard Shaw; family and friends; Christian Scientists; and anyone to whom she happened to take a fancy, particularly Virginians abroad.

Astor had very definite ideas on almost every subject, both foreign and domestic. She believed in an Anglo-American alliance for the improvement of the rest of the world. She inclined to pacifism, believing that one had to accept the existence of dictators, however personally unpleasant they might be. In 1931, she, Waldorf, Shaw, and others visited the Soviet Union, which at the time was a very unusual thing for a Western politician to do. Shaw was sympathetic to the Communist system, but Astor terrified the interpreters by boldly asking Joseph Stalin why he had killed so many of his own people. (Stalin's answer, after he ordered a translation of her question, was that many deaths were necessary to establish the Communist state.)

Although neither of the Astors came home converted to communism, this trip created bad publicity in Great Britain, particularly for Nancy. Her greatest political mistake, however, was in not recognizing the cruel insanity of Adolf Hitler, whom she never met, before World War II began. Like Neville Chamberlain, she learned too late the impossibility of dealing with a tyrannical madman. Her support of appeasement led to numerous accusations that the Astors and their friends, the so-called Cliveden set, were forming a pro-Nazi secret government. Once the conflict began, she would throw herself into war work with her usual energy, but Astor's political star was fading, even as that of her rival, Churchill, was beginning rapidly to rise.

Plymouth was hit by the Blitz in March, 1941, and again in 1943 and 1944, suffering some of the worst air raids of any British city during the war. Waldorf was lord mayor of Plymouth from 1939 to 1944, and much of the time he and Nancy stayed in the city, doing what they could.

Both Nancy and Waldorf were sixty-five in 1944, and the strains of war had affected them deeply, though in different ways. With the war's ending, the British people wanted new leaders and new ideas. The Cliveden set myth had never been entirely forgotten. Waldorf was ill with asthma and a heart condition. Nancy's tactlessness had increased, making her enemies both within and without her party. She was becoming a political liability.

Nancy seemed unaware of any difficulties, but Waldorf feared she would lose the next election. He and their children persuaded her not to stand again, but she accepted retirement with obvious reluctance. After twenty-six years, her remarkable political career had come to an abrupt end, and not by her own choice. She blamed Waldorf, and for several years they drifted apart, but they grew closer again as his health declined. He died in September, 1952. Nancy Astor lived another twelve years but without ever finding another vocation. She traveled widely. She attempted an autobiography but abandoned it. Gradually her health failed, and she died on May 2, 1964, at the age of eighty-four.

Summary

Nancy Astor was a pioneer in British politics and a great hostess; she was also a phenomenon, an atypical woman who inspired affection or hatred but almost never indifference. Yet she had many of the virtues and faults of her social class: She was honest, determined, and a loyal friend, but also tyrannical, rude, and unrealistic. She was a mass of contradictions. A wealthy woman, she was a spokesman for the poor; a society figure, she crusaded for temperance; a combative individual, she tried to work for world peace. History has not passed its final judgment on Nancy Astor—perhaps it never will.

Bibliography

Astor, Michael. *Tribal Feeling*. London: John Murray, 1963. Nancy Astor attempted an autobiography in the 1940's but for various reasons abandoned it. Her son Michael remedied this loss in his book of personal recollections, on which later biographers have heavily relied.

Collis, Maurice. *Nancy Astor, an Informal Biography*. New York: E. P. Dutton, 1960. Conceived and written in the late 1950's and published in 1960, this biography has the distinctions of being the first written about Astor and the only one published while she was still alive. There are both advantages and disadvantages in dealing with a living subject. Compared to later works, which have the benefit of time and more material available, it is more flattering and less detailed.

Grigg, John. *Nancy Astor: A Lady Unshamed*. Boston: Little, Brown, 1981. A short, concise, and generally favorable account of Astor's colorful career. Numerous pictures and good documentation of sources.

Halperin, John. *Eminent Georgians: The Lives of King George V, Elizabeth Bowen, St. John Philby, and Nancy Astor*. New York: St. Martin's Press, 1995.

Harrison, Rosina. *Rose: My Life in Service*. New York: Viking Press, 1975. Rose Harrison was a lady's maid to Astor for thirty-five years, and so her view is unique, though limited. Her account of this mistress-servant relationship adds depth and enlightenment to the often contradictory personality of Astor.

Langhorne, Elizabeth. *Nancy Astor and Her Friends*. New York: Praeger, 1974. The author, who is related to Astor by marriage, concentrated on the Astors' circle of friends, with an emphasis on British politics. Especially useful in describing events leading up to World War II.

Masters, Anthony. *Nancy Astor: A Biography*. London: Weidenfeld & Nicolson, 1981. This short biography breaks no new ground and offers a less favorable impression of Astor than most of the others.

Sykes, Christopher. *Nancy: The Life of Lady Astor*. New York: Harper & Row, 1972. Generally acknowledged to be the standard biography of Astor, this comprehensive study deals with an abundance of accounts, letters, and events in a clear and objective style. Covers the subject admirably and with restraint.

Winn, Alice. *Always a Virginian*. Lynchburg, Va.: J. P. Bell, 1975. A series of family reminiscences. Winn's accounts are detailed but episodic, and the reader, who unlike the author is not a Langhorne, has to search for dates. Like many family memoirs, however, it is lively and has many vivid descriptions of even small events.

Dorothy Potter

ANNIE BESANT

Born: October 1, 1847; London, England
Died: September 20, 1933; Adyar, India

After her early work promoting radical reform in England, Besant became leader of the Theosophical Society and was active in the nationalist movement in India.

Early Life

Annie Wood Besant was born on October 1, 1847, in London, England, the second of three children of William and Emily Morris Wood. Despite her English birth, Besant had a strong sense of Irish heritage, because her mother was Irish and her father half Irish. William Wood, although trained as a physician, engaged in commerce in London. He died when Besant was five, a loss the trauma of which was compounded by the death several months later of her baby brother.

When Besant was eight, her impoverished widowed mother moved the family to Harrow so that her ten-year-old son Henry could more cheaply attend that prestigious public school. Shortly after the move, Ellen Marryat, youngest sister of the novelist Frederick Marryat, offered to take Annie into her home in Devon to educate her. Although heartsick to be separated from her adored mother for the eight years she spent with Miss Marryat, Besant received excellent training, especially in literary skills, which enabled her to produce throughout her life a prodigious volume of writings for her many causes. During these adolescent years, she was intensely religious. Reading stories of early Christian martyrs, she longed to follow in their steps. She fasted regularly, tortured herself with self-flagellation, and engaged in other extremist behavior, a pattern which became characteristic of her personality. A person of deep if changing beliefs, she would always commit herself enthusiastically and wholeheartedly to her convictions, with the ever-present, self-proclaimed wish for martyrdom.

At age sixteen, Besant returned to her mother's home. She was a beautiful young woman, of small stature, with brown hair and eyes. She had, however, no romantic fantasies, for her emotional life was absorbed by her passionate love for Jesus Christ and for her mother.

She nevertheless married, in 1867, the Reverend Frank Besant, younger brother of the essayist Walter Besant, because she believed that she could best serve God as a clergyman's wife.

The marriage was a disaster. Annie, who married with no knowledge of sex, was shocked by her wedding night. Self-willed and rebellious, she also resented submitting to her domineering husband's authority. Her unhappiness was only somewhat alleviated by her success in selling several stories to the *Family Herald* and by the births of her son Digby, in 1869, and daughter Mabel, in 1870. She also found satisfaction in parish work when Frank Besant became vicar at Sibsey, a village in Lincolnshire. The marriage ended when Annie lost her religious faith after the grave illness of her children, whose sufferings made her doubt her belief in a loving and merciful God. The Besants were legally separated in 1873. She moved to London to make her way on her own with her daughter, while her son remained in the custody of the Reverend Mr. Besant.

Life's Work

Annie Besant's public career went through many distinct stages. After her loss of Christian faith and separation from her husband, she came under the influence of England's leading freethinker, Charles Bradlaugh. In 1874, she joined the National Secular Society and soon became one of its vice presidents. She edited with Bradlaugh the freethinking *National Reformer*, and, from 1883 to 1889, she also edited the magazine *Our Corner*. In these journals, she wrote in support of atheism, women's rights, Irish home rule, land-tenure reform, and against British imperialism. Besant propagated her beliefs not only in written form but also as a public speaker, an activity not considered respectable for women at that time. Her rich, vibrant voice made her a great success, and she took intense pleasure in the power she had over her audiences. Ever eager to absorb new knowledge, the energetic Besant also found time to enroll in courses in science at London University.

Besant's most controversial work with Bradlaugh was their republication in 1877 of Charles Knowlton's 1832 treatise on birth control, *Fruits of Philosophy*. They were arrested, and, in a sensational trial, they were convicted of publishing obscene literature, although their conviction was dismissed on appeal on a technicality. The defiant Besant then published her own birth control pamphlet, *Law of Population: Its Conse-*

Annie Besant *(Library of Congress)*

quence and Its Bearing upon Human Conduct and Morals (1881). She was the first English woman to advocate publicly the use of birth control methods. Even though she was not prosecuted for her pamphlet, the controversy did cause her to lose custody of her daughter.

Besant's humanitarian concerns led her in 1885 to become a socialist. Joining the moderate Fabian Society, she contributed an article to the influential 1889 *Fabian Essays in Socialism*, edited by her close friend George Bernard Shaw. She later also joined the revolutionary Marxist Social Democratic Federation. Ever concerned with theatrical display, she began to dress in proletarian garb and always wore a piece of red clothing to show her Socialist affiliation. This latest cause separated her from Bradlaugh, who was a strong antisocialist individualist. They remained personal friends, but she resigned as coeditor of the *National Reformer*.

As a socialist, Besant fought tirelessly to help working people, especially in trade union activity. Her most significant achievement was her organization of match-girl workers into a union, after helping them in a successful strike against the Bryant and May Match Company in 1888. The Matchmaker's Union, considered the beginning of the new unionism of unskilled labor, was moreover the first successful effort to organize women workers, who had been ignored by the Trades Union Council. Besant also worked for socialist causes as a member of the London School Board, to which she was elected in 1889.

Despite her advocacy of atheism, Besant felt increasingly unsatisfied by it and later spoke of her desperate hunger for spiritual ideals. This need was fulfilled by Theosophy, to which she, to the shock of her friends and associates, converted in 1889 after reading Mme Helena Blavatsky's *The Secret Doctrine* (1888). A charismatic Russian émigrée, Mme Blavatsky founded the Theosophical Society in 1875 along with the American lawyer Colonel Henry Olcott. The society, which remains active, aims at fostering bonds among all humanity; studying comparative religions and philosophies, especially those from ancient Eastern civilizations; and investigating and communicating with the world of the occult. Although not identified with any specific religion, Theosophists accept the Hindu and Buddhist belief in karma and reincarnation.

Committing herself fully to her new faith, Besant withdrew from the National Secular Society and the socialist organizations. She became editor of the Theosophist publication *Lucifer* and the leader of the Theosophical Society in England after Mme Blavatsky's death in 1891. In 1907, she was elected President of the Theosophical Society worldwide, a position she held for the rest of her life. As a Theosophist, in 1891 she renounced Malthusianism and withdrew her *Law of Population* from circulation. Although anguished at the effect this might have on the lives of poor women, she accepted Mme Blavatsky's view that humans must rise above animal passion through self-control and ascetic self-denial. Besant later returned to a qualified endorsement of birth control.

Besant traveled extensively throughout the world, organizing and lecturing for the Theosophical Society. After her first trip to India in 1893, she thought of that country as her home and believed that in earlier incarnations she had been Indian. She adopted Indian dress and in public always wore a white sari, which matched her now-white hair. Strongly drawn toward Hinduism, she learned Sanskrit and in 1895 translated the *Bhagavad-Gita* (first or second century A.D.).

Always the reformer, Besant was concerned to revitalize Indian civilization, to restore pride and self-respect in a people who had been made to feel inferior by British imperialists. She condemned child marriage, the seclusion of women, and eventually the caste system, but otherwise opposed efforts to westernize India. Disavowing at first political activity, Besant worked primarily for educational reform. Her major accomplishment was the establishment of the Central Hindu College in Benares in 1898, a college for Hindu boys based on ancient

Indian religion and culture as well as modern Western science. In 1904, she established the Central Hindu Girls' School, an important step in the emancipation of Indian women. The Hindu University, which absorbed the Central Hindu College in 1916, granted Besant an honorary degree in 1921, and thereafter she always styled herself Dr. Besant.

Besant eventually came to believe that efforts to strengthen Indian cultural pride were impossible as long as India was under British domination. In 1913, therefore, she entered the political arena by working actively for Indian home rule. As a vehicle for her campaign, she bought a Madras newspaper and renamed it *New India*. Founding the Home Rule for India League in 1916, she campaigned for self-government within the British Empire, which she envisioned as a partnership among equal nations. Her agitation against the British caused the government to intern her briefly during World War I, which only increased her popularity among Indians. In 1917, after her release, she was elected president of the Indian National Congress. She did not, however, remain long as leader of the Indian nationalists. She was soon eclipsed by the rise of the Mahatma Gandhi, with whose tactic of civil disobedience she disagreed, for fear that it would lead to violence. Considered too conservative in her insistence on law and order, she lost much of her political following in India.

Besant continued working for Indian home rule, and in 1925 she had an abortive Commonwealth of India Bill introduced into England's House of Commons. Her primary focus in the last part of her life, however, was in the promotion of her Hindu protégé, Jiddu Krishnamurti, as the new Messiah. Believing that in times of world crisis the Divine Spirit enters a human body to help humankind toward higher spiritual consciousness, she was convinced that Krishnamurti was the chosen vehicle. He ultimately disappointed her by renouncing his role in the divine plan. Besant nevertheless continued working for her beliefs almost until her death on September 20, 1933, in Adyar, India, the international headquarters of the Theosophical Society. A portion of her ashes was sprinkled in the holy Ganges River, the rest deposited in a Garden of Remembrance at Adyar.

Summary

An enthusiast for many causes, the leader of diverse movements, Annie Besant remained throughout her life committed to the principles of compassion, freedom, tolerance, and human equality. As a young woman, she had the courage to challenge such icons of Victorian respectability as the Church of England, patriarchy, propriety, capitalism, and imperialism. Although ultimately unsuccessful in her later years as a leader of the Indian home rule movement, she nevertheless made a significant contribution to Indian nationalism in helping to restore the pride of Indians in their own cultural heritage and in sensitizing the British to the narrowness and bigotry of their attitude of superiority toward India.

In her work as a Theosophist, to which she gave her most loyal and lasting allegiance, she incorporated the humanitarian concerns that had informed her other campaigns. Through her leadership she enabled the society to survive scandals, power struggles, and schisms. Although professing beliefs that the conventional world considered bizarre, she remained a personage of influence and respect and left as her legacy the vision of one world, seen and unseen, undivided by race, class, or sex, and bound together by love.

Bibliography

Besant, Annie. *An Autobiography*. London: T. Fisher Unwin, 1893. A passionate, frank account of her life up to 1891. A revision of her 1885 *Autobiographical Sketches*.

_____. *A Selection of the Social and Political Pamphlets of Annie Besant*. New York: Augustus M. Kelley, 1970. A collection of twenty-seven of Besant's pamphlets on English radical reform, published from 1874 to 1889, with a preface and bibliographical notes by John Saville.

Besant, Annie, and Charles Knowlton. *"A Dirty, Filthy Book": The Writings of Charles Knowlton and Annie Besant on Reproductive Physiology and Birth Control and an Account of the Bradlaugh-Besant Trial*. Edited by Sripati Chandrasekhar. Berkeley: University of California Press, 1981. Includes Besant's *Law of Population* and her recantation *Theosophy and the Law of Population* (1891), as well as Knowlton's *Fruits of Philosophy*. The texts are prefaced by a useful introduction.

Nethercot, Arthur H. *The First Five Lives of Annie Besant*. London: Rupert Hart-Davis, 1960. A balanced, detailed life of Besant up to 1893. Although relying sometimes too uncritically on Besant's autobiographical writings, it, along with the second volume (below), is the most complete and reliable biography.

_____. *The Last Four Lives of Annie Besant*. London: Rupert Hart-Davis, 1963. Besant's life and work in India from 1893 to her death. Based on extensive research in archives of the Theosophical Society and on interviews with Besant's family members and associates. An indispensable source.

Taylor, Anne. *Annie Besant: A Biography*. Oxford, England: Oxford University Press, 1992.

West, Geoffrey. *The Life of Annie Besant*. London: Gerald Howe, 1929. A lively, opinionated biography, written by a contemporary who admired Besant's achievements but was skeptical of Theosophy.

Williams, Gertrude Marvin. *The Passionate Pilgrim: A Life of Annie Besant*. New York: Coward-McCann, 1931. A readable popular biography. No footnotes, but a good bibliography.

Nancy Fix Anderson

BENAZIR BHUTTO

Born: June 21, 1953; Karachi, Pakistan

Daughter of assassinated Pakistani leader Zulfikar Ali Bhutto, Benazir Bhutto assumed the leadership of her late father's political party and became prime minister of Pakistan from 1988 to 1990 and again from 1993 to 1996. As a result, she became the first woman to head a predominantly Muslim nation in the modern era and, at thirty-five, the youngest chief executive ever in international politics.

Early Life

Benazir Bhutto was born on June 21, 1953, in Karachi, Pakistan. Named after an aunt who had died as a young woman, she was the oldest of the four children born to Zulfikar Ali Bhutto and his second wife, Begum Nusrat Bhutto. Benazir's father was a Sunnite Muslim (the dominant branch in Pakistan) while her mother, the daughter of an Iranian merchant, is a Shiite. The Bhutto family gained their political power through ownership of a large block of land in the Sind Province. Zulfikar's political career kept him and Nusrat in Islamabad, while Benazir and her siblings were cared for by an English governess.

Despite her Muslim faith, Benazir attended Roman Catholic convent schools. At the age of sixteen, Benazir followed in the footsteps of most wealthy male Pakistanis and left her home country to attend college; in doing so, she became the first Pakistani woman to attend a Western college. In 1969, she ventured to Radcliffe College, then the women's undergraduate arm of Harvard, to pursue a bachelor's degree in government. While an undergraduate, Benazir, despite the looming threat of deportation, participated in demonstrations against American involvement in the Vietnam War.

In December, 1971, with Benazir still in the United States, Bangladesh (then East Pakistan) won its independence with the help of India. As a result, Pakistan's military regime was discredited and forced to step down from power. Zulfikar Ali Bhutto's Pakistani People's Party (PPP) won a majority of the seats in Parliament, and Bhutto became president of Pakistan. Two years later, a new Pakistani constitution was put into place, and Zulfikar Ali Bhutto remained in control of Pakistan as its prime minister.

In 1973, Benazir traveled to England to pursue postgraduate work in politics, philosophy, and economic theory at Oxford University. She was graduated with honors in 1976, then put in another year of postgraduate work at Oxford completing a foreign service program in International Law and Diplomacy. She would also be elected president of the prestigious debating society known as the Oxford Union.

Life's Work

In 1977, Benazir Bhutto returned to Pakistan. The PPP had just won an enormous victory in the March parliamentary elections. Within only a few days of her return, however, Zulfikar Ali Bhutto's government was overthrown by General Muhammad Zia ul-Haq. Bhutto's opponents charged that the PPP had rigged the election. These charges led to riots that left hundreds dead before Zia's military forces seized power. Zulfikar Ali Bhutto was imprisoned and charged with conspiring to murder a colleague. He was found guilty and hanged in April, 1979.

Meanwhile, Benazir had also been arrested in 1977; she was held for protesting her father's arrest. She was repeatedly jailed for her political activities until April, 1980, not having been allowed even to attend her father's funeral. During this turmoil, her mother became the symbolic leader of the now outlawed PPP, but Benazir was the individual whom PPP supporters saw as the true heir to her father's power.

Benazir's two brothers, Shawanaz and Mir Ghulam Murtaza, were studying abroad when their father was arrested. Instead of returning to fight Zia's regime, they stayed abroad and formed Al-Zulfikar, a rebel organization based in Afghanistan. In 1981, the group hijacked a Pakistani International Airliner, rerouting the plane to Syria and forcing Zia to release a number of jailed Bhutto supporters. In retaliation, Zia again jailed Benazir. It would be January, 1984, before Benazir Bhutto was freed and allowed to leave Pakistan for London.

In July, 1985, Benazir's youngest brother, Shawanaz, died under questionable circumstances. Bhutto flew with her brother's body from the French Riviera back to Pakistan where she was, once again, arrested for her political activities. It would be November before she was allowed to return to London.

In December, 1985, Zia ended martial law after eight years. As a result, military courts were relieved of their involvement in civilian matters, allowing, by 1986, political rallies to be held legally within Pakistan. As the military's control ebbed, Benazir Bhutto returned to Pakistan on April 10, 1986. She was greeted by hundreds of thousands upon her return to Lahore. It is argued that this event was the largest political rally held in Pakistan since it gained its independence in 1947. Bhutto's address to her followers called for Zia to step down and for national elections be held to name his successor. She spoke of her father during this rally, telling the crowd, "He told me at our last meeting in Rawalpindi jail that I must sacrifice everything for my country. This is a mission I shall live or die for."

While her return to Pakistani politics did not force Zia out, it enabled Bhutto and her mother to be elected cochairs of the PPP in May, 1986. Bhutto's attempts to organize civil disobedience protesting Zia were not as successful as she had hoped; by August, she was again arrested while preparing to lead a rally. Released three weeks later, she pledged to continue to protest the government even if such actions were again outlawed.

In 1987, in an arranged marriage, Benazir Bhutto married Asif Ali Zardari. Zardari was also from Sind Province, where his family had been successful in banking, insurance, real estate, and the hotel industry. Despite Zardari's wealth and Pakistani traditions, she maintained her maiden name as she pursued her very public goals.

In June, 1988, one of Zia's supporters, Nawaz Sharif, was appointed chief minister of the Punjab Province. This move would come back to haunt the political futures of Bhutto and the PPP. In August, 1988, Pakistani president Zia ul-Haq was killed in a plane crash that is considered mysterious. Zia's followers blamed the United States' Central Intelligence Agency (CIA) for the crash. Zia's sudden death left a chasm at the center of Pakistani politics. In the elections that followed that November, the PPP garnered a sweeping victory, winning the single largest bloc of National Assembly seats. Benazir Bhutto was named prime minister on December 1, 1988. Later that month, Sharif formed a government in the Punjab Province.

Bhutto immediately began a policy of returning democratic rights to the Pakistani people. She freed political prisoners, restored civil rights, and reallocated resources to long-neglected social programs. Despite her attempts, she was unable to make much headway against the long-standing legacy of poverty, crime, and corruption. One key failure came in March, 1989, when Bhutto was unable to topple Sharif's government in Punjab after arranging for a vote of no confidence. This critical failure led to a dwindling of support for Bhutto in the National Assembly.

After only twenty months in office—less than half the term for which she had been elected, but during which time she became the first leader of a modern country to give birth while in office—Ghulam Ishaq Khan, the president of Pakistan, dismissed Bhutto from office. Her dismissal was predicated on charges of corruption. Khan then called for new elections in October, 1990. In those elections, the PPP was defeated by the Islamic Jamhoori Ittehad, and Nawaz Sharif succeeded Bhutto as prime minister.

Bhutto refused to leave the political arena and served as the leader of the parliamentary opposition against Sharif. In November, 1992, at the Silver Jubilee of the PPP, Bhutto announced her New Social Contract, which called for instilling a market economy, privatizing the means of production, downsizing the government, and decentralizing local and provincial governments.

Bhutto remained leader of the opposition until the next general election in October, 1993, when the PPP again won the majority of seats. Bhutto gained power as a result of a failed power play by Sharif. When Muslim League president Kahn Juneo died in March, 1993, Sharif worked to gain the nomination as party leader. His nomination fractionalized the Muslim League, allowing President Kahn to sack Sharif as prime minister. Despite a Pakistani supreme court ruling overturning Kahn's order, both Kahn and Sharif were forced to resign in May. This infighting allowed the PPP to win a majority of seats both in the National Assembly and in the Punjab and Sind Provinces. Once again, Benazir Bhutto was the prime minister of Pakistan.

In her second term as prime minister, her policies focused on the modernization of the Pakistani infrastructure. During the next three years, nearly twenty-five thousand elementary and secondary schools were built in Pakistan, electricity was brought to even the remotest villages across Pakistan's four provinces, and computers were introduced into the schools and the government.

Bhutto's government was dismissed again in November, 1996, when Bhutto's handpicked choice for Pakistani president, Farooq A. K.

Leghari, filed a dissolution order citing, among other charges, the failure of the Bhutto government to stop widespread corruption, attacks on the independence of the courts, and illegal wiretaps of political enemies. Nawaz Sharif again succeeded Bhutto as prime minister. Bhutto continued to serve as leader of the PPP and leader of the parliamentary opposition until she and her husband were arrested in 1998 on charges of corruption.

On April 15, 1999, both Benazir Bhutto and her husband, Asif Zardari, were found guilty of receiving kickbacks and commissions from two Swiss preshipment companies while in office. Both were sentenced to five years in jail, barred from participating in Pakistani politics, and fined thirteen million dollars. Bhutto fled to Dubai while filing initial appeals, but the Pakistani supreme court ruled that she must return to Pakistan to lodge any appeals in person. Bhutto claimed the charges were politically motivated and vowed to appeal the decision. She stated the following in a May, 1999, speech to the Woodrow Wilson International Center for Scholars:

> The charges against me are concocted. I would like the judgment passed against me to be scrutinized by any independent judicial body, legal opinion, human rights organizations, so that I can prove that what is occurring to me in Pakistan is not a case of corruption, but rather the [Sharif] regime threatening democracy.

Summary

In many respects, Benazir Bhutto spent the majority of her adult life breaking new ground not only for Muslim women but also for women of all faiths. Rising from a political and social system in which women's rights are traditionally limited, Bhutto rose above traditional roles to become the first woman to lead a predominantly Muslim nation. In doing so, she brought democratic reforms, human rights, and the information age to Pakistan. She also began to reform the traditional role of women in Pakistan working to provide them with more freedom as well as personal and political rights. Benazir Bhutto continued the political legacies of her father, symbolically gaining revenge for his assassination at Zia's hands. Despite her legal battles, Bhutto's political agenda was rewarded, as she received numerous human rights awards, including the Bruno Kriesty Human Rights Award, the Highest Moroccan Award, the Highest French Award, and UNIFEM.

Bibliography

"Benazir Bhutto." *Current Biography Yearbook* (1986): 39-42.

Bhutto, Benazir. *Daughter of Destiny.* New York: Simon & Schuster, 1989. Bhutto's politically charged autobiography.

Chitkara, M. G., ed. *Benazir: A Profile.* Columbia, Mo.: South Asia Books, 1996. A straightforward account of Bhutto's political career.

Doherty, Katherine M., and Craig A. Doherty. *Benazir Bhutto.* Danbury, Conn.: Franklin Watts, 1990. A relatively uncritical retelling of Bhutto's life and career aimed at younger readers.

Zakaria. *Women and Politics in Islam: The Trial of Benazir Bhutto.* New York: Apex Press, 1990. Examines the impact of a female leader in a Muslim, country through the eyes of an imaginary court composed of Islamic philosophers.

B. Keith Murphy

ANNE BOLEYN

Born: c. 1500-1501; probably at Blickling in Norfolk, England
Died: May 19, 1536; London, England

The desire of England's King Henry VIII to marry Boleyn led to the establishment of the Church of England.

Early Life

Future English queen Anne Boleyn was born into an ambitious family at a time when ambitions were realized through interactions with the court and marriage into the nobility. Young women from such families were expected to marry as their families dictated. Anne's great-grandfather, Geoffrey Boleyn, a tradesman lacking in social status, rose to become lord mayor of London in 1457 but improved his position further through marriage; Sir William Boleyn, her grandfather, made an even more impressive marriage to Margaret Butler, daughter of an Irish earl. Thomas Boleyn, Anne's father, was the eldest of their four sons. A highly successful courtier and diplomat, he married Elizabeth Howard, daughter of Thomas Howard, earl of Surrey; Elizabeth Howard was descended from King Edward I, thus bestowing a touch of royal blood upon her children.

While Elizabeth Howard was frequently pregnant, only Mary, Anne, and George survived to adulthood. To prepare Anne for an advantageous marriage, she was sent abroad, first, in 1513, to the court of Margaret of Austria, regent of the Netherlands. When Mary Tudor, sister of Henry VIII, married King Louis XII of France in 1514, Anne was moved to their court, where she joined her sister Mary. When Louis died, the sisters remained at court serving Claude of Valois, wife of the new king, Francis I, whose court was conspicuously vice-ridden. Mary Boleyn's reputation became tarnished; Anne remained aloof, although she developed the charm, wit, and love of French manners and fashions expected of her in that sophisticated environment.

She returned to England in 1521 or 1522, gaining a place in the household of Henry VIII's queen Catherine of Aragon, where her social skills brought her immediate attention. Her sister Mary was then

Anne Boleyn *(Library of Congress)*

mistress of the king, which may have facilitated Sir Thomas Boleyn's ennoblement as Viscount Rochford. During this period, Anne attempted to marry Henry Percy, heir to the earldom of Northumberland. Her desire to arrange her own marriage was itself shocking; her plans were thwarted by Cardinal Thomas Wolsey, archbishop of York and lord chancellor of England. Anne temporarily left court.

Life's Work

Anne returned to court in 1524 or 1525. His affair with her sister ended, King Henry VIII was attracted to Anne. She resisted his approaches, either because she was genuinely repelled or because she was unwilling to settle for a role as a mistress. Since 1509, Henry had been married to Catherine, daughter of Isabella of Castile and Ferdinand of Aragon, rulers of Spain, but the king was increasingly frustrated by Catherine's inability to bear a male heir. A series of pregnancies had resulted in only one child, Mary, who survived infancy. While miscarriages and high infant mortality rates were common, Henry was concerned that he have a legitimate successor to protect England against a recurrence of the previous century's civil wars. Moreover, the birth of his illegitimate son to Elizabeth Blount had proved to his satisfaction that he could sire sons. In 1527, Henry sought a "divorce"—essentially a modern annulment, since rather than dissolving the marriage, it would show that a legitimate marriage had never taken place. The king's argument was that despite the papal dispensation for his marriage to Catherine, his marriage was forbidden by the Bible, specifically by Leviticus 20:21, which forbids marriage with a brother's wife. In November, 1501, Catherine had married Henry's elder brother Arthur, who died in April, 1502, probably without consummating the marriage. Catherine's failure to bear a son was proof, Henry believed, of divine displeasure with the marriage.

Such divorces were frequent. The duke of Suffolk, who had married Henry's sister Mary in 1515, had secured two; Henry's older sister, Queen Margaret of Scotland, similarly secured one and remarried in 1527. Henry expected the process to be rapid, entrusting Cardinal Wolsey with what came to be called the "King's Great Matter." In 1527, however, the troops of Holy Roman Emperor Charles V had invaded Rome; the emperor was Queen Catherine's nephew. Pope Clement VII was now his prisoner and was unwilling to take steps against the emperor's aunt. He began a series of delaying actions.

Anne's role as rival with Catherine for Henry's affection was known by early 1526. Flirtatious, volatile, outspoken, arrogant, and sophisticated where the queen was grave, mild-mannered, modest, and restrained, Anne was intelligent in an age that rarely acknowledged the value of female intelligence. Anne gained few friends. Many could not understand Henry's attraction to her. She was no beauty. She was dark-haired; the ideal of the day was blond. She was thin, and her skin was sallow. She was said to have a rudimentary extra nail on one hand. To much of the court and the public, she became a stereotypical image of the temptress, although her frequent absences from court may have been serious attempts to avoid the king's attentions. Anne was blamed for Wolsey's fall from power. Henry, accustomed to having his way, replaced Wolsey with Thomas Cromwell, a man more in sympathy with Anne. Anne was accused of avenging herself for Wolsey's earlier interference in her romance with Henry Percy. By 1529, however, she could not have saved herself from the king's plans had she chosen to do so.

Henry was not in sympathy with the Protestant movement, which had swept through northern Europe since Martin Luther had posted his designs for church reform on a church door at Wittenberg in 1517. Henry considered himself a good Catholic and had been given the title "Defender of the Faith" for his opposition to Luther. Nevertheless, in 1529, determined to impose his will and gain a male heir, Henry convened a Parliament that was to bring about a religious revolution, as Pope Clement continued to thwart Henry's plans. In 1530, Clement told Henry to dismiss Anne from the court; in 1531, he banned the king's remarriage while the divorce case was being heard, apparently indefinitely, in Rome.

Anne, however, had allowed Henry increasing intimacy, and by the end of 1532 they had become lovers. By December, 1532, she was pregnant, and, probably sometime in January, 1533, Anne and Henry were secretly married. Henry's logic, apparently, was that he had a right to this second marriage because the marriage to Catherine had never been valid. On June 1, 1533, Anne Boleyn, visibly pregnant, was crowned queen of England in an elaborate ceremony that was to be the high point of her life. Despite the public pageantry, crowds were quiet and occasionally hostile as the new queen passed. Queen Catherine's many charities and conventional domesticity won for her friends that the new queen could never possess.

In July, Pope Clement VII ordered Henry to renounce Anne and declared any child of the new marriage illegitimate. That child, the future Elizabeth I, was born on September 7, 1533. She was the wrong sex for an heir, but Henry and Anne assumed that Anne would continue to bear healthy children, although Anne by then was about thirty-three years of age, well into middle age at a time of low life expectancy. In 1534, Anne gave birth to two stillborn infants. Understanding the importance to her well-being of a healthy son, she continued to become pregnant. The increasing insecurity of her position did not improve her disposition.

A depiction of the "Condemnation of Anne Boleyn." *(Library of Congress)*

Bent on having his way, Henry, via an Act of Royal Supremacy, made himself, not the pope, the spiritual father of the English people, thus separating England from the Roman Catholic Church. From February, 1535, it would be high treason to deny Henry's supremacy. He had already begun the series of executions that would taint his reputation for the remainder of his reign. He purged those who defied him, including his old friend the humanist scholar Sir Thomas More, who was beheaded in 1535, and the aged John Fisher, bishop of Rochester. They and many others could not accept the Act of Supremacy. Unwilling to accept any challenge to his will, he was also tiring of Anne's quick tongue and her apparent unwillingness to accept his unfaithfulness as had Catherine; like Catherine, Anne also failed to provide him with a son.

In January, 1536, Catherine of Aragon died. Henry was unlikely to marry for a third time while Catherine and Anne both lived, but he was pursuing Jane Seymour by November, 1535. Catherine's death freed him to rid himself of Anne and start anew. He maintained that Anne had bewitched him into marriage; he claimed she was a sorceress and was guilty of adultery. He also claimed that she had discussed what would happen when the king died, and such discussions constituted high treason. On May 2, Anne was arrested and taken to the Tower of London. There, where she had been received on the eve of her coronation three years before, she was made a prisoner.

Despite public hatred of Anne, few believed she was guilty. According to the case prepared by Thomas Cromwell, she had committed incest with her brother, George Boleyn (Lord Rochford). Three prominent courtiers, Sir Henry Norris, Sir Francis Weston, and William Brereton, as well as her musician, Mark Smeaton, were arrested as her partners in adultery. Smeaton was not a nobleman; as a commoner, he could be and apparently was tortured into a confession. Charges included conspiracy to murder the king.

The duke of Norfolk, Anne's uncle Thomas Howard, presided over the trials of Norris, Weston, Brereton, and Smeaton on May 12; all were condemned to death. Anne and her brother were tried separately on May 14; again, Anne's uncle presided. Actual evidence against them was lacking, and the case was poorly prepared, but the results were foreordained. Both were condemned. On May 17, Archbishop Thomas Cranmer convened a court at Lambeth to annul Henry's marriage to

Anne, thus preparing the way for Henry's marriage to Jane Seymour on May 30 as, essentially, his first valid marriage. Anne Boleyn was beheaded on May 19 at the Tower of London; her remains were buried in the Royal Chapel of St. Peter ad Vincula of the Tower.

Summary

Scholars have argued over the degree to which Anne Boleyn was a Protestant rebel against the Church of Rome. She encouraged individual reading of the Bible and the reading of works banned by the Church, but there is little other evidence that she was a conscious Protestant. Nevertheless, because she was, willingly or otherwise, a pawn in the King's Great Matter, she was at the heart of the separation of England from the Roman Catholic Church and of the despoliation of convents and monasteries that was to follow. Her independence of spirit and attempts at autonomy, despite the great powers that controlled her destiny, seem to ally her with the Protestant movement, whatever her intent, and cause modern feminist historians to view her with sympathetic eyes.

Bibliography

Chapman, Hester. *The Challenge of Anne Boleyn*. New York: Coward, McCann & Geoghegan, 1974. Places Boleyn in the context of a politically ambitious family in an age of melodramatic excess; pays particular attention to the courts in which Boleyn was trained.

Erickson, Carolly. *Mistress Anne: The Life and Times of Anne Boleyn*. New York: Summit Books, 1984. In one of a series of Tudor biographies that include *Bloody Mary* (1978) and *Great Harry* (1980), Erickson vividly re-creates the world in which these people lived; her work is scholarly, but her style is popular. Her portrait of Anne is not generally sympathetic.

Fraser, Antonia. *The Wives of Henry VIII*. New York: Alfred A. Knopf, 1993. Originally published in London as *The Six Wives of Henry VIII* (1992). Fraser balances anti-Boleyn propaganda with information from other sources to achieve a convincing portrayal, in part sympathetic.

Lindsey, Karen. *Divorced, Beheaded, Survived*. Reading, Mass.: Addison-Wesley, 1995. A feminist interpretation of Boleyn's life, this work emphasizes Boleyn's role as victim of an all-powerful monarch determined to conquer her. Cites as evidence a poem by Sir Thomas Wyatt, who knew Anne well.

Loades, David M. *Henry VIII and His Queens*. West Sussex, England: Sutton, 1997. This short and highly readable work by a respected British historian provides a useful introduction to the topic.

Warnike, Retha M. *The Rise and Fall of Anne Boleyn: Family Politics at the Court of Henry VIII*. Cambridge, England: Cambridge University Press, 1989. Focusing on Anne's society and its conventions, Warnike argues that Anne's failure to produce a male heir doomed her.

Weir, Alison. *The Six Wives of Henry VIII*. London: The Bodley Head, 1991. Heavily dependent on the virulently anti-Boleyn commentary of Spanish ambassador Eustace (or Eustache) Chapuys, Weir presents an almost totally unsympathetic portrait of Boleyn as manipulative seductress.

Betty Richardson

MARGARET BONDFIELD

Born: March 17, 1873; Furnam, Somerset, England
Died: June 16, 1953; Sanderstead, Surrey, England

From humble shop assistant, Bondfield became assistant secretary of the Shop Assistants' Union and chair of the Adult Suffrage Society. Elected to Parliament from Northampton in 1923, she became the first woman chair of the Trades Union Congress in that same year, and the first woman in a British cabinet, in 1929 as minister of labour.

Early Life

Margaret Grace Bondfield was born March 17, 1873, in Furnam, near Chard, Somerset. She was the tenth of eleven children, and her family was politically active. Her father, William, a foreman and designer for a lace firm, was a Chartist and a member of the Anti-Corn Law League. Her mother, née Ann Taylor, was the daughter of an energetic Congregationalist minister, George Taylor.

After Margaret attended the local elementary school, she served as a pupil teacher. In 1886, she left for Brighton, where a sister and brother lived with an aunt. As a shop assistant, she lived in a dormitory above her employer's shop and worked a sixty-five-hour week, earning twenty-five pounds a year plus her room and board. In Brighton she was befriended by Mrs. Hilda Martindale, a Liberal and a women's rights advocate who furthered her education. In 1894 the young Bondfield moved to London to join her brother Frank, a printer and trade unionist, who introduced her to Amelia Hicks. Hicks was active in the rope and box makers' union; through her, Bondfield met Henry Mayers Hyndman, Harry Quelch, and other members of the Social Democratic Federation but was later repelled by class-war theories. Later, at the Ideal Club, she met Sidney and Beatrice Webb and George Bernard Shaw and became a member of the Fabian Society. Eventually she joined the Independent Labour Party, where she became a friend of Margaret Gladstone, soon to marry future prime minister Ramsay MacDonald. Through her brother, she also met James McPherson, secretary of the Shop Assistants' Union, and in 1897, at the age of twenty-four, she was elected to its National Executive Council.

Life's Work

The Shop Assistants' Union was founded in the 1890's and admitted members irrespective of craft or sex as long as they were employed in the industry of distribution. The union was affiliated with the Women's Trade Union League (WTUL), and Bondfield served on its General Committee. She became a confidante to its leader, Lady Emilia Dilke, who had just engineered a shift in its policy from opposition to one that favored legislative restrictions on the conditions of labor and so got more male trade-union support.

From 1896 to 1898, Bondfield joined with Edith Hogg in surveying shop assistants' working conditions for the Women's Industrial Council. Its findings led to passage of the Early Closing Act of 1904, supported by Sir John Lubbock (later Lord Avebury), although Bondfield had favored Lord Dilke's bill, which exempted local option. She lobbied for the abolition of the living-in system with the Shop Hours Act of 1906 and the inclusion of maternity benefits in the 1911 Health Insurance Act. Because of her knowledge of shop assistants' grievances and her clear, resonant voice, she was chosen assistant secretary of the Shop Assistants' Union from 1898 to 1908, with a salary of 124 pounds a year. She contributed articles to its journal, the *Shop Assistant* (founded in 1890), under the pseudonym Grace Dare. Membership in the Shop Assistants' Union grew from 2,897 in 1898 to 20,218 in 1907.

In 1899, Bondfield was the only women's delegate to Trades Union Congress (TUC) conference at Plymouth and during this period traveled widely, recruiting members for the Shop Assistants' Union. It was during one of these trips to the Glasgow area that she accomplished the conversion of Mary MacArthur to the cause of trade unions. They became inseparable friends, and when the WTUL needed a new secretary, Bondfield recommended MacArthur. In 1906, MacArthur helped found the National Federation of Women Workers (NFWW), the first general union for women. Together with MacArthur and Margaret Llewellyn Davies, and through the Women's Co-operative League, Bondfield lobbied for the passage of the Trade Boards Act of 1909. It fixed minimum wages in four of the most sweated trades employing women.

As a feminist, Bondfield also became active in the suffrage movement. From 1906 to 1909, she served as president of the Adult Suffrage Society, a group that differed with suffragettes who were willing to

Margaret Bondfield *(Library of Congress)*

accept a more limited enfranchisement of both men and women. As an ardent member of both the Independent Labour Party (ILP) and the Labour Party, Bondfield opposed limited suffrage because it might hamper the cause of socialism. In 1907, she debated Teresa Billington-Grieg, a leading member of the Women's Freedom League, which supported limited suffrage. Twice, in 1910 and 1913, Bondfield, as an ILP candidate, unsuccessfully contested a seat on the London County Council from Woolrich. Eventually she supported the Suffrage Act of 1918, even though it granted only heads-of-household suffrage to women over the age of thirty. Later, in 1928, Bondfield and Anne Godwin lobbied to extend the vote to women over twenty-one.

These activities took their toll, and in 1908, exhausted and depressed, she took a holiday in Switzerland. Bondfield loved travel and in 1910 spent five months studying labor and social problems in Lawrence, Massachusetts, and in Chicago. On both trips she was accompanied by Maud Ward, a cooking expert, with whom she shared a home in Hampstead for most of her life. Upon her return to England she resumed lecturing, and while in Lancashire, she collapsed during a speech. She subsequently resigned her position with the Shop Assistants' Union. After two years' total rest, she returned to social service activities in October, 1912. As a lobbyist for the Women's Industrial Council and aided by Clementina Black, she researched the conditions of work of married women in the Yorkshire woolen industry. Between 1912 and the outbreak of World War I, she became organizing secretary of the Women's Labour League and participated in the campaigns of the Women's Cooperative League for minimum wage, maternity, and child welfare schemes.

In August, 1914, when war threatened, Bondfield opposed British involvement. She arrived at her pacifism through characteristic self-education after reading J. A. Hobson's *Imperialism* (1902), Norman Angell's *Europe's Optical Illusion* (1909), and Henry N. Brailsford's *The War of Steel and Gold* (1915). She also joined E. D. Morrell's Union of Democratic Control. On August 6, 1914, Bondfield, along with Mac-Arthur, Marion Philips, and Susan Lawrence, formed the War Emergency Workers' National Committee to protect working-class interests during hostilities. Bondfield was also a member of the Central Committee on Women's Employment and the Trade Union Advisory Committee of the Ministry of Munitions. The first provided workshops for approximately nine thousand unemployed women, while the latter, established July 17, 1917, by Winston Churchill, tried to ease friction between the government and the NFWW, the Workers' Union, and the National Union of General Workers. Bondfield's main energies during the war, however, were devoted to the work of organizing secretary of the NFWW.

Shortly after the war began in March of 1915, Bondfield resumed her peace efforts and with Philips attended the Women's International of Socialists and Labor Organizations, in Berne, Switzerland. It called for peace without annexation and self-determination for all minorities. Later, in 1917, as attitudes toward the war hardened, the government refused her permission to travel to the Stockholm peace conference; to an American Federation of Labour conference in the United States; and to the Women's International League for Peace and Freedom Conference at The Hague. This probably resulted from her close association with MacDonald's call for a negotiated peace and opposition to consumption.

After World War I, Bondfield resumed her international travels and attended the initial conference of the International Labour Organization in Washington, D.C. In 1920, she was a member of the joint delegation of the TUC and Labour Party to the Soviet Union. While her experiences led her to oppose British intervention in the civil war there, the trip revealed to her the dictatorial nature of Communism, and in 1920 she opposed the application of the British Communist Party for affiliation with the Labour Party. After 1923 she felt ideologically estranged from most of the new leaders of the Independent Labour Party.

Also after the war, the NFWW merged with the National Union of General and Municipal Workers (NUGMW). When Mary MacArthur, her closest friend, died in January, 1921, Bondfield assumed the post of chief women's officer (a post that MacArthur had been slated to fill) and held it until 1938. The amalgamation of the NFWW saw women gradually squeezed out of most leadership positions by men. When confronted by the NUGMW's abolition both of its separate Women's District and provision for a woman on the General Council (thus reducing her to figurehead status), Bondfield threatened to resign. She was dissuaded only by being given "complete control of all national women's questions."

Ironically, in September, 1923, by the rota system, Bondfield became the first female chair of the TUC General Council, a post she relinquished when, after two previous failures to win a seat in Parliament at Northampton, she succeeded in 1923. She then served as parliamentary secretary to Thomas Shaw, minister of labour for the first Labour government. In the election of October, 1924, she was defeated. Later, as a member of the TUC General Council, she supported the General Strike of 1926 and also Ernest Bevin's decision to call it off. In 1926, at Wallsend, she was returned to Parliament and at that time signed the Blanesburgh Committee's report recommending the lowering of benefits and abolition of extended benefits, but the extension of the "not genuinely seeking work" clause. This led to her censure by the NUGMW and the Shop Assistants' Union and the greatest battle of her political life. She successfully fought off the attack of a minority of extremists before the TUC, the Labour Party, and her local constituency.

In 1929, Bondfield was reelected to Parliament by defeating Wal Hannington and a Tory candidate. Hannington even lost his deposit. Ramsay MacDonald appointed her minister of labour, making her the first female cabinet minister and privy councillor. In the face of the depression in July, 1930, and after March unemployment figures rose to 1.7 million, Bondfield called for an increase in the insurance funds borrowing power to sixty million pounds. With the help of the Morris Committee, she managed to eliminate the "genuinely seeking work" clause, although the "Anomalies" [Unemployment Insurance No. 3] Bill in 1931 did deprive some married persons of benefits in order to reduce public expenditures. When MacDonald formed the National government, Bondfield stayed with the Labour Party and lost her seat in 1931; she was defeated again in 1935. She also lost her seat on the TUC General Council and, in 1938, retired as Chief Woman Officer of the NUGMW.

Bondfield continued her interest in women's economic and social problems, and in 1938 she helped found the Women's Group on Public Welfare and was its chairperson from 1938 to 1945. In 1938, she lectured in the United States, and when World War II began, she made another tour, sponsored by the British Information Services. She also organized voluntary services for civilian evacuation. She died June 16, 1953, at age eighty.

Summary
Margaret Bondfield's worldview was influenced by her early religious beliefs and later socialist education. Sincere and good-natured, she was a team player and was content to play second fiddle to MacArthur in the WTUL. Bondfield also had the courage of her convictions, as when she differed with the suffragettes in support of adult suffrage. She also was a realist, making the best of a hopeless situation when the NFWW was amalgamated with the NUGMW. Her views as a cabinet minister were made in the light of international monetary reality, not narrow sectarian interest or the grandstand play. She received many honors, including an honorary doctor of laws degree from Bristol University in 1929 and the Freedom of Chard, her hometown, in 1930. Few women achieved as many positions of power and accomplished as much social amelioration starting from such humble beginnings.

Bibliography
Banks, Olive. *Faces of Feminism: A Study of a Social Movement*. New York: St. Martin's Press, 1981. The best balanced treatment of the subject.

Bondfield, Margaret. *A Life's Work*. London: Hutchinson, 1949. A useful autobiography filled with vignettes of early trade-union personalities, but one which is reticent about flaws and silent on some subjects.

Boston, Sarah. *Women Workers and the Trade Union Movement*. London: Davis Poynter, 1980. A consistently sympathetic and uncritical treatment of the topic and particularly valuable after World War II.

Caine, Barbara. *English Feminism, 1780-1980*. Oxford, England: Oxford University Press, 1997.

Clegg, H. A. *General Union in a Changing Society: A Short History of the National Union of General and Municipal Workers, 1889-1964*. Oxford, England: Basil Blackwell, 1964. Good on the consolidation of the NFWW with the NUGMW.

Hamilton, Mary Agnes. *Margaret Bondfield*. London: Leonard Parsons, 1924. Written by a friend and contemporary, before Bondfield had to make hard choices.

Lewenbak, Shiela. *Women and Trade Unions*. London: Ernest Benn, 1977. Excellent history of women's trade unions, but almost entirely omits textile industry.

Liddington, Jill, and Jill Norris. *One Hand Tied Behind Us: The Rise of the*

Women's Suffrage Movement. London: Virago, 1983. A lively, incisive treatment which re-creates the past.

Soldon, Norbert C. *Women in British Trade Unions, 1874-1976.* Dublin: Gill and Macmillan, 1978. A balanced and comprehensive treatment of the subject.

Norbert C. Soldon

BOUDICCA

Born: First century A.D.; Britain
Died: A.D. 60; Central Britain

Having endured flogging and the violation of her daughters, Boudicca led a rebellion of the Britons against the Roman invaders. Although the Romans were caught by surprise and lost three cities burned by the rebels, the uprising was quelled, and Boudicca herself died by taking poison.

Early Life

Boudicca was born and grew up in iron-age Britain, which was in the process of subjugation and colonization by imperial Rome. Her place and date of birth and her parentage are not known; nor in fact are any details of her early life except that she married Prasutagus, who was allowed by the Romans to rule his tribe, the Iceni, as a client king. By him, she had two daughters who were probably teenagers by A.D. 60. It seems likely that Boudicca was born circa A.D. 20 to A.D. 30. Two classical authors provide the known extended written accounts of Boudicca: The Agricola and Annals (c. A.D. 100) of Tacitus and the History of Rome by Dio Cassius (late second century A.D.). Many archaeological finds have tended to confirm the written accounts: coins, pottery, and ruins of forts and buildings. Tacitus is generally accepted as the more reliable historian, because he wrote only forty years after the events and because his father-in-law, Julius Agricola, was a high official in the colonial administration at the time of Boudicca's revolt. Also, the work of Dio Cassius has survived only in the form of a summary, or "epitome," made by the monk Xiphilinus of Trapezus in the eleventh century.

The first Roman military adventure in Britain was that of Julius Caesar in 55 B.C. After several skirmishes with the Britons in which the Romans were largely victorious, Caesar withdrew, only to return again the next year with additional troops and cavalry. Some Britons, fearing destruction, made peace and agreed to pay tribute to Rome; others in more remote regions held out fiercely. Distracted by signs of trouble in Gaul, Caesar withdrew again, leaving further conquests to others in the reign of the emperor Claudius, more than a hundred years later.

In A.D. 43, Roman legions led by Aulus Plautius landed in Britain and campaigned against the many tribes of the island in order to bring them under Roman rule. In awe of Roman might, and seeking advantage over other tribes, some leaders made deals with Rome and were allowed to rule as client kings. Others withdrew to the west into Wales to wage guerrilla warfare.

The most effective leader of resistance against the Romans was Caratacus, who continued to rally support for his cause even after a decisive Roman victory near the river Medway. These events occurred during the girlhood and young womanhood of Boudicca. Her husband Prasutagus was allowed to rule his tribe, the Iceni, as a client king, a sort of intermediary between the Romans, who were the real rulers, and the people.

When Aulus Plautius retired, he was replaced by the experienced and stern general Publius Ostorius Scapula, who arrived in Britain just in time to confront serious uprisings in the West, led by Caratacus. In order to prevent an attack from behind while chasing Caratacus, Scapula ordered all the British tribes to be disarmed, and he established a colony of retired military men at Camulodunum (modern Colchester) that he hoped would be a stabilizing influence. These measures were resented by the Britons, more so because the Romans of the colony lorded it over them, taking their property and treating them as slaves. Eventually, Caratacus fled to the north and was betrayed to the Romans by Queen Cartimandua, who needed to curry Roman favor in return for protection against other tribes. In A.D. 51, Caratacus was taken to Rome in chains. About this time, Scapula died and was succeeded by Didius Gallus, who remained as governor until A.D. 58.

Gallus had to deal with uprisings in the north and with continual trouble with the Silures, a tribe in Wales. Upon the death of Emperor Claudius, Gallus retired in favor of Veranius, who died within a year, but not before waging a vigorous campaign against the Silures. His efforts were continued and expanded by the next governor, Suetonius Paulinus, who had served with distinction in North Africa and who was a specialist in mountain warfare. The death of Prasutagus in A.D. 59 brought on the events for which his widow Boudicca has become famous.

Life's Work

Prasutagus had become wealthy and knew of the Romans' greed and contempt for the rights of the Britons. He made a will leaving half of his estate to the Emperor Nero, thinking thus to protect the enforcement of the will and to preserve some of the estate for his wife and daughters. Nevertheless, the local Roman officials, under command of the procurator Catus Decianus, sought to plunder the estate for their own benefit. Boudicca's objections were met with brutality; she herself was scourged, and her daughters were raped.

Far from the quietus they had sought, the Romans soon found they had stirred a hornet's nest. The Iceni and their allies gathered in a horde that may have numbered in the tens of thousands. They descended on the hated encampment of Camulodunum, where a huge temple to the recently deified Claudius was under construction, built with British taxes and British slave labor. In spite of the arrival of two hundred Roman troops, the defenders of Camulodunum were driven into the temple of Claudius and annihilated, their whole town burned and looted. A legion commanded by Petillius Cerealis marched to the relief of Camulodunum but was ambushed and suffered severe losses, Cerealis barely escaping with his life.

The Britons, excited by victory and looting, approached London, which was little more than a village with few defenses. Meanwhile, Suetonius Paulinus had been in the far west on the island of Mona (Anglesey), where his forces had destroyed a druid stronghold and cut down the sacred groves of the cult. He sped to London to see what could be done, but he decided that the city had to be abandoned to the rebels. Catus Decianus fled to Gaul to save himself from the common fate.

Boudicca and her forces burned London to the ground and killed everyone they found there, including Britons they regarded as turncoats. Even today, there is a layer of ashes about 17 feet beneath the surface in London testifying to the holocaust. The rebels then turned to Verulamium (St. Albans) and sacked it, massacring the occupants, mostly Britons who had befriended the Romans.

Meanwhile, Suetonius Paulinus withdrew to the west and north of London because he needed time to gather provisions. He also sought reinforcements from the legion commanded by Poenius Posthumus stationed near Exeter. Preparing for the approach of the Britons, Paulinus moved his forces to a carefully chosen battlefield in a canyon with a forest behind it. The exact location is unknown, but it may have been near Mancetter, where the horde of Britons confronted the ordered ranks of the Romans. So confident were the Britons that all of their families were drawn up behind them in wagons to watch the battle. Boudicca rode on a chariot with her daughters and exhorted the men and women of her army, reciting her grievances against the Romans and urging the Britons to fight for freedom.

Tall and serious in mien, Boudicca was an impressive figure, with fair, waist-long hair and dressed in a multicolored tunic and long cloak. Suetonius Paulinus told his men to ignore the cries of the attacking savages and to press on with their spears and swords, forgetting thoughts of plunder but intent on victory and the glory it would bring.

The Britons attacked with wild, warlike shouting and trumpet blasts, brandishing their yard-long swords, some of them naked with their skins painted with intricate designs in blue. The Romans waited in orderly ranks, wearing armor of steel and leather strips and equipped with shields, spears, and short, thick swords.

The Romans carried the day by superior discipline and benefit of the terrain. After showering the rebels with spears, the Roman phalanx drove ahead, forcing the Britons back into their wagons. In the rout that followed, the Romans put to death anyone they could catch, including the pack animals. Boudicca took poison and died rather than accept capture and humiliation. The Roman reinforcements from Exeter failed to arrive in time for the battle, depriving them and their commander Poenius Posthumus from a share in the glory of victory. It is not known whether Posthumus delayed because he feared being ambushed on the way or because he was involved in other military actions. In any event, he felt sufficient shame that he killed himself by falling on his sword. It is asserted that eighty thousand people died in the battle.

In revenge for the uprising, Paulinus and his army swept through the lands of the Iceni, burning crops, looting, and killing anyone they suspected of aiding the rebels. Boudicca was reportedly buried in a magnificent tomb, which has never been found.

Summary

Boudicca's rebellion and its aftermath were probably the bloodiest events ever to occur on British soil. The Romans were forced to the realization that their terror tactics had led to unacceptable losses and that a more diplomatic policy was needed. Many more years were required for the pacification of Britain, and the Caledonians in the north were never completely subdued. Increased trade and the wealth it brought to cooperative Britons was a major factor in pacification.

The memory of Boudicca turned to the stuff of legend, and she became the symbol of freedom and independence for the British. Her story was retold many times in literature by such authors as Ben Jonson, William Cowper, Alfred, Lord Tennyson, and others. An opera has also been written by Gillian Carcas.

Queen Elizabeth I and Queen Victoria were both compared with Boudicca, and it is thought that the name "Boudicca" (also spelled Boadicea and Boudica) probably means "victory" in the Celtic language. A statue of Boudicca in London made by Thomas Thornycroft was placed near the Houses of Parliament in 1902. It depicts the heroine and her daughters on a huge chariot quite unlike the small Celtic war chariots described by Julius Caesar.

Bibliography

Dio Cassius. *Dio's Roman History*. Translated by E. Cary. Cambridge, Mass.: Harvard University Press, 1961. Boudicca's revolt is discussed in volume 8.

Dudley, D. R., and G. Webster. *The Rebellion of Boudicca*. New York: Barnes & Noble, 1962. This and Webster's 1978 book (cited below) are major works devoted solely to Boudicca. Legends and traditions are covered as well as history. Portions of Tacitus's *Annals* and *Agricola* describing the rebellion are quoted at length in an appendix, both in the original Latin and in translation.

Fraser, Antonia. *The Warrior Queens*. New York: Alfred A. Knopf, 1989. Interesting account of women who assumed roles of power usually reserved for men. Boudicca is considered the archetypal "warrior queen" and is discussed alongside Cleopatra, Golda Meir, Margaret Thatcher, and others.

Ireland, S. *Roman Britain: A Sourcebook*. London: Routledge, 1996. Translations are provided for selections from Tacitus and Dio Cassius.

Mikalachki, Jodi. *The Legacy of Boadicea: Gender and Nation in Early Modern England*. New York: Routledge, 1998. Examines ancient British history and the role of women as soldiers in literature, such as in William Shakespeare's plays *Cymbeline* (pr. c. 1609-1610) and *King Lear* (pr. c. 1605-1606).

Salway, Peter. *Roman Britain*. Oxford, England: Clarendon Press, 1981. Part of the *Oxford History of England* series. Scholarly account of history (55 B.C. to A.D. 449), culture, economy, and religion. Extensive bibliography and maps.

Tacitus. *Tacitus on Britain and Germany*. Translated by H. Mattingly. West Drayton, England: Penguin Books, 1948. Pages 64-67 treat the revolt of Boudicca.

_____. *Tacitus on Imperial Rome*. Translated by M. Grant. Baltimore: Penguin Books, 1956. Pages 317-321 provide the most reliable classical source for Boudicca's revolt.

Webster, Graham. *Boudica*. Totowa, N.J.: Rowman & Littlefield, 1978. The 1962 book by Webster and Dudley cited above has been updated to incorporate extensive new archaeological findings from excavations at London, Verulamium, and Colchester. Includes photographs of coins, inscriptions, and other artifacts and views of sites observed from aircraft.

John R. Phillips

JANE BYRNE

Born: May 24, 1934; Chicago, Illinois

Active in Democratic politics since 1960 and in Chicago city administration since 1964, Byrne was the first woman to be elected mayor of Chicago.

Early Life

Jane Byrne was born Jane Margaret Burke on May 24, 1934, when her family resided at 6503 N. Claremont in Chicago. Her parents, William and Katharine (Nolan) Burke, had married in 1929; despite the Depression, their modest circumstances soon improved, and they moved their "lace curtain Irish" household to Sauganash, a fashionable neighborhood on Chicago's northwest side. The warm, bright, ambitious son of a blacksmith, Bill Burke worked his way up from clerk to vice president of Inland Steel. In 1940, he formed Gordon-Burke Steel and later became the Steel Warehousemen Association's national president. Burke was a successful member of the "North Side Irish" elite.

"Janie" was the second of six children. Their mother, Katharine Nolan Burke, was strong-willed and well-read; she reared them by strict principles, within an insular Roman Catholic family structure. Janie attended Queen of All Saints Parish grammar school and all-girl St. Scholastica high school, graduating in 1951; she was an exemplary, serious student, though shy. At St. Mary-of-the-Woods College in Terre Haute, Indiana, she majored in biology and premedical studies, but grew homesick.

Transferring to all-female Barat College of the Sacred Heart, in wealthy north suburban Lake Forest, Jane Burke fit in well. She had impressive Catholic social credentials: Jane's uncle, the Right Reverend Monsignor Edward M. Burke, was the chancellor of Chicago's archdiocese; uncle Joseph Burke was also a priest. Jane had traveled with her uncle Ed to Rome in 1950, enjoying an audience with Pope Pius XII. She debuted at Samuel Cardinal Stritch's Presentation Ball of 1955.

Notably studious, shy, and ambitious, Jane made weekend treks to Notre Dame, where "Barat girls" hunted upwardly mobile Catholic husbands. During her junior year, Jane fell in love with William P. Byrne, a Naval ROTC student. They were graduated in 1955; Byrne was commissioned a Marine Corps officer, and from 1955 to 1956, Jane taught fourth grade at St. Juliana Grade School in Chicago. Rejecting a medical career, Jane Burke married Bill Byrne on New Year's Eve, 1956, satisfying 1950's social expectations.

The Byrnes were posted to Florida, Texas, and North Carolina. Jane delivered their daughter, Katharine Crane Byrne, in Chicago on December 31, 1957. Shortly before his scheduled discharge, Bill Byrne was killed on the foggy night of May 30, 1959, when his plane crashed at Glenview Naval Air Station. Jane Byrne was a widow at age twenty-five, with a seventeen-month-old daughter. This tragedy rerouted the course of Jane Margaret Burke Byrne's life: She would not follow her beloved mother's domestic footsteps.

Life's Work

Jane Byrne assuaged her grief by joining her sister Carol on John F. Kennedy's 1960 presidential campaign. As a secretary for Margaret Zuehlke, executive director of Illinois Citizens for Kennedy, Byrne made important contacts with local and national Democratic Party supporters. After Kennedy was elected by a historically close margin— put over the top by Daley's Chicago machine—Jane Byrne attended education classes, received her master's degree from the University of Illinois at Chicago, and again taught grade school. A 1964 encounter with Chicago Mayor Richard J. Daley nudged Byrne back into politics.

Daley told Byrne to do political work in Sauganash, the city's Thirty-ninth Ward. As a reward for paying these political dues, Daley promised to secure a patronage position for Byrne. In the summer of 1964, Jane Byrne was hired at Head Start, controlled by the Chicago Commission on Urban Opportunity (CCUO), an agency created by Lyndon Johnson's Economic Opportunity Act. Byrne soon left Head Start for a personnel slot in the CCUO itself. She also continued her work on behalf of the city's Democratic machine, in part, organizing socials.

In March of 1968, Daley appointed Byrne to serve as commissioner of the small Chicago Department of Consumer Sales, Weights, and Measures. Some commentators believed her to be unqualified; she seemed Daley's "token woman." Commissioner Byrne controlled city inspection and regulation of consumer affairs, such as retail unit pricing, retail advertising, and toy safety. Byrne immediately leveled gender-based pay differentials among inspectors and began eliminating department corruption. She enforced fair inspection of retailers in poor neighborhoods, where grocery price gouging ran rampant; she pushed through a landmark ordinance banning phosphates in detergents. In 1973, her department prompted the Federal Trade Commission to undertake an antitrust investigation of Checker and Yellow Cabs, divisions of one company which controlled 80 percent of Chicago taxis. Consumer rights activist Ralph Nader applauded Byrne's efforts.

Byrne rode the consumerism wave of the 1970's to public visibility. As a relatively "clean" commissioner within the corrupt machine, her political clout rose. After the 1972 national convention, Mayor Daley made Byrne the new Illinois member of the Democratic National Committee, where she chaired the powerful Resolutions Committee. Daley appointed Byrne cochair of the Cook County Democratic Central Committee in January of 1975, clearly signalling Byrne's ascendance in the machine hierarchy.

Richard J. Daley died in December, 1976. Despite her status as a Daley protégé, Jane Byrne was maneuvered aside by male members of Chicago's Democratic political machine. Michael Bilandic became interim mayor; George Dunne replaced Byrne as cochair of the County Committee. Byrne, however, was still head of a second-class cog, the Democratic Women of Cook County and Chicago, and she remained in office as commissioner of the Department of Consumer Sales, Weights, and Measures. Oversight of the city's public vehicle licenses had been transferred to Byrne's department under Daley; when Bilandic sponsored a questionable cab fare increase in November, 1977, Byrne blew the whistle. The post-Daley machine cut Byrne off: Her dismissal exploded into a media spectacle.

The public appreciated "Fighting Jane" Byrne's gutsy demeanor, and her speaking engagements established grassroots support for a mayoral run. On St. Patrick's Day in 1978, Byrne married Chicago journalist Jay McMullen. Shortly thereafter, Byrne announced her candidacy for the office of mayor. Byrne's shoestring campaign used constant personal contact with the voters to advantage. Byrne preached "change" and reform, criticized "business as usual" in City Hall, and forged a multicultural voter coalition. Luck helped, since the frigid winter of 1979 burdened Chicago with catastrophic, record snowfalls. Bilandic's administration failed miserably at snow removal, and Byrne lambasted Bilandic and his machine for incompetence.

Byrne won the February primary after a record turnout; she won the general election on April 3, 1979, with a startling 82 percent of the vote.

Jane Byrne was sworn in as mayor of the city of Chicago on April 15, 1979, the first female mayor of any major American city. Mayor Byrne faced grave problems. She had promised to improve Chicago's neighborhoods and aging infrastructure; she learned "the city that works" was verging on bankruptcy as 1970's inflation peaked in 1980. A transit strike loomed; Byrne had promised all city workers union contracts. The Democratic machine remained in place and was only semicooperative; State's Attorney Richard M. Daley (son of the late mayor) soon targeted Byrne's administration with investigations. Byrne's aggressive public persona both aided and hindered her progress.

Chicago Transit Authority workers went on strike in December of 1979, exposing Byrne's lack of a contingency plan, but shortly returned to work after succumbing to pressure from business interests. Chicago's end-of-year deficit of $102 million denied Byrne an easy solution to a $101 million shortfall in the public school system budget. The state of Illinois split bailout costs with the city, but in January of 1980, the teachers went out on strike. Byrne played a major role in the final settlement of the education crisis, but the city faced greater difficulties when it confronted what one historian has called a "strike-a-month schedule." Politically conservative firefighters struck in February, 1980, endangering the public safety during midwinter, and public opinion helped Byrne propel the firefighters back to work without a contract. The media often criticized Byrne for indecision and an acidic style during these three major strikes in her first mayoral year, yet she settled them by displaying a remarkable "sense of fiscal responsibility," according to Melvin G. Holli.

Byrne balanced the city budget every full year of her term (1980-1982); an unanticipated fifteen-million-dollar deficit occurred in 1983, when she left office at midyear. The balanced budgets were accomplished by adopting unpopular austerity measures, such as initiating city worker layoffs, and some tax increases. To her credit, Byrne had not juggled the books or raided earmarked funds as previous administrations had. The city's bond ratings dropped, then improved. Byrne even launched some major development initiatives, such as 1981 revitalization plans for the city's North Loop district, a transit extension to and major renovation plan for O'Hare International Airport, an extension of the Chicago Transit Authority's rail service on the city's southwest side, and basic infrastructure improvements. She continued to support ChicagoFest, begun by Michael Bilandic, while initiating Taste of Chicago and various neighborhood festivals.

Byrne believed in public drama and spectacle, gaining popular approval. Her battles with the Chicago media were legendary. Byrne's political postures could flip-flop dizzyingly: She apparently offered Jimmy Carter her support at a 1980 election fund-raiser, but announced support of Edward Kennedy two weeks later. Political drama sometimes backfired. In 1981, Byrne's two-week tenancy in Cabrini-Green, a Chicago housing project suffering protracted gang violence, was widely praised for boldness and widely ridiculed as "grandstanding." She increased police, maintenance, and education provisions in public housing, with only short-term consequences. She also increased, then cut minority hiring. One study noted that 47 percent of employees hired between 1980 and 1981 were black in a city with an African American population at 40 percent; 28 percent of new hires in 1982 were black. Byrne seemed racist defending her white Chicago Housing Authority (CHA) head against a 1982 federal agency power grab, realigning the CHA board's racial balance with controversial white appointees.

Poor ethnic relations hindered Byrne's reelection bid. The 1983 Democratic primary pitted Byrne against African American Congressman Harold Washington and white State's Attorney Richard M. Daley; the contest was racially polarized. Incumbent Byrne was a woman, with a mixed record, with limited (white) machine support and flagging minority support. Harold Washington won the Democratic primary with 36 percent of the vote; Byrne received 34 percent, and Daley netted 30 percent. Byrne withdrew her brief write-in candidacy; Washington won the bitterly fought general election.

Twice more, Jane Byrne ran unsuccessfully for mayor. She and Washington squared off in the March, 1987, Democratic primary, in which Washington polled a scant majority of the record turnout. After his election, Washington attempted to slate Byrne for clerk of the circuit court, but the machine refused. Byrne challenged Richard M. Daley in the February, 1991, Democratic primary, but came in a distant third. Jane Byrne also served as a political commentator; in 1992, she published her autobiography, *My Chicago*.

Summary

Jane Byrne's political career was startling in its contradictions. A privileged child, she became a civil servant. A machine functionary, she ran a "clean" city department. A 1979 mayoral long shot, she became the first woman to hold that office, yet she failed to support the Equal Rights Amendment. A coalition-builder, she became a divisive figure in City Hall despite her various administrative achievements. In the final analysis, although her credentials as an Irish-Catholic Democrat were impeccable, she could not maintain the power for which Richard J. Daley groomed her.

Because Jane Byrne was a woman, she faced constant opposition from male Democrats and the press. Her inability to present a stable, competent public image—regardless of actual performance quality—led to her rapid political downfall. One survey rating six recent Chicago mayors ranked Byrne fifth overall, but third for "accomplishments." Her most visible legacies are the Chicago Transit Authority and infrastructure projects as well as the summer festivals; her handling of "hard" issues— major strikes, budgeting, race relations—may acquire future cachet, but her later "perennial candidacy" seriously tarnished her reputation.

Bibliography

Byrne, Jane. *My Chicago*. New York: W. W. Norton, 1992. A sometimes self-serving, but readable, anecdotal autobiography that encompasses the history of Chicago, Byrne's genealogy, and her entire political career, especially her association with Richard J. Daley and her own term as mayor. Its Chicago-centered bibliography is wide-ranging.

_____. "One Minute: Citizen Jane." Interview by Rebecca Cutler. *Chicago* 48, no. 4 (April, 1999): 19. Byrne discusses former Chicago mayor Richard Daley and her activities after leaving office.

FitzGerald, Kathleen Whalen. *Brass: Jane Byrne and the Pursuit of Power*. Chicago: Contemporary Books, 1981. Relying heavily on personal interviews of Byrne's friends and family, this extremely sympathetic biography is notable mainly for its germane explication of Byrne's Catholic, "lace curtain" Irish background and worldview.

Gove, Samuel K., and Louis H. Masotti, eds. *After Daley: Chicago Politics in Transition*. Urbana: University of Illinois Press, 1982. Essays by

Samuel Gove and Milton Rakove in this academic collection address Jane Byrne's mayoralty, complementing other essays addressing Chicago concerns. Rakove's explicit analysis is interesting, though undocumented.

Granger, Bill, and Lori Granger. *Fighting Jane: Mayor Jane Byrne and the Chicago Machine*. New York: Dial Press, 1980. This critical, occasionally hostile, biased account coauthored by a well-known, reactionary Chicago newspaper columnist details the Byrne mayoralty through 1980, incorporating Byrne's biography.

Green, Paul M., and Melvin G. Holli, eds. *The Mayors: The Chicago Political Tradition*. Carbondale: Southern Illinois University Press, 1987. Holli's essay analyzing Byrne's mayoral administration offers an astute, concise account of major events and objectively assesses its positive and negative outcomes; his expert survey rating recent mayors provides perspective.

Rivlin, Gary. *Fire on the Prairie: Chicago's Harold Washington and the Politics of Race*. New York: Henry Holt, 1992. In explaining how Harold Washington, Chicago's first African American mayor, succeeded Byrne, Rivlin lends significant perspective on Byrne's tenure and on her unsuccessful campaigns after 1983, particularly emphasizing minority communities and racial problems.

Penelope J. Engelbrecht

KIM CAMPBELL

Born: March 10, 1947; Port Alberni, British Columbia, Canada

As Canada's first female prime minister, Campbell advanced the quest of North American women for high political office.

Early Life

Avril Phaedra "Kim" Campbell was born on March 10, 1947, in Port Alberni, British Columbia. Her father, George, was a Canadian soldier in World War II who later became a lawyer. George Campbell married Lissa Cook in 1944. Their first child, Alix, was born in 1945, followed by Avril Phaedra two years later.

After struggling to establish himself professionally for several years, George became a successful lawyer and moved his family into the suburbs. A liberal, enlightened father, he encouraged his younger daughter to excel at her studies and explore her interests in the arts. By the time she entered high school, she was recognized as the most talented and intelligent student in her class. Yet behind the veil of serene success, there was trouble at home. The Campbells were divorcing, and in the aftermath of the split Lissa did not see her daughters for ten years. It was during this period that Avril Phaedra assumed the nickname "Kim."

Kim Campbell was valedictorian of her high school class in 1964. Despite her obvious promise, her life remained tentative and provisional during her early adulthood. Campbell earned an honors degree in political science from the University of British Columbia in Vancouver. Even though the late 1960's were the height of radical agitation in North America over involvement in the Vietnam War, Campbell's politics had already taken on a moderate-conservative coloring.

In 1967, Campbell began to date Nathan Divinsky, a mathematics professor twenty-two years her senior. Divinsky, a brilliant but erratic intellectual, introduced Campbell to a wider world of thought and discourse. The couple began living together as Campbell pursued her master's degree in international relations at the University of British Columbia. With Divinsky's aid, Campbell won a scholarship to study at the London School of Economics. Here, her conservative political views were cemented. In 1972, she married Divinsky, and they returned to Canada shortly thereafter. Campbell tried to look for teaching jobs, but since she had not completed any advanced degree she could only get the most lowly and temporary positions.

Life's Work

Kim Campbell decided to abandon a teaching career in academia and, like her father, earn a law degree. Once again, she excelled as a student, and her achievement began to awaken thoughts of a political career. In 1980, Campbell won a seat on the Vancouver school board.

By 1983, Campbell was chair of the school board. Her increasing public prominence strained her marriage to Divinsky, and in that year the couple divorced. As school board chair, Campbell earned notoriety for her vociferous attacks on trade unions. At the same time that she was accepted as an associate at a prestigious Vancouver law firm, she tried to move up in politics, running for the provincial parliament. Even though she lost, Campbell had found her true vocation.

Campbell abandoned her career as a private attorney when she was hired to work in the office of William Bennett, the premier of British Columbia. When Bennett resigned, Campbell entered the race to replace him. As a total unknown, she lagged far behind the leaders, but her effort nevertheless garnered her a seat in the provincial legislature in October, 1986.

Campbell generated controversy and earned acclaim as an advocate of women's rights when she opposed the antiabortion views of the new premier. As a consequence, she alienated the right-wing leaders of the Social Credit Party, known for its advocacy of conservative political views in British Columbia. Realizing that her climb up the political ladder would be severely restricted if she remained in provincial politics, Campbell began to cast her eye toward the federal arena.

Meeting with important local leaders of the ruling national Progressive Conservative (Tory) Party, Campbell impressed them with her drive and ambition. When a parliamentary seat opened up some months later, Campbell decided to run. Although initially reluctant to leave British Columbia, Campbell soon thrived in the political atmosphere of Ottawa. Strenuously championing Prime Minister Brian Mulroney's free trade agreement with the United States, Campbell won election by a narrow margin.

Campbell moved to Ottawa, where she began drawing attention. Campbell was soon named to Brian Mulroney's cabinet, as minister of state for northern affairs and political development. In the Canadian parliamentary system, unlike American politics, legislators must also be administrators. Campbell's smooth mastery of both challenges brought her much praise from senior Tories.

Campbell broke through to the leadership ranks of the federal party in 1990, when Mulroney appointed her to serve as Canada's first female attorney general. Campbell's agenda was primarily focused on one issue: gun control. Drafting a proposed bill that would fortify existing gun control laws, she devoted many months to shepherding her bill through a sullen and fractious Parliament. Her vigorous efforts were vindicated when the bill was successfully passed in September, 1991. Although staunch in her support of conservative law and order issues, Campbell emerged as an unconventional and unpredictable politician. Despite her conservative background, she argued that much of Canadian law was biased in favor of white males, and she overtly campaigned for women's rights.

The Mulroney government, like the administration of Ronald Reagan in the United States, had reaped political profit from the economic boom years of the 1980's. In the wake of the worldwide recession that began in 1990, Mulroney's popularity, which had been sufficient to ensure his reelection two years before, plummeted. By 1993, the Tories had been in power for nine years and were increasingly regarded as stale, outmoded, and likely to lose in the election that had to be called by autumn of 1993. As one of the few fresh faces in the party, Campbell saw her popularity and political eligibility soar. Her political strength was acknowledged when Mulroney asked Campbell to serve as defense minister in January of 1993. Once again, Campbell had broken a barrier, receiving an appointment to a post not traditionally occupied by women. No sooner, though, had she attained this post than Campbell began to be spoken of as a possible candidate to succeed Mulroney as prime minister.

After desperate attempts to secure, successively, the jobs of the secretary-general of the United Nations and the commissioner of the National Hockey League for himself, the dismally unpopular Mulroney resigned in March, 1993, and Campbell immediately entered the race to be his successor as Tory party leader. Since in Canada's parliamentary system the leader of the ruling party automatically becomes prime minister, if Campbell won the Tory race she would be prime minister as well. Campbell took an early lead in the polls, spurred by the novelty of a female prime minister and by her relative lack of association with the hated Mulroney regime. She was soon challenged, however, by an ambitious, articulate young politician from Quebec named Jean Charest. At the party convention, Campbell turned back Charest's unexpectedly strong challenge and became Canada's first female prime minster.

Things did not look rosy in the polls for the Tory party in 1993. The perceived failure of Mulroney's economic politics, and his inability to resolve the constitutional crisis precipitated by the wish of many in the French-speaking province of Quebec to withdraw from the Canadian confederation, had shriveled the party's formerly widespread support. Not only were the party's traditional rivals, the moderate-left Liberals and the socialist New Democrats, looking to gain seats, but there were two new entrants in Canadian electoral politics. One was the Reform Party, which was based in the traditionally conservative western provinces and called for free enterprise, assaults on government waste, and an end to the "special pleading" of the French Canadians for a distinct role in the country's society. The other was the Bloc Québécois, a Quebec nationalist party that siphoned off the support of many Tories in that province who had helped elect Mulroney.

Despite this severe erosion in the Tories' base of support, Campbell's first weeks in office were dynamic and impressive. She soon became the most personally popular of all the party leaders, and rallied the Tories from far behind to a respectable place in the polls. Campbell's casual, colloquial, apparently unrehearsed style was refreshing and appealing to many voters. Many women saw Campbell's prominence as a ratification of the gains of women in the workplace and in society over the past generation. Campbell generally made a good impression on Canadians and on the world during this period. Traveling to the G-7 economic summit in Tokyo to meet with the leaders of the six other major Western democracies, Campbell was compared with recently inaugurated U.S. President Bill Clinton as a member of the baby-boom generation who was bringing fresh ideas and energy into politics.

Campbell sought to capitalize on this exposure when the election was formally called in 1993. Her opponents did not think that her experience would be sufficient, intimating that Campbell's brief tenure as prime minister was only "a summer job." Campbell went on the offensive, reviling her principal opponent, Liberal Party leader Jean Chrétien, as "yesterday's man." Campbell was appealing to many Canadians not only because she was a woman but also because she was from British Columbia, an English-speaking province, and thus represented a change from the long hegemony of Quebec politicians as exemplified by Mulroney and Pierre Trudeau.

Campbell's dynamism, however, was not enough. Her performance in the televised debates between the party leaders had to be superb in order for her to make any dent in the polls, but it was only workman-like. Mulroney's legacy had saddled the Tories with an indelible stain of failure, and by the time election day came the question was not whether Campbell would lose but by how much. As fate would have it, the margin was wide. In probably the most humiliating defeat for a major party in the history of modern democratic government, the Tories lost all but two seats of the more than one hundred and fifty they had previously held. The heavy loss of support from traditional Tory voters, who had fled to either the Reform Party or the Bloc Québécois, meant that the liberal Chrétien would be the next prime minister. There was not even any personal consolation for Campbell, as she lost her own seat in Vancouver as well. Campbell, though, was still only forty-six as she left office, a mere youth as far as political careers go, and many were predicting that this was not the last time her voice would be heard in Canadian politics.

Summary

Kim Campbell's brief tenure as Canadian prime minister was truncated by the unpopularity of her predecessor, which she was powerless to change. Nevertheless, Campbell for a short time illuminated the often-drab face of Canadian politics with her individuality and irreverence. She overcame personal disappointments and family unhappiness, and her swift rise to political power demonstrated that high office in Western democracies had become as open to women as to men. Campbell's career serves as a hopeful sign of a day when Western societies will be fully democratic and everyone can be seen as having potential for leadership, whatever their background. After Campbell's stint as leader of one of the largest nations in the world, it is assured that the door will never be closed again to women seeking positions of political leadership and responsibility.

Bibliography

Campbell, Kim. *Time and Chance: The Political Memoirs of Canada's First Woman Prime Minister*. Toronto: Doubleday Canada, 1996.

Davey, Frank. *Reading "Kim" Right*. Vancouver: Talonbooks, 1993. This unusual book, by a respected Canadian poet and professor at the University of Western Ontario, examines Campbell, especially as a media image and political symbol, from the perspective of contemporary literary and cultural theory.

Dobbin, Murray, with Ellen Gould. *Kim Campbell: From School Trustee to Prime Minister*. Toronto: James Lorimer, 1993. The fullest book-length biography of Campbell, this work focuses attention on her early political career in the British Columbia of the 1980's.

Fife, Robert. *Kim Campbell: The Making of a Politician*. Toronto: HarperCollins, 1993. This book, written from the perspective of the political insider, examines Campbell in the context of the machinations of the federal government in Ottawa, especially with an eye toward evaluating her potential as a vote-getter.

Fulton, E. Kaye, and Mary Janigan. "The Real Kim Campbell." *Maclean's* 106 (May 17, 1993): 16-23. A long, detailed article that served as the primary source during the campaign for many Canadians' impression of Campbell's biography. Significant not only for what it says about Campbell but also for the image of her it presented to the voters.

Gray, Charlotte. "Singing in the Rain." *Saturday Night* 106 (October, 1991): 28-31. This early profile of Campbell on the national scene emphasizes her work as justice minister and is the best contemporary account of those years.

Swan, Susan. "The Verge." *Mirabella* 5 (August, 1993): 71-75. Written by a Toronto novelist, this profile of Campbell provides American readers with an overview of her career and explains her phenomenal success from a variety of perspectives. Mentions Campbell's provocative pose that appeared in Barbara Woodley's photographic collection, *Portraits: Canadian Women in Focus*.

Nicholas Birns

CATHERINE DE MÉDICIS

Born: April 13, 1519; Florence
Died: January 5, 1589; Blois, France

Catherine de Médicis contributed to maintaining a strong centralized monarchy in spite of challenges from noble and religious factions. Her attempts to balance Roman Catholic and Calvinist interests in France also encouraged at least a minimum of toleration in the seventeenth century.

Early Life

Catherine de Médicis's father, Lorenzo de' Medici, was *capo dello stato* in Florence, *gonfalonier* of the Church, and, after a victorious expedition, duke of Urbino. His uncle, Pope Leo X, hoping to restore the Medicis to their earlier status, arranged a marriage between Lorenzo and Madeleine de la Tour d'Auvergne, a distant relation of Francis I, king of France. The young couple were married at Amboise in 1518, and within a year their daughter was born. Two weeks later, Madeleine was dead of puerperal fever, and five days later Lorenzo also died.

The baby Catherine was the last legitimate heir of the family. Immediately, she became a tool in the hands of her guardian, Pope Leo X, and of his half brother Giulio, later Pope Clement VII, to recoup the Medici fortune. Catherine's childhood was spent in Rome and Florence, where she was at times ignored and at other times the center of attention. In 1527, during a Florentine revolution, she was the hostage of anti-Medici forces and handled her desperate situation with great diplomacy. At the age of ten, she returned to Rome, where Pope Clement VII negotiated a marriage between Catherine and Henry, the second son of Francis I.

On October 26, 1533, Catherine and Henry, both fourteen years of age, were married at Avignon. Small and thin, with strong rather than beautiful features and with the bulging eyes of the Medicis, Catherine was vivacious, self-assured, witty, bright, and eager to learn. As a new wife, she traveled everywhere with the French court and joined a group of young women, protégées of her father-in-law, to study Latin, Greek, French, mathematics, science, astronomy, and astrology. She hunted, danced, and rode using a sidesaddle she invented. Still a child

Catherine de Médicis *(Library of Congress)*

when she married Henry, she had to call upon all of her habits of diplomacy to handle two major crises. The first was her husband's attachment to his mistress Diane de Poitiers. Catherine handled this problem by being a patient and loving wife and by making an ally of her rival. The second difficulty was more critical and became especially important in 1536, when Henry's older brother died and Henry became the heir to the French throne. That difficulty was her seeming inability to bear children and the possibility that Henry would obtain a divorce to marry a fertile bride and leave Catherine without resources. Catherine's charm and vivacity saved her from this fate, and, after ten years of marriage, she presented Henry with an heir.

During the next thirteen years, Catherine bore ten children, including four sons, and settled into a mutually respectful relationship with Henry and Diane de Poitiers. When Francis died in 1547, Henry arranged a coronation ceremony for Catherine, an unusual innovation for sixteenth century French kings. In 1551, when Henry went to war in Burgundy, he left Catherine as his regent, and, although Diane was his chief adviser, he also consulted with his wife. In 1559, Catherine was one of the architects of the Treaty of Cateau-Cambrésis, which temporarily calmed the Franco-Spanish rivalry. The new amity was sealed with the marriage of Philip II of Spain and Catherine's daughter Elizabeth. A tournament was held to celebrate this alliance, and, during one event, a splinter from a broken lance pierced the French king's eye and he died.

Life's Work

Although she did not know it at the time, Catherine's life's work began with the death of her husband. Her son Francis became king at the age of fifteen. A year earlier, he had married Mary Stuart, queen of Scotland and niece of the Guises, a prominent French noble family. Mary's relatives assumed responsibility for advising the young king. If Francis II had lived, Catherine would not have become an important political figure in France. When he died, Charles IX, aged ten, assumed the throne. After observing the arrogant despotism of the Guises, Catherine determined to become regent to her son.

During her years as regent, Catherine responded to two major crises in the face of four significant enemies. One struggle was to preserve royal authority against two noble families—the Guises and the Bourbons—who were determined to dominate the king and the royal family. The Bourbons were the hereditary kings of Navarre and the next in line to inherit the throne after Catherine's sons. The other major crisis for Catherine was the religious conflict between Roman Catholics and Protestant Calvinists, called Huguenots, in France. To complicate her task, the Guises became associated with the Roman Catholic position and often looked to the Spanish for assistance, while the Bourbons, at least the queen of Navarre and her brother-in-law the fiery prince of Condé, openly adhered to the Protestant faith. Even before Francis II's death, the prince of Condé had mobilized Huguenot support against the Guises in a conspiracy aimed at kidnapping the king and executing his Guise advisers. His efforts failed, but the lines of conflict were drawn. Catherine also faced a powerful Spanish king, Philip II, who would act in his own dynastic interest even though he was Catherine's son-in-law. Finally, she had to deal with an inadequate treasury and the imminent bankruptcy of the Crown. As a woman and a foreigner, Catherine's task was doubly difficult.

The Queen Mother's response to the religious difficulties was to organize a national religious council to mediate between French Protestants and Catholics. The Colloquy of Poissy, which met in 1561, succeeded in getting the French religious parties to talk together, but it also polarized them. The Guises and other staunch Roman Catholics united and sought help from the Spanish king to challenge royal efforts at mediation. Religious passions intensified. In January, 1562, when Catherine issued the Edict of Toleration granting government protection to the Huguenots, the Catholics left the royal court, and the first of the French religious wars began.

During the next ten years, France was torn by three major civil wars motivated by religious and noble rivalry. Catherine tried desperately to maintain a balance among all these forces, but she failed. The third and most savage of the first set of religious wars ended in August, 1570, with the Peace of Saint-Germain and a backlash against the Guises and their Spanish allies. A new party, the Politique Party, grew out of this disgust with foreign influence. Composed of Roman Catholic and Huguenot moderates who believed that the integrity of the state was more important than religion, this party reflected Catherine's own position.

Catherine's diplomatic expertise became especially important in 1572, in negotiating defense treaties with the English and the Ottoman Turks against Philip II and in gaining the throne of Poland for her third son, Henry. As Henry departed for Poland, Europe was rocked by news of the Saint Bartholomew's Eve Massacre. The occasion was the wedding of Catherine's daughter Marguerite to Henry, king of Navarre, heir to the French throne after Catherine's sons. All the important nobles of France were gathered in the capital, including the Huguenot leaders. Whether Catherine and Charles IX intended to kill all the Protestants in Paris on August 23, 1572, or whether Catherine only meant to kill one or two of the Protestant leaders, the result was a massacre of Protestants by Catholics in the capital city and in other cities throughout the nation. War broke out again and, in spite of their losses, the Huguenots managed to retain several key fortresses. When Charles IX died in 1574, and Henry III returned from Poland, the new king was also unable to seize the Protestant strongholds and to subdue the opposition. In 1576, peace was negotiated on the basis of the status quo. Henry III, Catherine's favorite son, was an adult when he came to the throne, and Catherine no longer played an important policy-making role. Since the king was unmarried and preoccupied with war, his mother continued to direct the ambassadors and to send and receive letters from agents and diplomats throughout Europe.

In June, 1584, Catherine's youngest son died of influenza. Thus, the Protestant Henry of Navarre would inherit the throne if Henry III were to die. War raged, and, fearing the Spanish king would send in troops, Henry III was forced to put himself at the head of the Catholic League in order to control its excesses. The Estates General refused to grant the government more money to fight the wars they did not want. On December 23, 1588, Henry III summoned the cardinal of Guise to the royal chamber, where armed guards killed him. Shortly thereafter, Henry had the duke of Guise assassinated as well. Catherine was in the castle at Blois that evening on her deathbed when Henry carried the news of the Guises' deaths to her. She was not pleased: By destroying one faction, Henry had put himself in the hands of the other; he no longer had a weapon against the Bourbon and Protestant nobles. The collapse of Spain would give Geneva and the Calvinists the victory.

Catherine died less than two weeks later, on January 5, 1589, and her son was assassinated before the end of the year. Henry IV, the Protestant king of Navarre, officially inherited the throne, but the war continued until 1595, when he had reconquered the north and converted to Catholicism. Henry was able, however, to protect his Huguenot friends and relatives by issuing the Edict of Nantes that granted the Huguenots several armed cities and freedom to worship.

Summary

Catherine de Médicis set out to destroy the resistance to royal power, to secure for her sons the French throne, to build a government with a centralized power in the hands of the French monarchy, and to limit the authority of the nobles. She succeeded in gaining those ends even as she failed to achieve them peacefully and permanently. Accused by contemporaries and historians of being a Machiavellian, Catherine must at least plead guilty to being a realist in her exercise of power. She changed sides, made secret agreements, and even sent ambassadors to the infidel Turk to negotiate a treaty against the Spanish in 1570. She met with all parties and used every means available to achieve her ends. She condoned war and murder in the interest of her duty as the regent of France.

It may have been her failure to balance the dynastic and religious conflicts that brought on the civil wars, but it was her success at identifying the factions in the conflict and her attempts to balance them that allowed Henry IV to obtain his throne intact with Huguenots alive to tolerate. The religious civil wars were horrible, but some of the changes as a result of the wars moved France closer to the centralized, bureaucratic state that was more nearly modern than was the sixteenth century dynastic structure. The wars served to redistribute the land from the hands of a few large noble families to those of a number of smaller families who were loyal to the monarchy. The most significant result of the civil wars, however, was the creation of the Politique Party, a party that recognized the need for a strong monarchy regardless of religious affiliation and regardless of noble demands for power. Catherine's contribution to French government in the sixteenth century was the principle of centralized power in the hands of the monarchy.

Bibliography

Héritier, Jean. *Catherine de Medici.* Translated by Charlotte Haldane. New York: St. Martin's Press, 1963. Long biography of Catherine as a great national and moderate leader who preserved for Henry IV a kingdom which was battered but intact.

Knecht, R. J. *Catherine De' Medici.* New York: Longman, 1998. A book in the series Profiles in Power. Includes bibliographical references and an index.

Neale, J. E. *The Age of Catherine de Medici.* New York: Harper & Row, 1943. Short and colorful presentation of Catherine's rule as foolish, misguided, and middle class.

Roeder, Ralph. *Catherine de Medici and the Lost Revolution.* New York: Viking Press, 1937. Presents the problem of sixteenth century France as the inability of Catherine to balance the dynastic and religious conflicts of the age.

Sichel, Edith. *Catherine de' Medici and the French Reformation*. London: Constable, 1905. Presents Catherine as the evil nemesis of the political problems of France, never quite in control of her plans. Sichel also relates the art and literature of the period of the French Reformation to Catherine's reign.

Strage, Mark. *Women of Power: The Life and Times of Catherine de' Medici*. New York: Harcourt Brace Jovanovich, 1976. A conventional rehash of the story focusing on Catherine's relationship with Diane de Poitiers and Margaret of Valois.

Sutherland, N. M. "Catherine de Medici: The Legend of the Wicked Italian Queen." *Sixteenth Century Journal* 9 (1978): 45-56. An analysis of the attitudes of historians about Catherine de Médicis and her role in history from her contemporaries to the present day.

Van Dyke, Paul. *Catherine de Médicis*. 2 vols. New York: Charles Scribner's Sons, 1923. General study of Catherine within the context of her time. Catherine is held responsible for not solving the religious and political problems but not through inherent malice.

Loretta Turner Johnson

CATHERINE OF ARAGON

Born: December 16, 1485; Alcala de Henares, Spain
Died: January 7, 1536; Kimbolton, Huntingdonshire, England

Twice married to English princes, Catherine of Aragon, the first wife of Henry VIII, refused to accept a royal divorce, which led to Henry's expulsion of the Roman Catholic Church and the establishment of the Protestant church in England.

Early Life

Born Catalina (Catherine), an infanta of Spain, to their Most Catholic Majesties Queen Isabella of Castile and Leon and King Ferdinand of Aragon, this fifth surviving child and youngest daughter was named for her maternal English great-grandmother, Catherine of Lancaster. Catherine of Aragon was twice descended from English kings: maternally from Edward III and paternally from Henry II.

For the first fifteen years of her life, Catherine remained under the tutelage of her mother, Queen Isabella, who considered her own education so deficient that Catherine was tutored by scholars Peter Martyr and Antonio and Alessandro Geraldini. Catherine was instructed in the Bible, Latin histories, and Roman and Christian writers. She spoke fluent classical Latin, in addition to Spanish; studied heraldry, genealogy, and civil and canon law; and gained proficiency in music, dancing, drawing, and the domestic arts of spinning, weaving, and embroidery.

Contemporary accounts describe the young Catherine as having naturally pink cheeks, white skin, a fair complexion, and fairly thick hair with a reddish gold tint. Catherine's features were neat and regular in an oval face. Usually described as short, tiny, and plump, with a low voice, Catherine appeared to be a young infanta who would be a healthy producer of children.

The unification of Spain led Ferdinand and Isabella to use their children as marital pawns on the chessboard of European diplomacy. Their first- and third-born daughters wed Portuguese kings. The second daughter and the only son wed Austrian Habsburgs. Marriage negotiations between Madrid and London for Catherine to wed Prince Arthur of Wales, the eldest son of Henry VII, were opened in 1487 and formalized by the Treaty of Medina del Campo in 1489. A dowry settlement committing Spain to a payment of 200,000 crowns, plus plate and jewels valued at 35,000 crowns, formalized the Spanish-English alliance. Catherine (by proxy) and Arthur were first engaged in 1497 and then married in 1499.

Catherine's London arrival on November 12, 1501, and her official marriage to Prince Arthur two days later were greatly acclaimed by the English people. The usually parsimonious Henry VII gave Catherine and Arthur a lavish wedding at St. Paul's Cathedral. For Henry VII, the Spanish marriage publicly legitimatized the Tudor dynasty in England, contributed to the encirclement of England's enemy, France, and provided King Henry with a substantial dowry to use for his own political purposes.

Unfortunately, at Ludlow Castle in the Marches of Wales, the physically frail Arthur succumbed to illness on April 2, 1502. The cause of death remains unknown, but speculation has centered on tuberculosis or an undetermined plague. Catherine herself was too ill to attend her husband's funeral and burial at Worcester Cathedral. In widowhood, the young Catherine, now princess dowager of Wales, confessed to the bishop of Salisbury, Cardinal Lorenzo Campeggio, that her marriage had never been consummated. The couple had shared the marital bed only seven times.

Life's Work

During her years of her widowhood, 1502 to 1509, Catherine found herself a political pawn used by both her father and father-in-law. Catherine was first pledged in marriage to and then repudiated by both her widower father-in-law, Henry VII, and Henry VII's second son, Prince Henry. At issue was whether Catherine was still a virgin. If Catherine's marriage to Arthur had been consummated, an impediment of affinity prevented her from marrying another member of Prince Arthur's family. In 1506, Pope Julius II granted a dispensation and waived the issue of affinity, even if the marriage had been consummated.

Catherine's status remained unclear, however, because 100,000 crowns of her dowry remained unpaid by her father, who continuously pleaded poverty, and because her father-in-law repeatedly reevaluated Catherine's value as a future English royal bride in comparison with royal princesses in France and Austria. Increasing poverty forced Catherine to live in reduced state at Durham House, where she supported her household from her partial dowry and the sale of her plate and jewelry and suffered from frequent fevers.

Catherine of Aragon *(Library of Congress)*

Catherine's ambiguous status ended within two months of Henry VII's life when she wed her former brother-in-law, now Henry VIII, on June 11, 1509. Later, witnesses claimed that Henry VIII boasted his wife was a virgin when he took her to the marriage bed. Henry VIII's change of attitude toward Catherine was probably caused by his desire to retain her dowry and to keep Spain allied against France, and his need for an adult wife to found a dynasty. The possibility that Henry VIII actually loved Catherine should also not be discounted.

As queen, Catherine encouraged the arts, established her own library open to scholars, and befriended English writers. Queen Catherine contributed money to lectureships, supported poor scholars, and endowed the colleges of Ipswich and Oxford. She actively corresponded with leading humanists Thomas More, Erasmus, and Juan Vives. Catherine's greatest contribution to learning was as a pioneer of women's education. Catherine sponsored the publication of five handbooks on humanist instruction for women, including Vives's *The Instruction of a Christian Woman*.

Henry VIII appointed Catherine regent of England during his absences fighting the French on their territory. This action certainly demonstrates his appreciation and trust of Catherine's intelligence and diplomatic ability. While Henry was in France, Catherine gave the military orders launching an English army that defeated the invading Scots and killed their king, James IV (Henry's brother-in-law), at Flodden Field in 1513. Yet Catherine's promotion of a Spanish alliance and her continued involvement in policy making led her into conflict with Henry's lord chancellor, Cardinal Thomas Wolsey. Catherine would later blame Wolsey for Henry's desertion of her and his demands for a divorce.

The more important issue facing Catherine was her failure to produce a living male heir. The number of pregnancies and miscarriages suffered by Catherine has been the subject of much debate. Sir John Dewhurst, who has provided the best analysis of the existing period documents, concluded that there could have been only six pregnancies between the years 1509 and 1525: four stillbirths; a son, Henry, born January 1, 1511, who died seven weeks later; and their only surviving child, Mary, born February 18, 1516.

Exactly what caused Henry to announce his intention to divorce Catherine remains a topic of considerable debate. It seems that Henry's attitude toward Catherine changed abruptly after 1525, when the intended betrothal of their daughter Mary to Catherine's nephew, Charles V, king of Spain and Holy Roman emperor, was broken by Charles so that he could marry an older Portuguese cousin. The termination of this marriage plan ended Henry's dreams of an Anglo-Spanish alliance dominating Europe. It is also true that Henry was involved with Anne Boleyn by 1526.

Henry's May, 1527, decision to challenge the validity of his marriage to Catherine is known as the "King's Great Matter." Using the biblical passages Leviticus 20:21 and Deuteronomy 25:5-7, Henry claimed that a man marrying his brother's wife did so against God's will. Henry further argued that the papal dispensations granted by Julius II to remove the issue of affinity and allow the marriage were invalid.

Henry's actions divided the Roman Catholic Church in England. He failed to anticipate Catherine's refusal to go quietly and Charles V's seizure of Rome and imprisonment of Pope Clement VII. On March 6, 1529, Catherine appealed to Rome, asking the pope to take her case. Her only appearance before the Blackfriars Court on May 31, 1529, witnessed a queen defending the legality of her marriage and intent on saving it.

Both Clement VII and his English representative, Cardinal Campeggio, delayed clerical action, hoping for reconciliation. After 1530, Catherine's health began to decline. Henry last saw Catherine at Windsor on July 11, 1531, whereupon she was removed to increasingly remote locations and finally to Kimbolton. Pressure from the Boleyn supporters, Henry's increasing desire for a legitimate male heir, and clerical resistance to an annulment forced the king to begin the process of disestablishing the English Roman Church.

Attempts to encourage Catherine to lead a rebellion against her increasingly unpopular husband and the Boleyn party were rebuffed by the queen. Wars in Italy, Germany, and France prevented military intervention in support of Catherine by Charles V and the pope. Finally, almost five years after Catherine's initial appeal to Rome, on March 24, 1534, the pope declared the marriage valid in the eyes of God and the Church. By that time, however, Henry had taken matters into his own hands. The English Roman Church was disestablished (1532), Parliament annulled Henry's marriage to Catherine (1533) so that he could legalize his marriage to an already pregnant Anne Boleyn, and the king was enthroned as the head of the English Church (1534).

Increasing ill health led to Catherine's death on January 7, 1536. Henry celebrated with a ball at Greenwich. Although rumors circulated of Catherine's having been poisoned, she probably died from either cancer or a coronary thrombosis. In violation of Catherine's instructions, she was buried at Peterborough Cathedral with the honors of princess dowager.

Summary

First as an infanta of Spain, then as princess of Wales, and lastly as queen of England, Catherine of Aragon was sacrificed to diplomacy and statecraft by her parents, Ferdinand and Isabella of Spain, her father-in-law, Henry VII, and her husband, Henry VIII. In all her titled positions, Catherine represented the emerging Renaissance woman who was educated, spoke several languages, and was lauded by contemporary scholars for her support of humanism and culture.

Although contemporary and later historians have praised Catherine's virtue, trust, and high-mindedness, they have faulted her for her inability to use her popularity with the English people, the nobles, and the Church to maintain Catholicism in England or to lead an army into battle against Henry VIII in order to make their daughter, Mary, queen of England. Catherine's obedience to her husband, her willingness to accede to all of Henry's royal commands during the "King's Great Matter," and her absolute faith and devotion to the institutions of marriage and the Church enabled her to defend her marriage and keep her daughter in the Roman faith and in the line of succession, but those characteristics ultimately contributed to England's Protestant Reformation.

Bibliography

Albert, Marvin. *The Divorce*. New York: Simon & Schuster, 1965. A detailed study of the events leading to the divorce of Catherine of Aragon by Henry VIII. The reader becomes a participant in one of history's most celebrated divorce trials.

Dewhurst, John. "The Alleged Miscarriages of Catherine of Aragon and Anne Boleyn." *Medical History* 28 (1984): 49-56. The best medical analysis of historical documents to determine the number and outcomes of Catherine's pregnancies.

Dowling, Maria. "A Woman's Place? Learning and the Wives of Henry VIII." *History Today* 41 (June, 1991): 38-42. Dowling reintroduces the reader to the wives of Henry VIII as promoters of education, religion, and scholarship.

Fraser, Antonia. *The Wives of Henry VIII*. New York: Alfred A. Knopf, 1992. Fraser's careful analysis and reevaluation of archival and published works produces a thoughtful reinterpretation of Catherine's role in shaping England's entrance into the modern age.

Kipling, Gordon. *The Receyt of the Ladie Katheryne*. Oxford, England: Oxford University Press, 1990. A scholarly analysis of sixteenth century documents describing Catherine of Aragon's arrival in England, her entry into London, her marriage to Prince Arthur, and her subsequent widowhood.

Loades, David M. *Henry VIII and His Queens*. West Sussex, England: Sutton, 1997. This short and highly readable work by a respected British historian provides a useful introduction to the topic.

Mattingly, Garrett. *Catherine of Aragon*. Boston: Little, Brown, 1941. Mattingly's access to extensive archival material provides a detailed analysis of Catherine's character, the dynasties of Spain, England, Scotland, and France, and the politics of the Papacy in the turbulent sixteenth century. Still the definitive biography of Catherine.

Roll, Winifred. *The Pomegranate and the Rose: The Story of Katherine of Aragon*. Englewood Cliffs, N.J.: Prentice-Hall, 1970. A highly readable study of a young woman whose fate was determined by the statecraft of Spanish and English kings and the Roman Catholic Church.

Scarisbrick, J. J. *Henry VIII*. Berkeley: University of California Press, 1968. British historian Scarisbrick's extensive access to French, German, Latin, Spanish, and English primary sources and his careful analysis of Henry's character and relationship with his wives, ministers, and church officials reveals a king whose achievement fell below his potential greatness.

Travitsky, Betty S. "Reprinting Tudor History: The Case of Catherine of Aragon." *Renaissance Quarterly* 50, no. 1 (Spring, 1997): 164-174. Examines allusions to Catherine of Aragon in various editions of Juan Luis Vives's *Instruction of a Christian Woman*, the most influential conduct book for women in the sixteenth century.

William A. Paquette

CATHERINE THE GREAT

Born: May 2, 1729; Stettin, Pomerania, Prussia
Died: November 17, 1796; St. Petersburg, Russia

One of the early englightened monarchs, Catherine the Great attempted to create a uniform Russian government with a modern Westernized code of laws that represented all levels of Russian society with the exception of the serfs. In the forty-four years of her reign, she sculpted Russia into one of the great world powers of the time and laid the foundation for what would become modern Russia.

Early Life

Catherine the Great was born Sophie Friederike Auguste von Anhalt-Zerbst in Stettin, a seaport in Pomerania. Her parents, Prince Christian August and Princess Johanna Elizabeth of Holstein-Gottorp, were minor members of the German aristocracy. As a result of her strained relationship with her mother, Sophie developed into an independent young woman. Russian monarchs held the prerogative of choosing their successors, and her cousin Duke Karl Peter Ulrich of Holstein-Gottorp had been summoned to Russia by the childless Empress Elizabeth as the heir to the throne. It only remained to find him a wife. After several months of searching, Elizabeth decided on Sophie, and both she and her mother were invited to Russia in January, 1744.

Elizabeth was pleased with her choice, and Peter fell in love with the princess. On June 28, 1744, Sophie converted to Russian Orthodoxy, was given the name Catherine, and on the following day the couple were publicly engaged. From the time he arrived in Russia, Peter, whose health was never good, had a series of illnesses which left him permanently scarred and most probably sterile. Their marriage, which occurred on August 21, 1745, was not consummated immediately and probably not at all.

Married to a man who displayed a mania for Prussian militarism and who preferred to play with toy soldiers and conduct military parades than to be with her, Catherine was left to develop her own interests. She began to read, a pastime almost unheard of in the Russian court, and mastered the technique of riding astride, an activity in

Catherine the Great *(Library of Congress)*

which she took great pleasure, often going for long rides. Neither interest could overcome the lack of an heir, which, as the empress pointed out to her on more than one occasion, was Catherine's only reason for being. Starved for affection and more than a little aware that her position depended on producing a child, she took a lover, Sergei Saltykov. Twice she became pregnant and miscarried, but on September 20, 1754, Catherine delivered a male child, Paul Petrovich, who was probably the son of Saltykov.

The empress took control of the child from the moment he was delivered, and Catherine was once again left alone. Totally barred from any involvement in the political life of the court, she consoled herself with reading the works of such writers as Voltaire, Cornelius Tacitus, and Montesquieu. Saltykov was replaced by Count Stanislas August Ponistowski, and, in 1761, Catherine met and fell in love with Count Grigory Orlov. During this time, her husband's behavior became more and more eccentric. Russia was at war with Prussia, yet Peter made no secret of his pro-Prussian sentiments, even going so far as to supply Frederick II with information concerning Russian troop movements.

Elizabeth died in December, 1761, leaving Catherine's husband, Peter III, as the new emperor. Catherine was six months pregnant with Orlov's child at the time, a son who was born in April, 1762, but no one really noticed. Peter III immediately ended the war with Prussia and then allied himself with Prussia to make war on Denmark, declaring himself more than willing to serve Frederick II. Added to this insult to Russian patriotism, Peter outraged the Church by reviling Russian Orthodox ritual and by ordering the secularizing of church estates and the serfs bound to those estates. Most important to his final overthrow, he offended the elite Guards, dressing them in uniforms that were completely Prussian in appearance and constantly taunting the men.

In June, 1762, Catherine, with the support of the powerful Orlov family and the Guards, acted. In a bloodless coup, she seized the crown in St. Petersburg and published a manifesto claiming the throne. Dressed in a Guard's uniform and astride her stallion Brilliant, she led her troops against her deposed husband in his stronghold at Peterhoff. He offered his abdication, and, with its acceptance, Catherine became empress of Russia.

Life's Work

Catherine began her reign by declaring that she had acted only because it was the will of the people. Aware that she had come to the throne by the might of the powerful Orlov family and with the backing of the Guards, she realized the need not to antagonize the nobility or the Church. As a result, her manifesto justifying her seizure of the throne explained her actions as needed to establish the correct form of government, an autocracy acting in accord with Russian Orthodoxy, national custom, and the sentiment of the Russian people. While her words were a welcome relief from the brief reign of Peter III, her actions were not unilaterally accepted—after all she was a German by birth and had no blood claim to the throne, even if she was ultimately claiming it for her son. To complicate matters, Peter III died, in all probability murdered at the behest of the Orlovs, and in 1764 Ivan VI, himself deposed by Elizabeth, was killed in his prison cell during an abortive rescue attempt. Catherine was forced to deal with a throne which many thought she had murdered the legitimate claimants to gain.

At the time she took the throne, she still retained much of her early beauty. She had a clear, very white complexion, which was set off by her brown hair and dark eyebrows. Her eyes were hazel, and in a certain light they appeared bright blue. She had a long neck and a proud carriage, and in her youth she was noted for her shapely figure. As she aged, she grew increasingly heavy: When she collapsed immediately before her death, it took several men to carry her to her bed.

Despite her rather tenuous hold on the throne, the new empress rapidly took charge. She ended the hated war against Denmark and quickly went to work trying to reform Russia into what Peter the Great had envisioned for it. An advocate of economic growth and expansion and an opponent of trade restrictions, she abolished most state monopolies and authorized grain exports. Under her reign, Russia had some of the most liberal tariff policies in Europe. Determined to improve agriculture, in 1765 she established the Free Economic Society for the Encouragement of Agriculture and Husbandry.

Faced with the chaos of the Russian legal system, Catherine was determined to create an effective centralized government. She set to work codifying the laws of Russia, and in 1766 she published a work in which she drew freely from writers such as Montesquieu, Cesare Bonesana Beccaria, and Denis Diderot. It confirmed the need for an autocratic ruler as the best form of government to fill the needs of Russia; yet it developed the idea that the government was responsible to the needs of the people. All subjects, except the serfs, were entitled to equal treatment under the law, and all had the right to petition the sovereign. The standard use of torture in conjunction with legal proceedings and the common use of capital punishment were shunned, the only exception being in the case of national security.

Not content with this venture alone, she set to work on a series of legal codes to cover nearly all aspects of the Russian social order. In 1782, she published a work which gave minute instructions for the administration of the urban population. This was followed in the same year by two charters which delineated the rights and obligations of the various levels of society. Despite these laws, she did not deal with the one level of society that by the end of the century made up 90 percent of the population—the peasantry. Russian serfs were bound to the nobles, who had complete control over them. The wealth of a noble was based on how many serfs, or souls, he owned, not on how much land he controlled. Catherine maintained her position by the support of the nobility. To create any law that interfered with the nobles' rights over their serfs would alienate the nobility and without any question would lead to her being deposed in favor of her son. For this reason, while she remained acutely aware of the serfs' plight, she did nothing to change their status as property and refused them the basic right to petition the monarch, a right held by all other levels of society.

Two major problems that plagued her reign were wars and the frequent threat of impostors making claims on her throne. In 1768, the Ottoman Empire declared war on Russia over the question of Russian troops in Poland, and the war continued until the Ottomans surrendered in 1774. Russian territory was greatly increased in the settlement, but in 1787 the Ottoman Empire again declared war on Russia, a conflict which lasted until 1791. In 1782-1783, the Crimea was under siege but was subdued and incorporated into Russia in 1784. In 1788, while Russia was at war with the Turks, war with Sweden erupted and lasted until 1790. In 1793, Catherine annexed part of Poland, and in 1794 a full-scale rebellion erupted in that country but was finally crushed by Russian troops, leaving the area firmly in Russian control.

From the beginning of her reign, rumors abounded that Peter III was not dead, and at intervals impostors came forward to claim the Crown. Some of these amassed considerable followings, especially in the case of the Pugachov Revolt of 1773-1774, but all were quickly eliminated. Most of the impostors spent the rest of their lives in banishment in Siberia. Catherine was always aware of the fragility of her hold on the throne, and in later years she reacted in fear to the news of the French Revolution, taking stern measures to ensure that no such ideas developed in Russia. In 1793, she broke all relations with France, including the importation of any French goods, and, despite her earlier support of publishers, in 1796 she imposed rigid book censorship and limited the number of presses to those completely under government control. Any hint of republican thinking was quickly investigated, and anyone even remotely suspect was quickly banished.

At the height of this fear of French republicanism, and having outlived nearly all of her friends and advisers, she suffered a stroke in November, 1796, and died at the Winter Palace in St. Petersburg. Her relationship with her son had always been strained, and there were rumors that she intended to remove him as her heir in favor of his son Alexander. If she left a testament to this effect it was never found, although forgeries of such a document continued to appear. The new emperor, Paul I, had his murdered father's body exhumed, and, after crowning the remains with his own hands, he had the bodies of both of his parents buried together at the Peter and Paul Cathedral in St. Petersburg.

Summary

Under Catherine the Great, Russia was changed from a chaotic, badly managed nation to one of the major forces in Europe. Laws were codified and a powerful centralized government was formed. As a result of numerous wars, the lands of the nation were greatly increased. There was also a great increase in national wealth.

Despite her failure to deal with the question of the serfs, Catherine can be viewed as one of the first enlightened monarchs, attempting to create a moral society and eliminating corruption in government. She introduced smallpox inoculation to Russia in 1768, and in 1786 she published a statute setting up general education in the twenty-six provincial capitals. In a highly illiterate nation, this was a radical step forward. She encouraged advancement in agriculture and made every effort to improve the life of the Russian people.

Bibliography

Alexander, John T. *Catherine the Great: Life and Legend*. New York: Oxford University Press, 1989. This work gives a largely unbiased portrait of a complex and powerful woman. Alexander considers all aspects of Catherine's life and manages to deal honestly with the reality of her legendary love life. Excellent bibliography.

Bergamini, John D. *The Tragic Dynasty: A History of the Romanovs*. New York: G. P. Putnam's Sons, 1969. A generally detailed look at the life of Catherine although greater emphasis is given to her sexual appetites and her relationship with her two famous lovers than to the political aspects of her reign.

Cowles, Virginia. *The Romanovs*. New York: Harper & Row, 1971. Cowles deals with Catherine's love of opulence and the scandals of her life, emphasizing her love of grandeur and her numerous lovers.

Erickson, Carolly. *Great Catherine*. New York: Simon & Schuster, 1994.

Grey, Ian. *The Romanovs: The Rise and Fall of a Dynasty*. New York: Doubleday, 1970. Catherine is depicted as a ruthless sovereign who plotted her way to the throne even before the death of Empress Elizabeth.

MacKenzie, David, and Michael W. Curran. *A History of Russia and the Soviet Union*. Chicago: Dorsey Press, 1978. A text covering the history of Russia. Contains several detailed chapters on Catherine which show her life in a historical perspective. Excellent bibliography of historical texts on the period.

C. D. Akerley

LINDA CHAVEZ

Born: June 17, 1947; Albuquerque, New Mexico

As a Latina conservative activist and public official, Chavez broadened the role of women and minorities in American politics.

Early Life

Linda Chavez was born in Albuquerque, New Mexico, on June 17, 1947, the daughter of Rudy and Velma Chavez. Rudy Chavez was the descendent of Spanish immigrants who had settled New Mexico in the early 1600's; his wife Velma was of Anglo-American heritage. The Chavezes were devout Roman Catholics and provided their daughter with a sturdy middle-class childhood. A veteran of World War II, Rudy Chavez possessed a sense of patriotism and a quiet pride in his Hispanic heritage—qualities that had a major influence on his daughter's later conservative political beliefs.

When Linda was nine years old, she moved with her family from New Mexico, where Latinos were comfortably established as a majority ethnic group, to Denver, Colorado, where racial prejudice against Latinos and other minorities was more prevalent. During her teenage years, Linda reacted to this discrimination by developing a fierce determination to excel; she also marched against segregation and became involved in a range of social causes supporting civil rights for women and African Americans.

After she graduated from high school, Linda Chavez enrolled at the University of Colorado in 1965. As an undergraduate, Chavez became involved in teaching through tutoring Mexican American students in remedial studies. Although she was discouraged by patterns of discrimination she witnessed and the lack of motivation on the part of her tutorial students, Chavez remained committed to her ambition to become a teacher. Although the teaching profession was considered a conventional aspiration for women, Chavez believed the field of education presented women with a challenging opportunity to effect significant social change.

Near the middle of her undergraduate years, Chavez was married to fellow student Christopher Gersten in 1967 and chose to retain her maiden name after the ceremony. After graduating from the University of Colorado with a bachelor's degree in 1970, she pursued graduate studies in English literature at the University of California at Los Angeles (UCLA). As a graduate assistant, Chavez was persuaded to present a course on Chicano literature. Although she harbored serious reservations because of the lack of sufficient published material on which to base the course, Chavez bowed to academic pressure. She found that many of the students were unwilling to read the material she presented and were disrespectful during her lectures; some who were given failing marks retaliated by vandalizing Chavez's home. Discouraged by her experiences with teachers, colleagues, and students who made stereotypical assumptions about her because of her Hispanic heritage, Chavez left UCLA in 1972 and moved with her husband to Washington, D.C.

Life's Work

Despite her discouraging experience at UCLA, Linda Chavez did not abandon her interest in education. In Washington, D.C., Chavez became affiliated with the National Education Association (NEA), the largest union of schoolteachers in the United States, and worked for the Democratic National Committee in support of various liberal causes. She became increasingly discouraged by the way many organizations were courting her as an ethnic representative and lobbyist for Latino causes rather than respecting her opinions as an individual. After serving as an educational consultant for the Department of Health, Education, and Welfare, Chavez joined the staff of the American Federation of Teachers (AFT). As the second-largest national teachers' union, the AFT was known for its influence in policy making, and Chavez found an outlet for her own views while serving as editor of the union's quarterly journal, *American Educator*. Her series of articles in support of a return to traditional educational values and goals brought her to the attention of conservative politicians in Washington.

As the decade of the 1970's drew to a close, Chavez had reversed her previous liberal political stance after becoming alienated by liberal Democratic rhetoric that portrayed Latinos as defenseless, victimized minorities who depended on the financial assistance of wealthy upper-class whites. Her own vision placed Latinos in control of their own destiny—their success could be attained through hard work and personal dedication rather than the bureaucratic largesse represented by government handouts. Her opinions meshed with the growing national conservatism of the new decade that brought about the election of Ronald Reagan as president in 1980, and she began working as a consultant for the Reagan administration in 1981.

Appreciative of her contributions, President Reagan appointed Chavez to serve as director of the U.S. Commission on Civil Rights in 1983. A nonpartisan agency, the commission was charged with the responsibility of monitoring the federal government's progress in enforcing civil rights legislation. Echoing the administration's position, Chavez began to denounce many traditional civil rights measures, including affirmative action programs and racial hiring quotas. Chavez also authorized a federal study to investigate the negative effects of affirmative action on members of minority groups. Although she asserted that she was helping to direct the agency toward the stated goal of establishing a color-blind society in which minorities would advance based on merit rather than ethnic identity or gender, many civil rights activists criticized Chavez for transforming the agency into a partisan arm of the Reagan administration. Chavez also found that the ideological differences between her and many Latino activists prevented her from persuading them to support her policy positions.

In 1985, Chavez was promoted to the position of director of the Office of the White House Public Liaison. As the highest-ranking woman on the White House staff, Chavez found that her new post gave her more direct access to President Reagan. She switched her political affiliation to the Republican Party and lobbied hard to promote the administration's policies within Congress as well as among various public groups. After ten months, however, Chavez decided to leave the post to run for political office.

The Republican Party encouraged Chavez to become a candidate for the U.S. Senate seat in Maryland in 1986. Eager to retain their majority within the Senate, many prominent Republicans demonstrated their support for Chavez and helped her win the Republican primary race. Banking on her conservative credentials, her close ties to President Reagan, her solid middle-class background, and her potential appeal with women and Latino voters, the Republican Party launched a large-scale fund-raising effort and poured substantial funds into Chavez's election campaign.

Despite this demonstration of partisan support, Chavez found herself at a distinct disadvantage against Democratic challenger Barbara Mikulski. An ethnic, working-class populist who had represented her Baltimore district in the U.S. House of Representatives for many years, Mikulski had spent her life in the state, had close ties within the state's urban communities, and had deep support among the state's substantial majority of registered Democrats. All these credentials negated Chavez's perceived strengths, and her ratings in the political polls trailed far behind Mikulski's as the fall election approached.

Placed in the difficult position of having to counter criticism of her shifting political allegiance and her brief residence in the state of Maryland, Chavez adopted a campaign strategy of attacking Mikulski. The strategy backfired when Chavez, who was the mother of three children, called attention to the fact that Mikulski had never been married and accused her of being "anti-male." Chavez's campaign staffers exacerbated the situation by attempting to link Mikulski with several lesbian groups in the greater Baltimore area. In a clear rejection of these accusations, Maryland voters endorsed Mikulski for the Senate seat by a substantial margin.

Shaking off her loss, Chavez realized that the electoral fray was unlikely to yield concrete rewards for her in the foreseeable future. Instead, she became president of U.S. English, a private nonprofit organization lobbying to establish English as the official national language. She soon resigned her post in late 1988, citing her distaste for the anti-Latino and anti-Catholic bias exemplified in sentiments expressed by the group's founder. Upon leaving the organization, Chavez became a fellow at a conservative Washington-based think tank known as the Manhattan Institute for Policy Research. She also became a freelance political commentator and wrote columns and editorials for various periodicals.

Capitalizing on her growing prominence as a policy expert, Chavez published a work entitled *Out of the Barrio: Toward a New Politics of Hispanic Assimilation* (1991). Arguing against the representation of the Hispanics as a part of a monolithic community, Chavez reiterated her belief that affirmative action programs and hiring quotas effectively segregated Hispanics. According to Chavez, the organized Hispanic movement's tendency to focus most of its attention on the plight of those who are impoverished and disadvantaged not only has prevented Latinos from taking credit for the enormous gains made by those who have achieved middle-class status but also has reinforced a skewed perception of the Latino population by American society. The book was widely reviewed, and its success ensured Chavez a new level of visibility as a commentator during the early 1990's on shows such as *The McNeil/Lehrer NewsHour*.

Summary

Despite her failed bid for a seat in the U.S. Senate, Linda Chavez managed to establish impressive credentials during the course of her political career. A widely noticed and well-regarded commentator on American domestic affairs, Chavez worked to break down the limitations imposed by stereotypical perceptions of Latinos. As differences within their community became more evident, Hispanic Americans began to be courted as an important political constituency by both the Democratic and Republican parties. Riding the crest of this attention, Chavez received prominent political appointments, and her success within the Republican Party helped inspire other Latinos, such as Richard Pombo of California and Ileana Ros-Lehtinen and Lincoln Diaz-Balart of Florida, to campaign as Republicans and succeed in winning election to the U.S. House of Representatives. Although the election of Democratic candidate Bill Clinton to the presidency in 1992 shifted control of the executive branch of government out of the hands of the Republican Party, many Latinos continued to pursue elective office as Republicans.

As the 1990's ushered in new debates about multiculturalism and political correctness in the United States, Chavez continued to express her opinions regarding the advancement of Latinos. Affirming the long-cherished American ideal of respecting the political beliefs of those whose views run contrary to those of the political majority, Chavez argued passionately for a new vision of Hispanic Americans. Chavez's greatest importance for women and for Latinos was her willingness to challenge predictable stereotypes, regardless of the popularity of her beliefs.

Bibliography

Arias, Anna Maria. "Making People Mad." *Hispanic* (August, 1992): 11-16. This article, written by a Latina journalist, captures both

Chavez's polemical fervor and the underlying seriousness of her conservative political convictions.

Brimelow, Peter. "The Fracturing of America." *Forbes* 149 (March 30, 1992): 74-75. An influential and sympathetic analysis of Chavez's opinions on a variety of political topics, including her views on Hispanic Americans and minority status.

Chavez, Linda. *Out of the Barrio: Toward a New Politics of Hispanic Assimilation.* New York: Basic Books, 1991. Chavez's own exposition of her views serves as an excellent introduction to her political thought and a vital primer on her influence on the shifting American cultural scene of the 1980's and 1990's.

Grenier, Jeannin. "The Woman Versus Woman Race." *Ms.* 15 (November, 1986): 27. Grenier's piece centers on Chavez's contest with Barbara Mikulski, although it also includes some treatment of Chavez's earlier career and background. The author particularly highlights the issues of race, gender, and homophobia in the rhetoric of the two candidates and how their political views affected their campaign strategies.

Hernandez, Macarena. "Conservative and Hispanic, Linda Chavez Carves Out Leadership Role." *The New York Times*, August 19, 1998, p. A28. Discusses Chavez's efforts to end bilingual education in American schools.

Noonan, Peggy. *What I Saw at the Revolution.* New York: Random House, 1990. Although it contains no direct information about Chavez, this memoir, written by a speechwriter for Ronald Reagan, provides insights into Chavez's encounter with Reagan-style conservatism. Noonan echoes some of Chavez's views, suggesting that, contrary to the settled conviction of most American liberals, Reagan's brand of political conservatism was an empowering, democratic force rather than a product of racist, reactionary tendencies.

Telgen, Diane, and Jim Kamp, eds. *Notable Hispanic American Women.* Detroit: Gale Research, 1993. Filling a gap in the coverage of minority women in available reference works, this collection profiles more than two hundred women of Hispanic descent. The entry on Chavez provides a thorough overview of her career through the early 1990's and is accompanied by a useful list of periodical sources.

Nicholas Birns

Shirley Chisholm

Born: November 30, 1924; Brooklyn, New York

As the first African American woman elected to the U.S. Congress and the first to run as a candidate for the presidency, Chisholm was an outspoken advocate for women, children, and ethnic minorities.

Early Life

Shirley Anita St. Hill was born in 1924 in the Bedford-Stuyvesant section of Brooklyn to West Indian emigrants, Charles Christopher St. Hill and Ruby Seale St. Hill. Seeking relief from the 1920 famine that besieged their Caribbean home on the island of Barbados, both parents migrated to New York City. Unable to save enough money from her work as a seamstress in the garment district or his work as an unskilled laborer in a burlap bag factory, the St. Hills sent three-year-old Shirley, along with her two younger sisters, Muriel and Odessa, back to Barbados to live on a farm with their maternal grandmother, Emmeline Seale.

The next seven years under the stern, disciplined eye of Grandma Seale, a towering woman who was more than 6 feet tall, shaped Shirley's compassion and concern for the well-being of others and further strengthened her understanding that commitment to one's principles, while rewarding, might be a lonely existence. The foundation of Shirley's future academic success would be based on the structured academic environment of the British-styled schools of Barbados.

The transition back into American life in 1934 at the height of the Depression was difficult for eleven-year-old Shirley. The meager resources of the St. Hill family were further divided with the arrival of baby sister Selma. The stark contrast between the warm, balmy climate of Barbados as compared to the harsh cold reality of New York winters made the adjustment even more painful.

The family moved from the predominantly Jewish neighborhood of Brownsville to the more ethnically diverse community of Bedford-Stuyvesant in Brooklyn. This half-black neighborhood would help sharpen Shirley's developing political awareness, especially as the economic conditions of the neighborhood worsened.

Shirley's fertile teenage mind was challenged by the daily lectures and discussions with her father, a largely self-educated man. Charles St. Hill, a voracious reader, daily devoured several publications. Like many working-class blacks, he was an avid follower of Pan-Africanist leader Marcus Garvey. Garvey's Universal Negro Improvement Association (UNIA) encouraged self-sufficiency and promoted racial pride, and was one of the most significant political, cultural black movements during the early part of the twentieth century in America.

Upon returning to the New York school system, Shirley was held back in a lower grade because of her ignorance of U.S. civic history. After receiving tutoring lessons, she was promoted to her appropriate grade level and quickly surpassed the efforts of many of her classmates. Chisholm would always retain one trait from her years in the Caribbean—a slight, melodious West Indian accent. A petite young woman, Chisholm soon learned that her size tended to disguise her surprisingly forceful, straightforward manner.

Shirley Chisholm *(Library of Congress)*

Upon graduation from high school, Shirley received offers to attend college at Vassar and Oberlin. Because of her family's limited economic resources and her own desire to remain close to home, however, she accepted a scholarship to study sociology at Brooklyn College. Shirley's involvement in several campus organizations and the debating society caught the attention of one Brooklyn College professor, who encouraged her to pursue a political career. In the end, Chisholm chose to become a teacher, a more realistic career choice for African American women of her day.

In 1946, she graduated cum laude from Brooklyn College with a degree in social work. She immediately began work on a master's degree in elementary education at Columbia University's night school. During the day, she was employed at a local nursery school. At about this time, she met a recent Jamaican transplant, Conrad Chisholm, who was working as a waiter. They were married on October 8, 1950, and settled in Brooklyn. Conrad returned to school and then became an investigator for the New York City Department of Hospital Services.

For the next several years, Shirley worked for a number of schools, including Friends Day Nursery in Brownsville and the Mount Calvary Child Care Center in Harlem. From 1953 to 1959, she served as director of the Hamilton-Madison Child Care Center in Lower Manhattan. She further distinguished herself as a bilingual educator, because of her ability to communicate fluently in Spanish. Gradually, her reputation as a leading early-childhood specialist spread, resulting in increased demands for her services as a consultant to such organizations as the New York City Bureau of Child Welfare.

Life's Work
Shirley Chisholm's growing interest in the political world began in the mid-1950's when she stepped up her involvement in several organizations, including the Bedford-Stuyvesant Political League, the National Association for the Advancement of Colored People (NAACP), the Democratic Women's Workshop, and the League of Women Voters. The organization that most directly sparked Chisholm's activism was the Seventeenth Assembly District Democratic Club. She became active in the district's party politics after meeting an old college associate, Wesley Holder. Holder had carved out a reputation for getting African American candidates elected while still remaining loyal to the white-dominated Democratic Party agenda. Shirley's distaste for such blind allegiance to the party machine, however, soon found her at odds with Holder and on the outside of the club's inner circle. This situation rendered Chisholm politically inactive for a number of years.

She reentered politics in 1960 when she helped form the Unity Democratic Club with the express goal of destroying the grip the party held over her district. In 1964, Chisholm succeeded in winning a seat to the New York state assembly for the Fifty-fifth District as the first black woman from Brooklyn to serve in the state legislature. During her four years in Albany, New York, she was the only woman and one of only eight African American representatives in the state assembly. As a state representative, Chisholm spearheaded the passage of a bill for unemployment insurance for domestic workers and also developed a program known as Search for Elevation, Education, and Knowledge (SEEK), which was designed to increase higher educational opportunities for disadvantaged youth.

Having cut her political teeth at the state level, Chisholm went on in 1968 to beat James Farmer, former leader of the Congress of Racial Equality (CORE), who was running as a Republican candidate for the newly created Twelfth Congressional District of Brooklyn. This new congressional district included her old Bedford-Stuyvesant neighborhood, a community comprising 70 percent black and Puerto Rican residents by the late 1960's. Her victory made her the first African American woman to win a seat to the U.S. Congress.

As a champion for the underdog, Chisholm made it clear that she would always align herself with the most able candidate. So in 1969, she crossed party lines when she supported Republican candidate John Lindsay in his successful New York City mayoral bid. During her fourteen years on Capitol Hill, Chisholm served on a number of congressional committees. She was originally appointed to the Agricultural Committee, but she aggressively lobbied to be removed from this committee because it did not serve the direct interests of her urban constituents. While on the Education and Labor Committee, Chisholm worked diligently to increase the minimum wage standard and increase federal subsidies for day care centers. Her proposed bill, however, was later vetoed by President Gerald Ford. Other noteworthy legislation introduced by Chisholm called for increasing the level of federal reimbursement of state welfare programs to 70 percent and the establishment of a Department of Consumer Affairs as a cabinet-level position.

Always active in the women's movement, Chisholm was involved in the early years of the National Organization for Women (NOW). She was a founding member of the National Women's Political Caucus, was a spokeswoman for the National Abortion Rights Action League (NARAL), and served as a guiding force in the formation of the National Political Congress of Black Women (NPCBW). From 1972 to 1976, Chisholm served on the Democratic National Committee.

Convinced that the status quo power structure of American politics needed to be changed, Chisholm decided in 1972 to run for the presidency. Returning to her old campaign slogan, "Unbought and Unbossed," Chisholm waged an uphill battle against the reigning power oligarchy and many old prejudices. Despite her lack of strong financial backing, Chisholm succeeded in mounting a groundbreaking campaign, assembling a coalition of African Americans, feminists, and other minority groups. Nevertheless, she failed to gain the largely symbolic yet influential support of the members of the Congressional Black Caucus. She arrived at the 1972 Democratic Convention with only 24 votes; later, she received an additional 151 votes released to her by Hubert H. Humphrey.

This particular campaign, more than any other venture, left a bitter taste in Chisholm's mouth as she came to grips with the unexpected opposition she encountered from two previously supportive sectors: women's groups and black civil rights organizations. Nevertheless, Chisholm remained convinced that her maiden journey had opened the door for future generations of women.

The year 1977 was a momentous time in Chisholm's life, highlighted by her appointment to the powerful House Rules Committee. This political success was nearly overshadowed by the dissolution of her marriage to Conrad Chisholm. After her divorce became final in 1978, she was married to Arthur Hardwick, Jr., a black businessman and an old acquaintance from her days in the New York state assembly. In 1979, Hardwick was involved in a serious car accident, sustaining injuries that necessitated a long recovery. This personal burden combined with the pressures of a changing political atmosphere in Washington, D.C., to place Chisholm at a challenging crossroad in her career. She retired from the U.S. House of Representatives in 1983. After her retirement, she essentially remained out of the political arena, limiting her involvement to endorsing and advising Jesse Jackson in his 1984 and 1988 presidential campaigns. In addition to serving as a popular speaker on the lecture circuit, Chisholm accepted an appointment as the Purington Professor at Mount Holyoke College, teaching classes in women's studies and political science from 1983 to 1987. She became a widow after Arthur Hardwick died from cancer in 1986. Although her outspoken nature created a stormy relationship between Chisholm and the Democratic Party during the 1990's, she was nominated to serve as U.S. ambassador to Jamaica by President Bill Clinton in 1993.

Summary

As an outspoken, charismatic maverick, Shirley Chisholm enjoyed a lengthy political career that witnessed many firsts. Chisholm's trail-blazing journey served to inspire others to overcome seemingly insurmountable hurdles as she became the first African American woman to win a seat in the U.S. Congress and the first African American woman to mount an official campaign for the presidency of the United States.

An advocate for the rights of women, children, and racial minorities, Chisholm served as a voice for many who could not speak for themselves. Her political agenda included the introduction of legislation that improved conditions for women and their children and created employment opportunities for inner-city residents. Undaunted and confident in her ability to wage "the good fight," Chisholm continued to pursue an independent course and was proud to remain unaccountable to either a party agenda or the narrow goals of special interests. After fourteen years on Capitol Hill, Chisholm succeeded in altering and realigning portions of the Democratic Party platform to reflect her own political beliefs. Even so, she was unable to placate some interest groups and often clashed with environmentalists, whose causes often placed obstacles in the way of her efforts to secure much-needed jobs for her constituents.

Chisholm's public career served to inspire other women to pursue careers in politics, and her achievements helped shape and influence an entire generation of African American political leaders, most notably California congresswoman Maxine Waters and presidential candidate Jesse Jackson. In spite of the obstacles and petty feuds she faced throughout her political career and particularly during her unconventional run for the presidency, Shirley Chisholm could look back on nearly forty years of public service as both a legislator and an educator with great pride.

Bibliography

Brownmiller, Susan. *Shirley Chisholm: A Biography*. Garden City, N.Y.: Doubleday, 1971. A short biography for young readers covering Chisholm's life from her return to New York City up through her successful bid for a congressional seat.

Chisholm, Shirley. *The Good Fight*. New York: Harper & Row, 1973. This memoir provides Chisholm's own perspective on the prejudices and obstacles she encountered in her unsuccessful 1972 bid for the American presidency.

_____. *Unbought and Unbossed*. Boston: Houghton Mifflin, 1970. Chisholm's first autobiography profiles her early life up through her election to the U.S. House of Representatives for New York's Twelfth Congressional District in 1968.

Drotning, Philip T., and Wesley W. South. *Up from the Ghetto*. New York: Cowles, 1970. An entire chapter of this book is devoted to Chisholm's effort to succeed against all odds. Places her struggle within the context of efforts by other African Americans to carve out productive careers in the face of racial prejudice and discrimination.

Duffy, Susan, comp. *Shirley Chisholm: A Bibliography of Writings by and About Her*. Metuchen, N.J.: Scarecrow Press, 1988. A useful source for locating writings by Chisholm, this work also serves as a good starting point for surveying the variety of sources of biographical information on Chisholm.

Rennert, Richard Scott, ed. *Female Leaders*. New York: Chelsea House, 1993. A work that surveys the lives and careers of several significant African American women, this multibiography places Chisholm's achievements within the context of her era and demonstrates how her efforts inspired women who followed, including Illinois Senator Carol Moseley Braun.

Scheader, Catherine. *Shirley Chisholm: Teacher and Congresswoman*. Hillsdale, N.J.: Enslow, 1990. A well-organized biography aimed at a juvenile audience, this work provides a straightforward overview of Chisholm's career and accomplishments and includes some discussion of her activities since leaving Congress.

Thomas, Cynthia. "Catching up with . . . Shirley Chisholm." *The Wall Street Journal*, June 7, 1999, p. 4. An overview of Chisholm's life and her years in retirement.

Donna Mungen

CHRISTINA

Born: December 8, 1626; Stockholm, Sweden
Died: April 19, 1689; Rome

Under Christina's short rule, Sweden benefited politically and socially through the Treaty of Westphalia, which brought an end to the devastating Thirty Years' War, and culturally by the importation of many works of art and manuscripts from cultural centers of Europe. During her residence in Rome, Christina was an enthusiastic patron of the arts, founding the learned society Accademia Reale in 1674, a precursor to the Accademia dell'Arcadia of eighteenth century Italy.

Early Life

Christina, Queen of Sweden from 1644 until her abdication in 1654, was born on December 8, 1626, daughter to the beloved King Gustavus II Adolphus of Sweden and his mentally unstable wife, Maria Eleonora, daughter of the elector of Brandenburg. Gustavus was not only a war hero of epic proportions but also the famed Protestant king and commander of the Swedish troops in the Thirty Years' War as well as the last male member of the Protestant branch of the royal Wasa family. Christina was the only one of the couple's children to survive beyond her first year and was convinced that she was hated by her mother because of her sex—both mother and father had hoped for a male heir to the throne. Yet Gustavus accorded all the ceremony and honor to his daughter that a prince would have received, and he made her his heiress before the Riksdag in 1630. When Gustavus was killed at the Battle of Lützen in 1632, his five-year-old princess became queen, although she did not begin ruling until she reached eighteen years of age.

The young Christina showed an intellectual bent unusual for females of her time; she spent long hours studying and, apparently, preferred this activity to all others. The young queen displayed the same talent for languages that her father had possessed; she learned German, French, and Latin rapidly, reading Livy, Terence, Cicero, and Sallust. Soon she developed a liking for Cornelius Tacitus, who was one of her father's favorite writers and not an easy one to comprehend.

Christina *(Library of Congress)*

Christina's appearance also set her apart from other women. Her gait was mannish; she spoke in a deep, booming voice; and she showed a lack of interest in fine clothing and adornment. This latter trait developed in later years into a penchant for wearing (often shabby or dirty) men's clothes with little or no jewelry. She was decidedly homely, though portraits reveal large, beautiful eyes. In addition, her exceptional skill in horseback riding surpassed that of most men of her court.

Major figures in the young queen's life included Chancellor Axel Oxenstierna, her tutor in statesmanship, who essentially ruled in her minority; Bishop John Matthiae, her religious instructor, who was primarily responsible for teaching her tolerance of other religions; and Countess Catherine Palatine, her paternal aunt, who came closest to providing the young girl with a normal mother figure until Christina's mother sent her away. Maria Eleonora seems to have been too warped by grief to be able to nurture her child properly; in addition, the Queen Mother kept dwarves and buffoons at court, characters that frightened Christina, who was also misshapen. Oxenstierna and other advisers to the late king removed Maria Eleonora to Uppsala, fearing that her instability and prolonged, ostentatious grief would prove harmful to her daughter. Christina's childhood was therefore essentially lonely and devoid of a proper family environment.

An early romantic interest blossomed for Christina in her early teens, and she and her cousin Charles Gustavus (later Charles X of Sweden) became secretly engaged. By the time she reached the throne, however, her feelings for him had cooled, possibly as a result of her passionate if unanswered affection for the courtier Magnus De la Gardie; they never married. During this time, she also made the acquaintance of Countess Ebba Sparre, her best female friend (Christina had otherwise little interest in women), who may have been Christina's lover.

Life's Work

Christina's adult life lends itself to a discussion of two distinct time periods: her Swedish reign and her postabdication travels and eventual permanent residence in Rome. She came to power in Sweden during a particularly difficult time. The Thirty Years' War had been raging for twenty-six years, a situation that had taxed the Swedish population in terms of both men and money. In addition, the politics at the court itself featured a strengthened nobility worried about possible land confiscations to improve the royal finances. Christina proved herself to be an astute politician and strategist but a profligate spender with little comprehension of economic affairs. She improved Sweden's diplomatic relations with France, to some degree through her personal friendship with the French minister (later ambassador) Pierre-Hector Chanut, and brought her country to temporary, welcome peace by the Treaty of Westphalia. She strengthened the power of the Crown vis-à-vis the nobility by means of clever strategies, aligning herself with the estates of the bourgeoisie and the peasantry. Yet the royal finances continued to deteriorate.

For all of her enjoyment of diplomatic intrigues and political power (things she did not cease to seek even after her abdication), her spiritual life was apparently lacking. She had been reared in the Lutheran faith but had been repelled by its austerity and sternness; her religious instructor, Matthiae, had taught her religious tolerance. The war booty from the Continent, which boasted sumptuous Italian paintings, vibrant tapestries, and volumes of literature, introduced her to the cultural wealth, lacking in her native land, that the more southerly countries of Europe had to offer. Although Christina called, among others, foreign artists, musicians, doctors, and philosophers (including René Descartes) to her court to try to fill the cultural void, she soon realized that she could not remain in spartan Sweden. She chose to abdicate, a decision to which her unrequited love for De la Gardie may have contributed. She prepared for this step with great care, ensuring that her own candidate for the succession, her cousin and former fiancé Charles Gustavus, was officially accepted by the Riksdag as the heir to her throne. During this time, she became attracted to the Catholic religion, a faith with greater appeal to her aesthetic sense than Protestantism (it is recorded that she actually subscribed to her own private religion), and received instruction in secret from Italian Jesuit priests, for Catholicism was still illegal in Sweden at the time. Although the Riksdag refused initially to accept her bid for abdication, she persisted, citing as grounds her intention never to marry, her "weaker" sex, and her wish to retreat into private life. She also probably allowed an inkling of her Catholic interest to be perceived. It would have been a terrible embarrassment to Sweden if the daughter of its Protestant hero had converted to the opposing religion. To retain her on the throne would have been unthinkable. Her decision was accepted, and she abdicated on June 6, 1654.

After her abdication, Christina left in disguise for the Spanish Netherlands; the sponsor of her conversion to Catholicism was Philip IV of Spain. After a stay in Brussels, she continued to Innsbruck, where she made her formal profession of the Catholic faith on November 3, 1655; Pope Alexander VII received her in Rome with lavish ceremonies on December 23 of the same year. There she met Cardinal Decio Azzolino, who later became her closest friend and, some believe, her paramour; he supported her with advice and friendship for the remainder of her life, dying two months after she did as her sole heir.

Christina was not content to live quietly in Rome, practicing her new faith. Her interest in politics kept her in touch with the most powerful figures of Europe; on a more prosaic level, she needed money to maintain her extravagant lifestyle. Although she thought that she had provided for steady financial support by securing for herself the income from Sweden's Baltic possessions and other lands, political unrest and poor or dishonest administration of these areas made her financial situation shaky at best. For these reasons, she went to France in 1656 and entered into secret negotiations with Cardinal Jules Mazarin to place her on the throne of Naples, a political dream that was foiled, partially through the treachery of a member of her entourage, Gian Rinaldo Monaldeschi. She had him murdered at Fontainebleau on November 10, 1657, an act which later prevented her from ascending the Polish throne (to which she actually had some claim) and which gave her a reputation for bloodthirstiness. In 1660 and 1667, Christina made trips to Sweden, primarily to protect her financial interests. Finally, in 1668, she returned to Rome, where she remained until her death.

In her adopted home, the now-round, stout queen, eccentric as ever, continued her involvement in politics and culture; she supported certain papal candidates during conclaves and founded learned societies, in particular the Accademia Reale. She invited singers and other musicians to her rented palace, the Palazzo Riario, and bought works of art which were displayed there. Christina worked on her autobiography (of which there are several drafts extant) and began writing aphorisms, which are often rather unoriginal but occasionally revelatory of her feelings toward Azzolino. She died in the aftermath of a stroke on April 19, 1689.

Summary

Christina has never quite died in terms of controversy over her reputation. She has been by turns slandered and revered, seen as a murderess of her lovers and as a saint who sacrificed her crown for religion. Clearly the fact that she was female and that she never married contributes to the fascination surrounding her. She was an anachronism in some ways; a woman with a strong personality and a sharp intellect would fit into the modern world much more smoothly than into the Baroque Age. It was perhaps partly her own inability to feel comfortable in her time that made her restlessly give up one crown, go on to seek two or three others, and change religions and homelands. Her attractive personality reaches across time to pull modern readers and historians into her sphere, as the physically plain queen was able to attract young courtiers, cardinals, and even noblewomen to her. Christina remains enigmatic, and perhaps this is why much of what has been written about her has focused on the questions of whether she had sexual relations with Sparre, Azzolino, Monaldeschi, or other members of her court, or on questions of her alleged hermaphroditism or lesbianism.

Yet Christina made a lasting contribution to Swedish and Italian cultural life. She commanded that libraries from the Continent be bought and shipped to Sweden, modeled the Swedish court on that of Louis XIV, and surrounded herself with many talented minds. In Rome, she continued to support the arts to the extent that her reduced means allowed, making her home a meeting place for culture and scholarship.

Bibliography

Goldsmith, Margaret. *Christina of Sweden: A Psychological Biography.* Garden City, N.Y.: Doubleday, Doran, 1933. A straightforward biography that is, despite the title, not of a particularly psychological orientation. The thesis and conclusion, that Christina left no mark on history, leads one to wonder why the author decided to write about this important figure. The bibliography is useful.

Gribble, Francis. *The Court of Christina of Sweden and the Later Adventures of the Queen in Exile.* New York: Mitchell Kennerley, 1913. Despite the title, this work is actually also a biography of Christina with a good discussion of her aphorisms presented in the last two chapters. The author sees, perhaps correctly, the relationship with Azzolino as the most important aspect of her life. Contains illustrations and an excellent annotated index.

Mackenzie, Faith Compton. *The Sibyl of the North: The Tale of Christina, Queen of Sweden*. London: Cassell, 1931. A nonscholarly biography, written in a chatty style, with a tendency to romanticize. Too much attention is paid to Christina's alleged love affairs. Contains a short bibliography, an annotated index, and four illustrations.

Masson, Georgina. *Queen Christina*. New York: Farrar, Straus & Giroux, 1968. An excellent, informative introduction that proceeds chronologically from a brief overview of Gustavus's career to the funding of a monument to Christina by Clement XI in 1701. Gives succinct and helpful explanations of the often-confusing historical events of the seventeenth century. Includes a well-organized bibliography, an annotated index, and interesting illustrations.

Rodén, Marie-Louise, ed. *Politics and Culture in the Age of Christina*. Stockholm: Swedish Institute in Rome, 1997.

Taylor, Ida A. *Christina of Sweden*. London: Hutchinson, 1909. An old-fashioned biography that, though engaging and basically accurate, suffers from its Victorian cast. Includes an annotated index and illustrations of major figures.

Woodhead, Henry. *Memoirs of Christina, Queen of Sweden*. London: Hurst and Blackett, 1863. This standard, two-volume treatment is indispensable for the serious student. It is well documented and gives a full picture of the political and historical climate surrounding Christina. The author takes the view that, despite her personal flaws, Christina made a considerable contribution to society. A selection of her aphorisms is given in English translation at the end.

Kathy Saranpa Anstine

CLEOPATRA VII

Born: 69 B.C.; Alexandria, Egypt
Died: 30 B.C.; Alexandria, Egypt

Cleopatra VII, as the last of the Ptolemaic Greek rulers of an independent Egypt, tried to come to terms with the ceaseless expansion of the Roman Empire throughout the Mediterranean and at her death left behind a rich, imperial province which continued to flourish as a center of commerce, science, and learning under Roman rule.

Early Life

Cleopatra VII was the daughter of Ptolemy XII Auletes and (possibly) of his sister and wife, Cleopatra Tryphaena. Such brother-sister marriages were common among the members of the Egyptian ruling house. It is believed that Cleopatra had three sisters, two older and one younger, and two younger brothers. Her representation with Negroid features by Michelangelo and her depiction as an Egyptian in cult paintings conceal her Macedonian ancestry; her family traced its lineage back to the Macedonian house of the Lagid Ptolemies, which had succeeded to the Egyptian throne after the untimely death of Alexander the Great in the early fourth century B.C. The Ptolemaic rule of Egypt was centered in Alexandria, the beautiful and populous city Alexander had founded to the west of the delta of the Nile when he invaded Egypt in 332 B.C.

Cleopatra was reared in a court beset by violence, murder, and corruption and dominated by the reality of Roman military might—all of which had played an important role in her father's accession to the throne. In 80 B.C., upon the death of Ptolemy Soter II, the only legitimate male Ptolemaic heir came to the throne as Ptolemy Alexander II. He was confirmed in power by the Romans but after murdering his wife, Berenice III, was himself murdered. Two illegitimate sons of Ptolemy Soter II were now claimants to the kingship.

The Romans put one brother in control of Cyprus. The other, Cleopatra's father, Ptolemy Theos Philopator Philadelphos Neos Dionysos—or, as he was known to the Alexandrians, Ptolemy XII Auletes (the Flute Player)—succeeded to the throne of Egypt. His relations with his subjects were difficult, in part because he recognized, unlike them, the growing power of Rome throughout the Mediterranean and realized that the only way to secure his position was to maintain close contact with the rulers of the world. During a visit to Rome, when he was hoping by means of massive bribes to secure the aid of the Roman army, his daughter, Berenice, in alliance with Archilaus, son of Mithridates, seized the throne, only to be put to death by her father upon his return.

When Ptolemy XII Auletes died in 51 B.C., after nearly thirty stormy years in office, he willed the kingdom of Egypt to his seventeen-year-old daughter and his ten-year-old son, who ruled jointly as Cleopatra VII and Ptolemy XIII Philopator. The young Ptolemy, however, soon fell under the influence of his advisers—Pothinus, a eunuch; Theodotus, a rhetorician; and Achillas the army commander—who must have found the boy king far more manipulable than his older sister, the intelligent, headstrong, energetic Cleopatra. As a result, Cleopatra was driven from Alexandria. When Julius Caesar arrived in Egypt, in pursuit of Pompey after the Battle of Pharsalus in 48, Cleopatra was in Pelusium, on the eastern frontier of Egypt, with her newly acquired army preparing to attack her brother and his associates.

Caesar, as Rome's official representative, was in a position to arbitrate between the siblings, and his plan to reconcile Cleopatra and Ptolemy might have worked had not Ptolemy's advisers decided that power should remain in their own grasp. In the resulting showdown, known as the Alexandrian War, Caesar was victorious—but not without a struggle. Pothinus, Achillas, and Ptolemy were all killed, and Cleopatra was restored by Caesar to the throne, this time with Ptolemy XIV, her younger brother, as consort. By 48 B.C., Cleopatra was in control of Egypt.

Life's Work

From this point onward, Cleopatra's future is inexorably intertwined with that of Rome and her leaders. In their writings, Plutarch and Suetonius dwell on the love affair that developed between Julius Caesar, then in his fifties, and the twenty-one-year-old Cleopatra. In spite of the arguments to the contrary, the child born to Cleopatra shortly after Caesar left Egypt on his eastern campaign was probably Caesar's son. At any rate, Cleopatra, by naming the child Caesarion, was claiming that her son was indeed the son of the Roman conqueror. Moreover, young Octavian, Caesar's heir, who had most to fear if Julius Caesar had a genuine son, had Caesarion put to death in 30 B.C., immediately after the death of Cleopatra.

Claudette Colbert portrays Cleopatra in Cecil B. DeMille's epic 1934 film, one of many modern representations of the legendary Egyptian queen. *(The Museum of Modern Art, Film Stills Archive)*

Little is known about Cleopatra's rule of Egypt, although there is evidence that she tried to win the favor of the farmers by reducing their taxes. From 46 B.C., she was living in Rome with Caesarion and Ptolemy XIV. The reason stated for her visit was that she had come to ask the senate for confirmation of her father's treaty of friendship; yet she was lodged by Caesar, along with Caesarion and Ptolemy XIV, in his villa in Trastevere, where she attempted to cultivate good relations with as many influential Romans as possible. Caesar also put a golden statue of Cleopatra in the temple of Venus Genetrix at Rome, thus associating her with the goddess who was in legend the mother of Aeneas and thus of the Julian line. He may have planned to gain special permission from the Roman people to contract a legal marriage with her, since his Roman wife was childless. The plans were frustrated by Caesar's assassination in 44 B.C., and Cleopatra probably left Rome shortly afterward.

Egypt's wealth did not pass unnoticed by the Romans, so it is not surprising that during Marc Antony's eastern campaign after the Battle of Philippi in 42 B.C. he saw the chance of subsidizing his wars by taxing Cleopatra's subjects. Cleopatra was shrewd enough to realize that her personal charms would be far more effective in preserving her kingdom than would open confrontation. Plutarch's account of the meeting between Antony and Cleopatra brilliantly describes both the fabulous wealth of the monarch and her grace. Just as Cleopatra had captivated Julius Caesar in her "salad days" when she "was green in judgment," she now in her maturity set out to win the heart of Antony.

After the formation of the so-called Second Triumvirate between Antony, Octavian, and Lepidus, which was sealed by Antony's marriage to Octavian's half sister Octavia, Cleopatra was left to rule Egypt. In 37 B.C., however, Antony's march eastward led to renewed friendship and an understanding between the two, which made available to Antony the resources of Egypt. From this time onward, Cleopatra's influence over Antony grew. She also now assumed Egyptian dress that represented the goddess Isis and is reported to have adopted the following oath: "As surely as I shall one day dispense judgment in the Roman Capitol." When Antony arranged for Caesarion and his own three children by Cleopatra to share in ruling both Egypt and Roman provinces in Asia Minor and formally divorced Octavia, Octavian declared war not against his fellow Roman Antony but against Cleopatra. He must have realized that Antony could not help but join Cleopatra.

At the Battle of Actium in 31 B.C., Cleopatra's Egyptian forces, together with Antony's Roman forces, faced Octavian's fleet, commanded by Marcus Vipsanius Agrippa. When Cleopatra retreated, she was quickly followed by Antony. Cleopatra's suicide in 30 B.C. marked the end of Ptolemaic rule and the beginning of direct Roman rule in what was now an imperial province.

Summary

The historical picture of Cleopatra VII is one-sided. Very little is known of her apart from her association with the two Roman generals Julius Caesar and Marc Antony. As one might expect, the Roman writers do little to enhance her reputation. In the work of Augustan poets, she is never mentioned by name, but merely as "the queen," "the woman," or "that one." She is chiefly seen as a crazy drunkard, surrounded by wrinkled eunuchs. Horace also pays tribute to her courage, but he, Vergil, and Sextus Propertius, whose livelihood depended upon Octavian's bounty, quite clearly toe the party line in suggesting that she received no more than she deserved. William Shakespeare's depiction of her as high-spirited, shrewd, sensuous, and fickle is based on that found in Plutarch, a Greek biographer, who mentions her only in association with his two heroes, Caesar and Antony. Yet Plutarch also depicts her as a highly intelligent woman who, unlike her Ptolemaic predecessors, actually went to the trouble of learning the language of her subjects. He reports, moreover, that she could converse easily with "Ethiopians, Troglodytes, Hebrews, Arabians, Syrians, Medes, or Parthians" in their own languages.

Although Cleopatra is often imagined as a ravishing beauty because of the ease with which she seduced experienced and mature soldiers such as Caesar and Antony, a few coins survive depicting her as large-nosed and sharp-chinned. She was also ruthless. After the Alexandrian War, Caesar thought it sufficient to expel Cleopatra's sister, Arsinoe, for her part in the uprising; Cleopatra later had her put to death.

Plutarch in fact describes not so much her beauty as her charm, humor, and ability to amuse and delight her company. She probably also made a powerful impression on the Romans by her intelligence and political ambition. The Roman political system was in a period of transition. Republican government had proved inadequate. Egypt in Cleopatra's time and afterward was essential as a source of wheat for the Roman populace, and its master, if properly armed, could dictate his terms to Italy and the Roman senate. As the creation of Alexander the Great and the place where he was buried, Alexandria provided an obvious starting point for the revival of his empire and its extension even as far as India. The capital of the Roman Empire would eventually be shifted to the east anyway, by Diocletian and Constantine the Great. Legend related that the Romans' ancestor Aeneas originated from Troy in Asia Minor. There may well be some truth in the stories that Caesar intended, if he had lived, to remove the capital to the old site of Troy, and Antony may have been captivated by his dead commander's vision. Cleopatra gambled that, with the aid of such Roman generals, she could make her dynasty a partner in a new eastern empire that would reduce Rome to second place. Like Caesar and Antony, she failed because she was ahead of her time. Her failure has fascinated many throughout the centuries—including Shakespeare and George Bernard Shaw—who have felt the romance and energy of her ambitions.

Bibliography

Bevan, Edwyn. *The House of Ptolemy: A History of Egypt Under the Ptolemaic Dynasty*. Chicago: Argonaut, 1927, rev. ed. 1968. In chapter 13, Bevan offers a brief account of the final days of Ptolemaic rule. Includes illustrations of coins depicting Cleopatra.

Flamarion, Edith. *Cleopatra: The Life and Death of a Pharoah*. Translated by Alexandra Bonfante-Warren. New York: Harry N. Abrams, 1997.

Fraser, P. M. *Ptolemaic Alexandria*. 3 vols. Oxford, England: Clarendon Press, 1972. The most comprehensive and scholarly treatment of the entire period of Ptolemaic rule. Especially valuable for the massively detailed citation of primary sources.

Hughes-Hallett, Lucy. *Cleopatra: Histories, Dreams, and Distortions*. New York: Harper & Row, 1990.

Lindsay, Jack. *Cleopatra*. New York: Coward-McCann, 1971. A complete treatment of Cleopatra's achievements, aspirations, and influence. Many details of political events of the period help to place Cleopatra's defeat in a Roman context. Lindsay includes full notes citing ancient sources and provides a bibliography.

Marlowe, John. *The Golden Age of Alexandria*. London: Victor Gollancz, 1971. A popular treatment of one of the most famous cities, from antiquity to its capture in the sixth century A.D. Includes a discussion of Cleopatra.

Plutarch. "Caesar." In *Fall of the Roman Republic*, translated by Rex Warner. Harmondsworth, England: Penguin Books, 1958. The meeting of Caesar and Cleopatra is recounted in chapters 48 and 49. Plutarch accepts Caesar's paternity of Caesarion.

_____. "Mark Antony." In *Makers of Rome*, translated by Ian Scott-Kilvert. Harmondsworth, England: Penguin Books, 1965. Offers by far the best depiction of the intelligence, vivaciousness, shrewdness, cunning, and ruthlessness of Cleopatra. This life of Antony was used to great effect by Shakespeare in his famous play.

Pomeroy, Sarah B. *Women in Hellenistic Egypt: From Alexander to Cleopatra*. New York: Schocken Books, 1984. Chapter 1, which discusses the queens of Ptolemaic Egypt, places Cleopatra in a historical context. Pomeroy's discussion of married women, slaves, and women of the capital city of Alexandria—and the overall role of women in the economy in Cleopatra's time—brilliantly depicts the female subjects of this great queen.

Volkmann, H. *Cleopatra: A Study in Politics and Propaganda*. Translated by T. J. Cadoux. New York: Sagamore Press, 1958. Volkmann's excellent treatment provides a full account of all periods of Cleopatra's life and reign and her influence on world history. His appendix gives a brief survey of modern and ancient literature, and his genealogical tables and maps are helpful.

Weigall, Arthur. *The Life and Times of Cleopatra Queen of Egypt*. New York: G. P. Putnam's Sons, 1924. Although dated, this book gives a shrewd assessment of Cleopatra's relationship with Caesar and Antony. Weigall argues that Caesar was quite clearly intending to move the center of Roman power to the east and that in Cleopatra he had found an ally uniquely qualified to help him realize his plans.

Frances Stickney Newman

HILLARY RODHAM CLINTON

Born: October 26, 1947; Chicago, Illinois

A highly regarded lawyer and activist for children's rights and comprehensive health care, Clinton also became her husband's most important adviser when he served as governor of Arkansas and president of the United States.

Early Life

Hillary Diane Rodham was born on October 26, 1947, in Chicago, Illinois. Her father Hugh was a textile merchant who married Dorothy Howell in 1942. Hugh's success in making draperies for hotels and corporate offices enabled the family to move to the upper-middle-class suburb of Park Ridge in 1950.

Growing up in a tightly knit family with her two brothers provided Hillary with what she later called her "core values." Along with her parents' unconditional love and support came their high expectations for achievement and a demand for responsible behavior and hard work. Hillary responded by becoming an honor student in high school who excelled at numerous extracurricular activities, including debate and student government. Her interest in politics led her to work as a volunteer in the 1964 presidential campaign for Barry Goldwater, a Republican candidate who reflected the conservative beliefs of her family and neighborhood.

The Methodist Church was another early influence in Hillary's life. The emphasis upon the social mission of the church as well its teachings on personal faith and growth appealed to her. Youth minister Don Jones was particularly influential. He took youth groups to meet inner-city teenagers, and he encouraged Hillary to help organize day care services for migrant farm workers. In 1962, Jones took a youth group to hear an address from the Reverend Martin Luther King, Jr., who spoke on the need to eradicate social injustice. Jones also introduced Hillary to the writings of liberal theologians Paul Tillich and Reinhold Niebuhr, works concerned with alienation and the search for meaning. Hillary later acknowledged that Jones not only whetted her intellectual curiosity but also demonstrated to her the necessity of helping those less fortunate than herself.

The evolution of her values was accelerated when Hillary Rodham entered Wellesley College near Boston, Massachusetts, in 1965. Amidst the turbulence of the late 1960's, she became a social activist. Rodham worked at a Head Start center in the Roxbury neighborhood of Boston, joined in an effort to recruit more minority students to Wellesley, organized teach-ins on the Vietnam War, and won election as president of Wellesley's student government.

The culmination of her undergraduate experience came when her classmates selected Rodham to deliver the first student commencement address at Wellesley. She offered a message common to that era, arguing that her generation was seeking an alternative to the "competitive corporate life" and wanted to find "more immediate, ecstatic, and penetrating modes of living." Her commencement message attracted national attention when *Life* magazine published a photograph of her and quotations from her address. The next logical step for Rodham, a political science major whose senior thesis was on poverty and community development, was Yale Law School, an institution known for its "social" approach to law.

Life's Work

Besides compiling an excellent academic record, Hillary Rodham met two important people during her time at Yale. In 1970, Marian Wright Edelman, who headed an advocacy group for poor children, made a speech on the campus. Rodham was so impressed by Edelman's appeal that she decided to work as an intern with her in Washington, D.C., during the summer of 1970. Eager to learn more about the problems of children, Rodham worked at the Yale Child Study Center upon her return to law school and began a study of child development and children's rights. From this research, she wrote an article entitled "Children Under the Law" that appeared in the *Harvard Educational Review* in 1974.

The other significant person Rodham met at Yale was a Rhodes scholar from Arkansas named Bill Clinton. Although he was initially intimidated by Rodham, Clinton quickly found that they were intellectually as well as romantically compatible. The two traveled to Texas in 1972 to work on George McGovern's presidential campaign. Following graduation the next year, however, Rodham became a staff attorney for Edelman's Children's Defense Fund in Cambridge, Massachusetts, and Clinton accepted a position on the faculty of the University of Arkansas Law School at Fayetteville.

In January, 1974, Rodham joined the legal team headed by John Doar, special counsel to the House Judiciary Committee, selected to conduct the impeachment investigation of President Richard Nixon. One of only three women among the forty-three lawyers picked, Rodham helped establish the procedural guidelines for the investigation.

Hillary Rodham Clinton *(Library of Congress)*

After President Nixon resigned in August, 1974, Hillary decided to join Bill Clinton on the faculty of the University of Arkansas Law School and helped organized his congressional campaign against long-time incumbent Republican John Paul Hammerschmidt. Although he lost in a close contest, Clinton made a name for himself in Arkansas politics and ran successfully two years later for the post of attorney general.

Bill and Hillary, who had married on October 11, 1975, moved to the state capital in Little Rock, Arkansas, in 1976. Both had worked in Jimmy Carter's presidential campaign that year, Bill in Arkansas and Hillary in Indiana. Impressed by her efforts in the campaign and her legal expertise, President Carter appointed Hillary in 1977 to serve on the board of the Legal Services Corporation, an agency that administered funds for legal services to the indigent. She also became the first female associate in the Rose Law Firm in Little Rock, where she specialized in family law and commercial litigation.

Beginning in 1978, Hillary Rodham was a crucial figure in her husband's six campaigns for governor, all of which he won except the 1980 race. An effective and tireless speaker, she also became a valued adviser on campaign tactics and issues. Despite her expertise, Hillary was perceived by some as a hindrance to the success of her husband's gubernatorial races. After her marriage, she kept her maiden name until 1982 because she had developed her professional reputation as Hillary Rodham. Traditionalists in Arkansas, however, disapproved. They also did not want the state's first lady to continue her career. More serious were charges that her continued affiliation with the Rose Law Firm brought the governor into a conflict of interest whenever the firm did legal work for the state.

Such concerns did not prevent Governor Clinton from appointing his wife to chair some significant statewide committees. The most important appointment came in 1983 when she headed the Arkansas Education Standards Committee. She tackled the challenge in a way that presaged her effort a decade later to reform health care. She spoke to civic groups around the state and held hearings in every Arkansas county. In all, she heard from thousands of citizens; from those exchanges, she crafted a package of reforms for the legislature's consideration. An improved curriculum, reduced class size, mandatory student testing, improved teacher salaries, and a sales tax increase to pay for the improvements were approved by the legislature and began to be implemented in 1987.

While Hillary Clinton impressed most with her organizational skills, excellent speeches, and an impressive two-hour presentation to the Arkansas House, she angered many teachers. Believing that demonstrating teacher competency was the only way to convince voters to support a tax increase, Hillary Clinton included mandatory tests for all public schoolteachers in Arkansas in the reform package approved by the legislators. Demanding accountability from those benefiting from reform became a hallmark of her efforts.

Clinton's life was not consumed entirely by campaigning and serving on committees. She devoted time to caring for her daughter Chelsea, who was born on February 27, 1980, and in carrying out some of the traditional ceremonial functions of the state's first lady. Hillary also found time to advance her career. After the Rose Law Firm made her partner in 1979, she branched out into patent infringement and other intellectual property cases. Acknowledging her growing influence, several enterprises, including the nation's leading retailer Wal-Mart, selected her to serve on their boards. Clinton's considerable accomplishments brought her numerous honors. Most notable, in both 1988 and 1991, the *National Law Journal* named her one of the hundred most influential lawyers in the nation.

When Bill Clinton joined the race for the 1992 Democratic presidential nomination, Hillary became a campaign issue. During the 1992 Republican Convention, for example, some speakers portrayed her as a radical feminist who represented a threat to the traditional family. Most damaging to the Clintons, however, were charges of Bill's infidelity. Rumors of marital problems had plagued the couple in the 1980's in Arkansas, but these rumors became headline stories when Gennifer Flowers, a former Arkansas television reporter and lounge singer, claimed she had had a twelve-year affair with Bill Clinton. While all the questions were not answered, Hillary Clinton played a major role in defusing the story in an appearance she made with her husband on the CBS news program *60 Minutes* in January, 1992. She not only vigorously defended her husband's character but also told a national audience that everyone, including political candidates, should "have some zone of privacy."

Following his inauguration, President Clinton demonstrated his faith in Hillary's abilities by naming her to head the most important commission of his new administration, the Task Force on National Health Care Reform. As she had done in the Arkansas legislature a decade earlier, Hillary Clinton impressed the national media and congressmen alike with her knowledge and poise in two days of hearings in the House of Representatives. Throughout 1993, she enjoyed high ratings in public opinion polls. The only significant concern with the First Lady's performance were questions about the legalities involved in the Clintons' investments in the Arkansas Whitewater Development Corporation. In April, 1994, she held a special press conference to answer questions and counter criticism that she had been less than forthcoming about her role in the corporation's activities.

While Hillary Clinton's legal problems persisted, in 1998 they were suddenly overshadowed by accusations that the president had given a false deposition in a sexual harrassment case. The case had been dismissed, but secretly tape-recorded conversations with Monica Lewinsky, a former White House intern and one of the witnesses in the case, revealed that the president had an "inappropriate relationship" with her. Both Lewinsky and the president at first denied the relationship, then claimed that it did not qualify as "sexual." The First Lady staunchly defended her husband, insisting that he was the victim of a right-wing witch-hunt. Throughout the impeachment process that followed, Hillary Clinton maintained a subdued but iron dignity. There was some criticism that she was too attached either to her husband or to public office, but overall her dedication to her family and her demeanor under public scrutiny earned for her the admiration of much of the country.

Some critics had derided Hillary Clinton's performance as First Lady because she had not been elected to office. In 1999, after much testing of public opinion, she decided to take a more active role in politics by declaring herself a candidate in the Senate race to replace retiring New York Democrat Daniel Patrick Moynihan.

Summary
In the eyes of many, Hillary Rodham Clinton became a role model in demonstrating the gains resulting from the changing status of women. While she refused to discard the roles of wife and mother, Hillary was not reluctant to embrace a career in both the private and public sectors.

That she was highly regarded in both areas was a testament to her intelligence, ambition, and skills as a politician. These achievements were not without costs. As they observed her rise to prominence, some portrayed Hillary as overbearing and arrogant, charges that ambitious, successful women often faced in the late twentieth century.

Most of her public struggles—for children's rights, better schools, and quality health care accessible to all—are best understood as an effort to help families fulfill their societal obligations. In pursuing these reforms, Hillary Clinton was doing more than following the social mission she learned as a teenager in the Methodist Church. She was also demonstrating that the old labels of liberal and conservative were no longer useful for many reformers in the late twentieth century. She advocated the use of government power to extend rights to citizens, but she also demanded that those citizens be accountable, that they demonstrate a sense of responsibility. In helping to redefine the relationship between government and the people, Hillary Rodham Clinton found the political meaning she had been seeking.

Bibliography

Andersen, Christopher. *Bill and Hillary: The Marriage*. New York: William Morrow, 1999.

Brock, David. *The Seduction of Hillary Rodham*. New York: Free Press, 1996.

Kelly, Michael. "Saint Hillary." *The New York Times Magazine*, May 23, 1993, 22-25, 63-66. Kelly offers a critical discussion of Clinton's efforts at reform. He sees her as one of a long line of do-gooders seeking to impose her view of morality on the populace.

Martin, Nina. "Who Is She?" *Mother Jones* 18 (November/December, 1993): 34-38, 43. In a largely complimentary article, Martin describes Hillary Rodham Clinton as a moderate reformer. More important, as she discusses Hillary's career, the author explores how marriage to Bill Clinton restricted Hillary's options.

Milton, Joyce. *The First Partner: Hillary Rodham Clinton*. New York: William Morrow, 1999.

Nelson, Rex, and Philip Martin. *The Hillary Factor*. New York: Gallen, 1993. This work by the political editor and a political columnist for the *Arkansas Democrat-Gazette* offers the perspective of reporters who covered Clinton during her almost two decades in Arkansas politics.

Olson, Barbara. *Hell to Pay: The Unfolding Story of Hillary Rodham Clinton.* Washington, D.C.: Regnery, 1999.

Radcliffe, Donnie. *Hillary Rodham Clinton: A First Lady for Our Time.* New York: Warner Books, 1993. The author, a *Washington Post* reporter, offers a full-length biography of Clinton. One of the virtues of the book is that the author was able to draw upon two extensive interviews with Clinton.

Sheehy, Gail. *Hillary's Choice.* London: Simon & Schuster, 1999.

Wills, Garry. "H. R. Clinton's Case." *New York Review of Books* 39 (March 5, 1992): 3-5. Through an examination of her articles and speeches, Wills offers an analysis of Clinton as an activist for children's rights. He concludes that she was one of the most important scholaractivists of the 1970's and 1980's.

Larry Gragg

DEBORAH

Born: c. 1200 B.C.-1125 B.C.; central Israel
Died: c. 1200 B.C.-1124 B.C.; central Israel

A Joan of Arc of the Bible, Deborah rallied Israelite tribes to defeat oppressors as she had prophesied; her victory poem is considered one of Scripture's most ancient texts.

Early Life

The biblical figure named Deborah is believed to have lived between 1125 B.C. and 1200 B.C. These years, falling between the death of Joshua and the institution of the monarchy in ancient Israel, are recounted in the biblical book of Judges. Tradition assigns Joshua as Moses' successor, charged with leading the loose federation of Hebrew tribes that were resettling ancestral lands in the area then known as Canaan. Whether or not the initial stage of resettlement proceeded as a unified military effort under Joshua, instability marked the years chronicled in Judges. Archaeological evidence supports a scenario of periods of war and crisis alternating with peaceful intervals during the twelfth and eleventh centuries B.C. Most towns in the region apparently suffered destruction, indicating a time of turmoil and uncertainty.

The Bible views the era as a cycle of lapses into idolatry punished by Yahweh through the agency of outside aggressors, followed by repentance and subsequent deliverance by divinely appointed leaders, or "judges." In Deborah's lifetime, the Israelites had become enslaved to Jabin, the king of Canaan. Scripture states that following the death of the judge Ehud, the people had fallen under the sway of gods other than Yahweh, who in turn, had given them up to their Canaanite oppressors.

The vulnerability of the Israelite population during Deborah's formative years would have highlighted her role as childbearer, particularly in a patriarchal society in which a man could sell his daughter as payment for debts. Yet the primacy of survival also required that women labor alongside men for the good of the community.

Deborah's development may have been affected by her tribal affiliation. Residing in the hill country in what is now central Israel, she was most likely a member of the tribe of Ephraim. The central position of their area of settlement, along with the fact that the religious center of Shiloh was located in their territory, engendered in the Ephraimites a proud and even militant spirit.

Life's Work

The fourth chapter of the biblical book of Judges introduces Deborah as a prophet to whom people came to settle controversies. She is described as bestowing her counsel under a palm tree, apparently a sacred site popularly associated with the burial place of Deborah, the nurse of the matriarch Rebecca.

Some see in this image the kahin (or *kahina*), known from nomadic Arabic tribes as a kind of magician or fortune-teller holding court and dispensing judgments in a sanctified place. A common phenomenon in antiquity, prophecy was essentially oracular; that is, it involved communication of the divine will regarding a specific matter. The prophet thus played a prominent role in the political life of a community by delivering messages in the name of a god. Nothing in the biblical account indicates that Deborah as a female functioned in the role of prophet any differently than a male. Nevertheless, it has been suggested that, as a woman whose priority was child rearing, her calling was at best part time during her childbearing years and may not even have begun until later in life.

As one to whom they came with their troubles and concerns, Deborah was no doubt keenly aware of her people's suffering under Jabin. Headed by Jabin's field commander, Sisera, the Canaanite army was equipped with iron chariots, giving them considerable military superiority over the Israelites, who were still technologically in the Bronze Age. This advantage enabled the Canaanites to control the passage through the valleys that separated the mountain tribes in the center of the land—including Ephraim, where Deborah resided—and those in the north, in Galilee, thus ensuring their subjugation of the Israelites.

Despite this obstacle, after twenty years of domination, Deborah initiated a war of liberation by summoning a military commander, a man named Barak, out of Kedesh-naphtali in the northern reaches of the territory. Because of the similarity of meaning between the name Barak ("lightning") and that of Deborah's apparent husband, Lapidoth ("torches"), some medieval commentators identify Barak as her spouse.

Most commentators, however, fail to find this identification borne out by the context. Based on the ambiguity stemming from the Hebrew word *esheth*, signifying either "woman" or "wife," and the question of whether *Lapidoth* is a proper noun, at least one commentator—Pseudo-Philo, the author of the first century *Biblical Antiquities*— interprets *esheth lapidoth* to mean "fiery woman," or "enlightener." The phrase therefore refers to Deborah herself and not her marital status, though given the social conventions of the time, it is doubtful that Deborah was unmarried, whether her husband is named in the biblical account.

In any event, in her role as prophet and now as judge, Deborah relayed Yahweh's command that Barak gather a force of ten thousand volunteers to Mount Tabor, at the boundary of the territories of the northern tribes of Zebulun, Naphtali, and Issachar. Barak, convinced of Deborah's power and influence, refused to act unless she accompanied him. She agreed, declaring that Sisera would suffer defeat at the hand of a woman.

True to Deborah's reckoning, Sisera and his army approached Mount Tabor from the south, along the valley of the river Kishon. The strategy of the poorly armed Israelite tribes was to exploit the flooding of the riverbed and lure Sisera and his nine hundred iron chariots into the muddy river valley. The Israelites descended the mountain and engaged the enemy in Taanach, by the waters of Megiddo, a Canaanite town located near a tributary of the Kishon. As the Israelites had planned, the Canaanites' chariots sank deep in the mire, leaving their troops to be routed by the Israelites. Not one of Sisera's camp escaped, though Sisera himself fled by foot to the tent of Jael, wife of Heber, a Kenite with whom Jabin was apparently at peace. Offering Sisera hospitality, Jael then proceeded to drive a nail into his head as he slept. There Barak tracked Sisera down, defeated as Deborah had said by a woman—by herself as well as Jael, many would argue. The victory over Sisera that Deborah had inspired ushered in a forty-year span of prosperity for Israel, twice the years of their oppression.

The narrative in Judges, chapter 4, names only the tribes of Naphtali and Zebulun as fighting in the battle against Sisera. The account of the victory in poetic form that follows in chapter 5, however, cites numerous tribes, either extolling their participation (Ephraim, Benjamin, and Issachar, as well as Naphtali and Zebulun) or condemning their absence (Reuben, Dan, and Asher). This hymn of triumph is said to be sung by Deborah and Barak, though the Hebrew verb is in the feminine form. Also in support of the claim that what has become known as the "Song of Deborah" was indeed authored by a woman, commentators note the presence of many feminine images. Chief among them is Deborah as "a mother in Israel." Her bold actions are understood to be that of a mother fiercely protective of her family—metaphorically, the family of her people. Female authorship is supported as well by the fact that more of the text is devoted to the actions of Jael and Sisera's mother—imagined as anxiously awaiting her son's return—than to a recapitulation of the battle.

Summary

The defeat of Sisera, instigated by Deborah, proved decisive in the decline of the Canaanite kingdom, thus easing the resettlement of the area by the Israelites. This proved significant in the history of religion, as both Judaism and Christianity developed from the nation that formed from Israelite expansion into the territory. Deborah's poetic reconstruction of the defeat has also made a mark in literary history. The Song of Deborah is intensively studied as one of the most ancient texts in Scripture, and it also forms part of the Jewish liturgy.

Commentators have noted how unremarkable Deborah's judgeship appears in the biblical text. Yet while the Scripture portrays Deborah as a woman of power and influence, interpreters of the biblical tradition have often blunted her impact. Flavius Josephus, in his first century account of Jewish history, omits any mention of Deborah's role as military strategist or judge, displaying a discomfort with a woman exercising authority over men that appears in rabbinical commentaries as well. The rabbis actually chastise Deborah for sending for Barak rather than going to him.

"We never hear sermons pointing women to the heroic virtues of Deborah as worthy of their imitation," bemoaned nineteenth century American suffragist Elizabeth Cady Stanton. Instead, she noted, "the lessons doled out to women" exhorted "meekness and self-abnegation." In the latter half of the twentieth century, the precedent set by Deborah has taken on new significance—in large part as a result of the rise of the women's movement and the rebirth of the state of Israel, whose fourth prime minister was a woman and whose women have, from the nation's beginning, served in its military.

Bibliography

Bird, Phyllis. "Images of Women in the Old Testament." In *Religion and Sexism: Images of Women in the Jewish and Christian Traditions*, edited by Rosemary Radford Ruether. New York: Simon & Schuster, 1974. Writing from a feminist perspective, Bird views Deborah as an exceptional women whose story is recounted in a book that portrays a man's world, that is, a world dominated by war and issues of power and control.

Brown, Cheryl Anne. *No Longer Be Silent: First Century Portraits of Biblical Women*. Gender and the Biblical Tradition Series. Louisville, Ky.: Westminster/John Knox Press, 1992. Examines references to Deborah in Pseudo-Philo's *Biblical Antiquities* and Flavius Josephus's *Jewish Antiquities*, retellings of the biblical narrative composed during Judaism's and Christianity's formative years. Brown's discussion demonstrates the variability of Deborah's image in Western religious tradition. A bibliography and index are provided, along with endnotes.

Deen, Edith. *All the Women of the Bible*. New York: Harper & Row, 1955. A highly reverential treatment of the biblical character, rife with speculation on her feelings and motivations. Contains a bibliography and index.

Fitzpatrick, Carol Flynn. *Deborah*. Uhrichsville, Ohio: Barbour Books, 1996. This book in the Young Reader's Christian Library is illustrated by Ken Save.

Lacks, Roslyn. *Women and Judaism: Myth, History, and Struggle*. New York: Doubleday, 1980. Concludes that Deborah's story counteracts conventional assumptions about women derived from elsewhere in the Bible as well as from rabbinic literature. Includes a bibliography, index, and endnotes.

Otwell, John H. *And Sarah Laughed: The Status of Woman in the Old Testament*. Philadelphia: Westminster Press, 1977. In two chapters, "Freedom of Action" and "Women in the Cult," Deborah's example is used to argue that women participated fully in the life of the ancient community of Israel. Provides a bibliography and index; because the index is of biblical passages, however, familiarity with Scripture is helpful.

Phipps, William E. *Assertive Biblical Women*. Contributions in Women's Studies 128. Westport, Conn.: Greenwood Press, 1992. Briefly examines Deborah in her various leadership roles. Contends that ancient society practiced gender egalitarianism to a greater degree than later generations. Offers endnotes as well as an index and select bibliography.

Williams, James G. *Women Recounted: Narrative Thinking and the God of Israel.* Bible and Literature Series. Sheffield, England: Almond Press, 1982. Views the biblical texts from a literary perspective, so that the figure of Deborah owes less to historical accuracy than to ancient literary conventions. Contains a bibliography, endnotes, and an index of biblical passages.

Amy Allison

DIANA, PRINCESS OF WALES

Born: July 1, 1961; Park House, near Sandringham, Norfolk, England
Died: August 31, 1997; Paris, France

Through her strong devotion to humanitarian causes, ranging from abolition of land mines to compassionate concern for the terminally ill, Diana revolutionized and uplifted the public image of British royalty in the 1990's.

Early Life

Diana Frances Spencer, the future wife of Prince Charles, was the youngest daughter of Viscount and Viscountess Althorp, later Earl Spencer and Mrs. Shand-Kydd. One sister, Jane, married Robert Fellowes, later private secretary to Queen Elizabeth. The other, Sarah, was one of Prince Charles's girlfriends before marrying Neil McCorquodale, a former army officer. Diana was especially close to her younger brother Charles, who fondly remembered her taking an almost maternal interest in him on his first day at school. Diana's early childhood years also provided her with the nickname "Duchess" (or "Dutch") by which close friends always knew her. Typical of the ironies that pervaded her life, it had no connection with royalty, being instead the name of the leading feline in Walt Disney's animated film *The Aristocats* (1970). It was, however, typical of Diana's childhood environment, emphasizing closeness with friends and animals. Although she grew up in a family with close ties to the monarchy (her birth home was on the queen's estate near Sandringham), she never developed a taste for country sports, especially fox hunting, which was later to prove a major difference between her and Prince Charles.

Diana first attended Riddlesworth Hall Preparatory School in Norfolk, then, starting in 1974, boarded at West Heath School southeast of London. In 1978, she attended the Institut Alpin Videmanette, a finishing school near Rougemont, Switzerland. Diana's critics often mentioned her twice failing the comprehensive tests taken by all students in their mid-teens. This lack of academic success has been attributed to both the British habit of preparing upper-class women to be breeders and homemakers and to a lack of self-esteem resulting from her parents' divorce.

Diana's first job after moving into a London flat in 1980 was to look after the infant son of an American couple. At this time, she also worked as a kindergarten teacher at the Young England School in Pimlico in south central London.

Life's Work
The defining event in Diana's life was her marriage to Prince Charles, heir to the British throne. Their friendship dated from a shooting party in November, 1977, to which Diana's sister Sarah had invited him. Later at a barbecue in July, 1980, Charles asked Diana to marry him after she expressed sympathy for the loneliness he felt over the assassination of his uncle, Lord Louis Mountbatten.

Romantic illusions aside, Charles had found what he required: a Protestant virgin with pedigree. Diana's marital goals were simpler; from early childhood she had stated her intents as falling in love, marrying, and having children with a husband to whom she could devote much time and support. However, some friends were concerned about her youth and lack of awareness about the demands of her official role and the different lifestyles of a royal such as Charles and a private upper-class girl such as Diana. The wedding on July 29, 1981, drew a media audience of millions of people, with 600,000 more lining the route from Buckingham Palace to St. Paul's Cathedral to view the first Englishwoman to marry an heir to the throne in three hundred years.

It seemed only appropriate that Diana's first official tour would be a visit to Wales, where she won the hearts of her hosts not only by her beauty and poise but also by delivering her speech in Welsh. However, the Welsh visit signaled a painful trend for which the prince had not been prepared: Diana's immense popularity. Traveling by car on public occasions, Charles could hear people complaining that they could see him but not her. Like other members of his family, Charles had been brought up to assume that the spotlight would nearly always be on him. Diana, meanwhile, was much distressed by his lack of sensitivity.

Diana produced a royal heir, Prince William, on January 21, 1982, and another son, Prince Henry (Harry), on September 15, 1984. The royal couple broke tradition when they brought Prince William with them on a tour of Australia and New Zealand in 1983. Solo overseas visits for Diana had begun in September, 1982, when she represented the queen at the funeral of Princess Grace of Monaco; later travels ranged from the United States to South Africa, Hungary, and Nepal.

After 1990, Diana's charitable work became highly visible, particularly patients with acquired immunodeficiency syndrome (AIDS) and many child welfare groups. Her campaign to ban land mines aided her colleague Jody Williams in receiving the 1997 Nobel Peace Prize. With respect to her sons, Diana's goals included teaching them to be responsive to the needs of all types of people. Thus they were taken to meet homeless people and patients suffering from cystic fibrosis and AIDS.

The evolution of Diana's relationship with fashion mirrored her movement from the unimaginative wardrobe of upper-class girls of 1980's London to an independent statement of personal values. Diana first embraced a romantic outburst of frills and flounces near her wedding. Realizing the need for resilience as her marital role grew more difficult, she learned to use clothing as a tool of power: A revealing black cocktail dress denoted sophistication, mature sexuality, and a rejection of conventional royal attire. By 1995, Diana had come far from the day when photographers maneuvered her into unconsciously revealing her legs through a long, flimsy skirt. Her later confidence showed in body-hugging, minimalist evening clothes, high hemlines and heels. She became a fashion icon for women of all ages and classes, and auctions of her designer dresses raised millions for her charities.

Diana's divorce from Prince Charles in 1992 forced her to resign as patron of many charities, but she continued with the English National Ballet and groups combating leprosy, AIDS, cancer, and children's diseases. Diana's biographers agree that her childhood had molded a woman who needed to be lavished with affection but that Charles, because of his upbringing, was incapable of responding to this need. Diana's initial response to the frustrations of her situation included attacks of bulimia and three attempts at suicide. The idea that the marriage was without love from the start has been rejected by biographers such as Charles Kay, who asserts that there were years when Charles and Diana's relationship was characterized by profound love and joy, especially the times near the birth of their children when they read poetry and listened to music by Russian composer Peter Tchaikovsky together.

The couple's marriage, however, was troubled by more than Diana's feelings of inadequacy; she was haunted by the frequent presence of Charles's previous girlfriend, Camilla Parker-Bowles, with whom he shared interests in riding, hunting, and other outdoor activities. Diana became convinced that she was not the sole object of his affection. Consequently Diana turned to other men for support, ranging from an acknowledged lover, James Hewitt, to a platonic close friend, James Gilbey, to her final involvement with Emad Mohamed "Dodi" al-Fayed, son of the owner of Harrods, London's elegant department store.

Though much debated, the precise relationship between Diana and Dodi al-Fayed may never be known. What is certain is that she much enjoyed his company and his warm, caring family who admired her for her individuality, not her position, and who also possessed the resources to protect her from invaders of privacy. Irony figured often in Diana's life: Named after the Roman goddess of hunting, she was relentlessly pursued by the media. The final irony may be that the Fayeds' wealth was not enough to avoid fatal errors of judgment, such as putting the couple into the care of a reserve chauffeur lacking specialized driving qualifications and who, on the fateful Saturday night of August 31, 1997, had drunk too much for safe driving. How much of a role press pursuit played in causing the vehicle containing the driver, a bodyguard, Dodi, and Diana to crash into a pillar of an underground expressway in Paris may never be determined.

The official time of Diana's death was 3:00 A.M., with the first floral tribute to her laid outside Buckingham Palace before 5:00 A.M. by a cab driver. By noon that Sunday, arrays of bouquets were in front of Harrods and Buckingham Palace. A carpet of blossoms, notes, teddy bears, and other gifts began swelling outside the gates of Kensington Palace, Diana's London home. In the week between Diana's death and funeral, the flower shops of Europe became denuded, and millions of people in Britain and abroad signed books of condolences in town halls, libraries, and even in supermarkets.

In death, Diana became, especially for those who had known her unstinting and genuine concern for others, a secular saint. Saints' resting places often become the object of pilgrimages. An awareness of this problem caused her family not to inter her in the parish church but on a private island at Althorp, the family estate, where her exact burial spot is known to very few. By the following July 1, Diana's followers had a means of objectifying their feelings when a museum honoring her achievements and memory was opened at Althorp. Also, the British government's announcement on July 31, 1998, of a total ban on land mines was timed to be implemented near the first anniversary of her death.

Summary

Diana's marriage to Prince Charles first focused media attention upon her beauty and nearly impeccable style in clothing. Her public demeanor seemed to fulfill the promise of a more accessible monarchy. The troubled marriage and subsequent divorce and Diana's openness with the British public about these matters caused many people to identify with her as a tragic figure, one capable of sharing the suffering and pain in their own lives. Her unexpected death paralyzed the world with grief for her and her sons. Questions about her relationship with Dodi al-Fayed and the possible involvement of press pursuit in causing the accident led to almost daily stories about Diana in newspapers around the world. Those who believed that Diana had been killed by the insatiable curiosity of the people to whom she had given so much continued to venerate her with nearly saintlike fervor. Many others remember Diana's keen, sometimes public, awareness of the problems of reconciling sensitive individualism and self-doubt with the impersonal image often demanded by her status. It was this awareness that identified her finally as the "People's Princess" and the "Queen of Hearts."

Bibliography

Burchill, Julie. *Diana*. London: Weidenfeld & Nicolson, 1998. Burchill, a novelist and social critic, views Diana's life as a fairy tale gone wrong, the story of a warm and witty woman trapped, used, and abused by Britain's royal dynasty. Includes a bibliography with over thirty items.

Campbell, Beatrix. *Sexual Politics and the Monarchy*. London: Women's Press, 1998. This strongly feminist account of Diana's life views her as a victim of sexual and social class expectations who was preyed upon by an insensitive husband and the insatiable media.

Holden, Anthony. *Diana: A Life and a Legacy*. London: Ebury Press, 1997. The brief text written by Holden, a veteran journalist who is well respected as Prince Charles's biographer, contributes much useful information and keen insights to a largely pictorial tribute. Contains 160 photographs.

Houman, Peter, and Derek McAdam. *Who Killed Diana?* London: Vision, 1998. The authors examine the circumstances of Diana's death, concluding that it was not an act of fate but of some person or group of people who allowed the crash to occur. They cite such possibilities as a mysterious group of men in the crowd around the Ritz Hotel before the disaster.

Kay, Richard, and Geoffrey Levy. *Diana: The Untold Story.* London: Boxtree, 1998. Kay and Levy deviate from the victim-oriented views of Diana in their assertion that her marriage, rather than being thoroughly painful, included many happy moments, especially with the births of their children.

Morton, Andrew. *Diana: Her True Story.* 1992. Rev. ed. London: Michael O'Mara, 1997. The author of several previous books about British royalty, Morton gained Diana's trust, which the princess exhibited by divulging much information about her situation, described by Morton as voiceless and powerless. Highly detailed with much material also provided by Diana's friends. This revised edition, published after Diana's death, includes additional selections from Morton's collection of taped interviews with Diana.

Robertson, Mary. *The Diana I Knew.* New York: HarperCollins, 1998. In early 1980, Diana worked for the Robertsons as a nanny for their infant son. Robertson remembers Diana as a sincere and committed woman who loathed formality and grew more extroverted and confident but was always in need of loving support and a strong home life.

Smith, Sally Bedell. *Diana in Search of Herself.* New York: Times Books, 1999.

Fran E. Chalfont

ELIZABETH DOLE

Born: July 29, 1936; Salisbury, North Carolina

As a dedicated government official, Dole served five American presidents in cabinet and other appointed positions before exploring a presidential run herself in 1999.

Early Life

Mary Elizabeth Hanford was the younger of John and Mary Cathey Hanford's two children. Her brother, John, was thirteen years her senior. Elizabeth's first name was not used, and she often called herself "Liddy" as a toddler because it was easier to pronounce. Liddy's father operated a successful wholesale floral business in Salisbury. Her mother gave up plans to study at the Juilliard School of Music to marry John Hanford. Cora Alexander Cathey, Liddy's maternal grandmother, influenced her greatly. Liddy admired her grandmother's positive attitude, selflessness, and strong faith.

Elizabeth's education began at Wiley and Boyston Schools in Salisbury and continued at Duke University and Harvard. She was an excellent student and was involved in many activities. She was a leader at an early age, and her classmates elected her president of the Third Grade Bird Club. She later started a Junior Book Club and named herself president. Liddy also wrote award-winning essays. For one, she received a trophy from the United Daughters of the Confederacy. In high school, she was involved in drama, the National Honor Society, and student government. Despite her campaign manager's attempts to compare her to Queen Elizabeth, Liddy lost an election for high-school class president.

In fall, 1954, Elizabeth Hanford decided to attend Duke University, where she majored in political science. In 1957, she was elected president of the Women's Student Government Association and was asked to join the White Duchy, an elite society that accepted only seven new members annually. Hanford graduated with honors from Duke in 1958 after being selected for membership in Phi Beta Kappa, a prestigious honor society for top students, and being named Leader of the Year.

After her graduation, Hanford rejected her brother's offer of a job in the family business. In fall, 1958, she began a job at the Harvard Law School library and enrolled in a master's degree program in education and government at Harvard in 1959.

In summer, 1960, she worked in the office of B. Everett Jordan, a senator from North Carolina. While working for Jordan, she networked with women in government, including Maine's Senator Margaret Chase Smith. Smith urged Hanford to earn a law degree. Elizabeth participated in her first national political campaign in 1960. She was a greeter in a whistle-stop campaign for vice presidential nominee Lyndon Baines Johnson.

In fall, 1960, Hanford took Margaret Chase Smith's advice and began law school at Harvard, despite her mother's concern and discouragement from her brother. Their initial resistance notwithstanding, Elizabeth's family eventually supported her decision. Besides grueling academic work, Hanford and the twenty-three other women in the 1965 Harvard Law School class of 550 endured a hostile environment. Some professors either refused to call on them or publicly embarrassed them.

Life's Work

After earning her law degree, Elizabeth Hanford moved to Washington, D.C., passed the bar exam for the District of Columbia in 1966, and obtained an entry position in the Department of Health, Education, and Welfare. When that job ended, she became a public defender, practicing law in Washington, D.C., from 1967 to 1968.

For the next six years, Hanford held several executive branch positions dealing with consumer interests. Under the Johnson administration, she became a consumer advocate. When Richard M. Nixon became president, many Johnson appointees resigned, but Hanford stayed. Her new boss, Virginia Knauer, a Nixon appointee, became her mentor.

In the early 1970's, Elizabeth Hanford began to receive rewards. She was named Washington's Outstanding Young Woman of the Year in 1970, and she received the Arthur S. Flemming Award for outstanding government service in 1972.

In 1972, Virginia Knauer urged Hanford to help her lobby Senator Robert Dole, head of the Republican Party, to include a consumerism plank in the party's platform. Bob and Elizabeth were impressed with each other when they first met, but Bob waited several months to call Elizabeth, reportedly concerned about their thirteen-year age difference. The two had much in common and enjoyed being together. Because of their demanding work schedules, theirs was often a telephone courtship.

Besides introducing Elizabeth to Bob, Knauer urged Nixon to nominate Hanford to fill a Federal Trade Commission (FTC) vacancy. Nixon agreed, but the director of the Senate committee that needed to confirm Elizabeth did not. Hanford asked the director what she needed to do to earn his support. He told her to get endorsements from consumer advocates, which she did.

Elizabeth Hanford was confirmed as a commissioner on December 3, 1973. At the FTC, she worked on many projects, some of which benefited women. The FTC investigated misleading claims about nursing home care and vigorously enforced the Equal Credit Opportunity Act, which was designed to help widowed or divorced women get credit. In 1975, Hanford helped start Executive Women in Government, a network intended to aid women's career advancement.

By fall, 1975, Bob and Elizabeth were serious about their relationship. They were married on December 6, 1975. Because of their high-profile positions, they were labeled a "power couple," a term that Elizabeth Dole disliked.

In 1979, Elizabeth resigned from the FTC to help Bob campaign for the Republican presidential nomination. Feminists criticized her for this, as they would in 1987 when she left a cabinet post for the same reason. Elizabeth disagreed with assessments made by women's groups that her decision was a letdown to her gender. She wanted to campaign for Bob and believed she should be free to make that choice.

Elizabeth Dole chaired Voters for Reagan-Bush in the 1980 presidential campaign. In 1981, Ronald Reagan appointed her assistant to the president for public liaison, a position she held until 1983. A longtime Equal Rights Amendment (ERA) proponent, Dole was serving in an administration that opposed that amendment. With limited success, she tried to convince women's groups that the Reagan administration would attack discrimination by urging governors to ban it in the states.

In January, 1983, Reagan named Elizabeth Dole secretary of transportation; she became the seventh woman to occupy a cabinet position. She was sworn in on February 7, 1983, and from then until October,

1987, she was in charge of more than one hundred thousand employees and a budget of twenty-seven billion dollars. Her vita boasts that the United States had the best safety record in its history while she headed the Department of Transportation (DOT). She was not, however, without critics. Some said that she irritated automakers but pleased consumers. The Center for Auto Safety, however, accused Dole of caving in to automakers.

Dole's major accomplishments at the DOT involved safety. She spearheaded a movement to raise the drinking age to twenty-one, backed random drug testing in public transportation, and improved traffic and air safety. While she was the head of the DOT, the agency passed a rule requiring airbags or automatic safety belts in 1990 model cars unless two-thirds of the country's population lived in states with strict seat-belt laws. To reduce the number of rear bumper collisions, another rule required a rear, eye-level brake light beginning with 1986 models. Regarding airline safety, Dole implemented tougher airport security and inspection measures and hired more federal marshals. She was criticized, however, for not developing a plan to cope with the aftermath of an earlier air traffic controllers' strike.

After the longest tenure of any secretary of transportation, Elizabeth resigned in 1987 to help Bob campaign for president. His unsuccessful bid did not diminish people's affection for Elizabeth Dole. In 1988, she received the Distinguished Alumni Award from Duke University and an award from the National Committee Against Drunk Driving. A Gallup poll named her one of the world's ten most admired women.

Newly elected President George Bush asked Elizabeth Dole to become secretary of labor. She accepted and was sworn in on January 30, 1989. This time she was in charge of 18,500 employees and a budget of thirty-one billion dollars. Dole was the lone woman in Bush's cabinet.

At the Department of Labor, Dole's priorities included upgrading workforce quality, improving workplace safety, fighting discrimination, encouraging labor-management cooperation, and urging adoption of voluntary policies to help employees balance work and family roles. Regarding the first priority, Dole's initiatives encouraged business to help at-risk youth develop basic skills. The Secretary's Committee on Achieving Necessary Skills was established to allow business, educators, and labor to define human skills needed to make that transition successfully.

Regarding safety, the Occupational Safety and Health Administration, a Labor Department subagency, increased enforcement and raised penalties during Dole's tenure. More than two hundred additional inspectors were hired, and more construction industry inspections were scheduled.

Dole started a glass-ceiling initiative to move qualified women and minorities beyond mid-management levels. This program ensured that companies provided training and development opportunities and appropriate rewards to help women and minorities advance.

The settlement of the Pittston Coal Strike was gratifying to Elizabeth Dole. She appointed a skilled mediator to resolve the dispute and was pictured joining hands with labor and management representatives on New Year's Eve, 1989, when they agreed to end the strike.

Favoring voluntary policies that would help all employees excel on the job, Dole established an information clearinghouse on programs to break employment barriers. She wanted to convince companies that voluntary programs to assist workers with family responsibilities made good business sense.

In early 1990, the American Red Cross asked Dole to consider becoming its president, but she was not quite ready to leave her cabinet post. Later that year, however, she accepted the Red Cross position. The first Bush cabinet member to depart, she stepped down on November 23, 1990.

In 1990, Elizabeth Dole received more honors, this time from the labor movement. She received the Labor Management Award from the Work in America Institute and the Construction Person of the Year Award.

At the Red Cross, Dole revamped the blood collection system to increase the safety of the nation's blood supply. She modernized disaster relief services, improved financial accountability, and initiated a cultural-diversity program. To symbolize unity with the volunteers, Dole accepted no salary during her first year as Red Cross president. Her staff in that organization numbered nearly thirty thousand, and there were more than a million and a half volunteers.

In 1996, Bob Dole made another serious bid for the White House, resigning his Senate position to concentrate on the election. This time, he won his party's nomination. Elizabeth Dole was an active campaigner for her husband and created a strong impression with a speech at the Republican National Convention in which she walked among the audience members. Nevertheless, Bob Dole could not oust President Bill Clinton from office. In 1999, however, it was Elizabeth's turn for a presidential run. Dole quit the Red Cross in January and began to look for political and financial support in February. She set up an exploratory committee, raised millions of dollars, and soon became a serious challenger to Texas governor George W. Bush and businessman Steve Forbes for the Republican nomination. Although Dole withdrew from the race in October because of a lack of funds, some saw her popular candidacy both as a stepping stone to higher office (such as the vice presidency) and as a milestone for women in politics.

Summary

During her career, Elizabeth Dole faced obstacles, as have many employed women, but she viewed them as challenges and overcame them. Dole advanced because she could pass through the narrow band of success as defined in 1987 by Ann M. Morrison, Randall P. White, and Ellen Van Velsor in *Breaking the Glass Ceiling*. To fit through the narrow band, a woman must not be viewed as too stereotypically masculine or feminine. She must be firm and demanding but nonthreatening and able to put others at ease. Elizabeth Dole fits that description. Although women should not have to pass through a narrow band to succeed, in Dole's generation, this situation was a reality. Throughout her career, she worked on issues that would benefit people—from a 1960's assignment to organize a conference for the deaf to a 1990's task to oversee disaster relief. Related to her concern for people, improving safety— whether of consumer products, workplace conditions, or transportation systems—became another of Dole's causes.

Dole served as a positive role model for women in government service. Her leadership style, including empowerment, consensus building, teamwork, and self-competition, proved an appealing one. Before running for the highest office in the United States herself, she worked for five presidents during the course of nearly twenty-five years, a lifetime of service to her country and its people.

Bibliography

Bartley, Diane. "Labor's Elizabeth Dole." *The Saturday Evening Post* 262 (May/June, 1990): 44-49. Briefly, Bartley reviews Dole's accomplishments as secretary of labor and gives information about her childhood and personal life.

Dole, Robert, and Elizabeth Dole. *The Doles: Unlimited Partners*. New York: Simon & Schuster, 1988. Elizabeth and Bob Dole alternated in the writing of this work. It describes Elizabeth's early background and work experiences through her stint as secretary of transportation.

Kozar, Richard F. *Elizabeth Dole*. Philadelphia: Chelsea House, 1999. A book in the Women of Achievement series that examines Dole's life of public service.

Miller, James A. "Portrait: Elizabeth Dole." *Life* 6 (July, 1983): 21, 24, 28. A sketchy review of Dole's leadership style, childhood, and dual-career relationship, this article touches on her role as secretary of transportation.

Mulford, Carolyn. *Elizabeth Dole: Public Servant*. Hillside, N.J.: Enslow, 1992. This book examines Dole's life thoroughly from childhood through her position at the American Red Cross.

Weiss, Philip. "Charming Her Way to the White House." *The Washington Monthly* 19 (September, 1987): 29-43. Weiss attacks Dole's performance as secretary of transportation. He highlights her early life and role in a dual-career couple.

Margaret Foegen Karsten

HELEN GAHAGAN DOUGLAS

Born: November 25, 1900; Boonton, New Jersey
Died: June 28, 1980; New York, New York

As a congresswoman from California and in her private life, Douglas was an outspoken advocate of civil liberties and opportunities for oppressed minorities.

Early Life

Mary Helen Gahagan (she was always called Helen) was born on November 25, 1900, in Boonton, New Jersey, where her parents briefly rented a home so that her father could supervise a construction project nearby. Her twin brothers had been born two years earlier, and a sister and brother would follow in 1902 and 1910. She grew up in Brooklyn, New York, in a comfortable household with strong-willed parents intent on imbuing their children with strong moral and educational ideals. Her father, Walter, was an engineer who founded his own construction company in 1899 and prospered from the outset. A graduate of the Massachusetts Institute of Technology, he read insatiably and filled the Gahagan house with shelves of books. Helen's mother Lillian had been reared on the Wisconsin frontier. She was a country schoolteacher before her marriage, and her beauty, optimistic outlook, and exquisite singing voice were inherited by her elder daughter.

Helen had the benefit of the accoutrements of affluence during her childhood. These included a summer home in Vermont, a family trip to Europe when she was twelve, accompanying her mother to the opera (which, ironically, Helen disliked intensely), and private schools. The first of these was the Berkeley School for Girls, which was located only a block from the Gahagans' home. It was at this school that her interest in acting blossomed under the direction of her drama teacher, Elizabeth Grimball. Her grades were mediocre in subjects unrelated to performing, but she studied intensely for a college preparatory school. She matriculated at Barnard College in New York in order to be close to the stage and her drama instructor.

She would spend only two years at Barnard College before her debut into the Broadway theatrical world. Her impressive perfor-

Helen Gahagan Douglas *(Library of Congress)*

mances in school productions and an Off-Broadway play led director William A. Brady, Jr., to cast her as the ingenue in *Dreams for Sale* in 1922. Over the extremely strong protests of her father, who insisted that she complete her education, Helen accepted.

She quickly became a star. Her generally favorable reviews led to contracts with Brady and other well-known producers and assured her a niche in the roster of leading ladies of the 1920's stage. Practically every new theatrical season brought a new role, and she toured the country in roles she established in New York. She was the subject of much press coverage, not only for her acting talent but also for her great beauty.

Gahagan's ambition to perform ultimately led in another direction. During the run of a New York play in 1926, she began to take vocal lessons from a Russian émigré, Madame Sophia Cehanovska. For the next several years, Gahagan would devote time, money, and trips to Europe to the pursuit of performing operatic roles with leading companies, a pursuit that was never as successful as her Broadway acting career.

Helen's performance in the 1930-1931 Broadway production of *Tonight or Never* was important for a number of reasons. The play was her only collaboration with the legendary David Belasco (he would die during its run), her father died during the same run, and she married her costar, Melvyn Douglas. By the end of 1931, she had moved from New York to the West Coast, where Melvyn began his career in motion pictures. Except for some brief performing engagements, Helen would not live in New York again until after her immersion in and forced withdrawal from another career of a very different type.

Life's Work

The first task for Helen Gahagan Douglas and her husband, upon reaching California, was to establish a new way of life in new surroundings. Melvyn had a studio contract with Metro-Goldwyn-Mayer (MGM), and Helen was busy with singing lessons and performances on the West Coast stage in both acting and singing roles. Although Helen would have the opportunity to read dozens of film scripts in search of suitable parts, her efforts to find strong roles or to receive reasonable financial offers were stymied. She appeared in only one picture, *She* (1935), a film later considered a "classic" for its overblown production and acting rather than for any positive contributions to the cinematic arts.

The hectic pace of life on the dramatic and sound stages for the couple soon led both to seek a respite. They accomplished this by traveling around the world in 1933. A few months after their return home, Helen gave birth to their first child, Peter. A daughter, Mary

Helen, would follow five years later. Helen continued her theatrical performances and vocal training, and the family settled into a new home built on three acres in the hills above the Hollywood Bowl.

Two significant events contributed to Helen's involvement in political causes. The first involved her awakening to conditions in Germany and Austria during a concert tour there in 1937. She ultimately canceled several engagements on the tour after encountering anti-Semitism directed against the pianist who was traveling with her. Although she was not Jewish, her husband Melvyn was, so she regarded these sentiments as a personal affront.

Back in California, Helen Gahagan Douglas became involved in Democratic Party campaign activities in 1938. Her husband had joined in the statewide gubernatorial and congressional campaign efforts; at first, she merely accompanied him to meetings. After becoming acquainted with social and economic conditions firsthand, however, she began to take the lead in organizing efforts to assist migrant workers. As a result of their activities on behalf of California Democrats, the Douglases were invited to visit President and Mrs. Franklin D. Roosevelt in the White House in 1939. Helen was greatly impressed by Eleanor Roosevelt, who became something of a political mentor and role model for the actress.

Helen's intelligence and capacity for hard work, as well as her friendship with Eleanor Roosevelt, led to her rapid rise within the leadership of the Democratic Party in California. In 1940, she was selected as the state's Democratic National Committeewoman. In that capacity, she attended the party's national convention, where she was an enthusiastic supporter of a third term for FDR. Following Roosevelt's reelection, she was appointed vice chair and head of the Women's Division for the California state Democratic Party. Her efforts for Southern California Democratic candidates in 1942 contributed to party successes there in spite of Republican victories throughout the rest of the state.

Helen Gahagan Douglas's high visibility in state Democratic politics made her a natural choice for the congressional race in the Fourteenth District in 1944, when popular Congressman Thomas Ford announced his retirement. Although she did not live in the largely working-class district in central Los Angeles, she campaigned thoroughly there and won the nomination in the May primary. Prior to the general election, Douglas delivered a principal address before the Democratic National Convention in Chicago, in which she reviewed the accomplishments of the Roosevelt administrations. In the fall campaign, she followed the lead of Democrats nationally in identifying her programs with FDR and the New Deal, a strategy that produced a narrow victory. She became only the third woman elected to Congress from California and the first who did not take over her seat from a deceased husband.

In Washington, D.C., Douglas adhered to the same formula that had produced political success in California. She maintained a grueling schedule, largely eschewed social events, and applied her keen mind to the process of absorbing all available information on issues pending before Congress. Her legislative interests lay in two areas, one involving foreign affairs, the other domestic. She secured an appointment to the House Foreign Affairs Committee, which is usually an unimportant body, since only the Senate ratifies treaties. Nevertheless, with negotiations under way for the postwar international organization that became the United Nations, Douglas believed that the House as well as the Senate would play an integral role in the increased nationwide commitment to internationalism. Membership on the House Foreign Affairs Committee would provide a forum for activities designed to ensure world peace. In domestic affairs, Douglas's natural inclinations were bolstered by the makeup of her congressional district. She lent support throughout the postwar period to legislation benefiting organized labor and African Americans and other minorities.

Through her diligence, her charismatic appeal, and her high visibility in the press, Douglas became a leading figure in California politics. Following her second reelection, in 1948, her congressional seat seemed to be secure; she and her supporters now looked to a greater challenge—the seat in the U.S. Senate held by the conservative Democrat Sheridan Downey. Following the incumbent's withdrawal from the 1950 primary, Douglas won the nomination in spite of vicious attacks on her internationalist position as being procommunist.

The smear tactics begun in the Democratic primary intensified in the general election, when Douglas faced Congressman Richard Nixon. In an election that has since become famous for the infamous dirty tricks of the Nixon campaign, Helen Gahagan Douglas was removed from public office. In her autobiography some thirty years later, she wryly remarked: "There's not much to say about the 1950 campaign except that a man ran for the Senate who wanted to get there, and didn't care how."

Douglas's life after politics was spent partly in the public eye, since she continued to speak in favor of causes such as world peace. She campaigned for Democratic presidential candidates Lyndon Baines Johnson in 1964 and George McGovern in 1972. During the last three decades before her death from cancer in 1980, she was certainly not forgotten, but neither was she occupying her accustomed place in the limelight.

Summary

In a number of respects, Helen Gahagan Douglas had an enviable life and a great deal of good fortune. She became a famous actress almost overnight, not only because of her talent but also because of her great beauty. Capitalizing on her acting fame, she became a force in politics through intelligence and hard work. Although her fame boosted her political career at the outset, it eventually became a liability to Douglas as a politician seriously intent on pursuing an important agenda. She constantly downplayed her glamour in order to be taken seriously.

She was able, in the end, to use the press attention focused on her in order to advance an international and domestic social program that was liberal, enlightened, and forward-looking. She did not hesitate to challenge bigotry, isolationism, and red-baiting. Although her public service was cut short because of Nixon's malicious campaign against her in 1950, she stood as a symbol for other intelligent, forthright, public-spirited women and men to emulate.

Bibliography

Douglas, Helen Gahagan. *The Eleanor Roosevelt We Remember*. New York: Hill & Wang, 1963. In her autobiography, Helen Douglas clearly indicated that Eleanor Roosevelt was a major influence in her decision to become a political activist. This book, a tribute to Roosevelt, contains photographs from a variety of sources and an admiring text by Douglas.

_____. *A Full Life*. Garden City, N.Y.: Doubleday, 1982. An engaging autobiography in which the author thoroughly discusses her family life, stage experiences, and involvement in political affairs.

Douglas, Melvyn, and Tom Arthur. *See You at the Movies: The Autobiography of Melvyn Douglas*. Lanham, Md.: University Press of America, 1986. A posthumously published autobiography that focuses on the author's acting career and includes occasional anecdotes about his wife's careers and their marriage.

Mitchell, Greg. *Tricky Dick and the Pink Lady: Richard Nixon vs. Helen Gahagan Douglas—Sexual Politics and the Red Scare, 1950*. New York: Random House, 1998. Mitchell examines the California Senate campaign of 1950.

Morris, Roger. *Richard Milhous Nixon: The Rise of an American Politician*. New York: Henry Holt, 1990. Includes the fullest description and analysis of the 1950 Senate campaign in California; it is especially valuable for establishing the context of California politics. Morris covers the Douglas and Nixon primary campaigns as well as the general election.

Scobie, Ingrid Winther. *Center Stage: Helen Gahagan Douglas, a Life*. New York: Oxford University Press, 1992. A thorough biography by a professional historian who conducted research in manuscript and oral history collections around the country. Scobie also met with and interviewed Helen and Melvyn Douglas.

Richard G. Frederick

ELEANOR OF AQUITAINE

Born: c. 1122; either at Bordeaux or at the nearby castle of Belin,
southern France
Died: April 1, 1204; the Abbey of Fontevrault

As queen of France, queen of England, and mother to two English kings,
Eleanor of Aquitaine was probably the most powerful woman of her time. In
addition, she promoted the literary and social style of courtly love and the
troubadours.

Early Life

The first important influence on Eleanor's childhood was William IX,
her grandfather. He was the earliest troubadour known by name and
ruled Aquitaine and Poitou from 1086 to 1127. Though he was known
for a scandalous private life and his defiance of the Church, he maintained control over his quarrelsome vassals and passed down to William X and ultimately to Eleanor a considerable inheritance. William X,
Eleanor's father, was also a cultured man and a patron of poets and
troubadours, though enormously quarrelsome and disrespectful of the
Church. Eleanor's mother, Aénor, who died when Eleanor was eight,
was the daughter of the notorious Dangerosa, the wife to the viscount
of Chatellerault, and the mistress to Eleanor's grandfather. William X
was fond of Eleanor, his eldest child, and took her with him wherever
he went. Medieval rulers could not reside quietly at some central
castle. In order to maintain control over their vassals and administer
justice throughout the land, they were almost always on the move from
one residence to another.

Eleanor's education was not confined to women's arts such as
needlework. She learned to read and write Latin, an unusual accomplishment for a layman, and probably to speak it as well. She also
learned to read and write Provençal, the language of the lyric poetry of
the troubadours. Eleanor herself became the inspiration of much troubadour poetry.

When Duke William X died in 1137, his daughter, under feudal law,
automatically became the ward of the French king Louis VI. She did
inherit her father's fief and the homage of his vassals, but she was

vulnerable to seizure by any powerful suitor who could forcibly marry her and enjoy her inheritance. Louis VI hastened to betroth her, therefore, to his only surviving son. Even before they were actually married, the monarch made his son, then sixteen years old, claim Poitiers and Aquitaine and receive the homage of Eleanor's vassals. At age fifteen, therefore, Eleanor became the bride of the young man destined to be Louis VII. The bridegroom had a much less worldly upbringing than Eleanor, having been destined from earliest childhood to be a monk. Only the accidental death of his older brother, the crown prince, brought the "child monk" out of the monastery of Saint-Denis.

Chroniclers agree that the young prince was appropriately smitten with adoration for this tall, beautiful girl who already carried herself like a queen. Even writers who did not always approve of her worldly tastes agreed that she was strikingly beautiful, with a superb figure that she never lost, fine features, and lustrous eyes. On July 25, 1137, Louis and Eleanor were married in the cathedral of Saint André at Bordeaux in the presence of many lords and church dignitaries. A few days later, on August 8, they were consecrated duke and duchess of Aquitaine in the cathedral at Poitiers. During the banquet that followed, the abbot Suger, who was a trusted counselor to both King Louis VI and his son, brought the news that the king had died. Young Eleanor was crowned queen of France on Christmas Day, 1137.

Life's Work

Eleanor apparently enjoyed the next few years of married life, making her court the most splendid in Western Christendom. She filled it with troubadours from southern France and trouvères, their northern counterparts, who wrote not only love songs but also the epic *chansons de geste*. In spite of his savage temper, Louis VII became known for his honesty and generosity and extended royal authority in France by issuing charters to the towns.

In 1147, Eleanor accompanied her husband on the Second Crusade. Edessa had fallen to the Saracens in 1144 and Christendom feared that the Holy Land might be lost, after having been won from the infidels at such great cost only a generation before. After attempting an overland trip through Bavaria, Hungary, and the Balkans, Eleanor and Louis were royally entertained in Constantinople by Emperor Manuel Comnenus. The refinements of ancient Greece and Rome were still in

A drawing of Eleanor of Aquitaine from 1901. *(Library of Congress)*

evidence in Constantinople, as well as the luxuries of the East: oriental silks, Russian furs, Persian carpets. This experience, combined with the royal reception later in the Latin principality of Antioch where her uncle Raymond of Poitiers was their host, confirmed Eleanor's taste for Byzantine splendor.

The actual contact with the Saracens, however, and some of the dreadful effects of weather were not so pleasant. Emperor Manuel had reported that the German king Conrad III, whose crusaders had preceded Louis, had already successfully engaged the Turks. Louis, wishing to share in such a triumph, moved hurriedly into dangerous territory. There he found that Conrad had actually suffered a disastrous defeat.

Louis and his band met with little better luck. On Christmas Day, heavy rains and floods destroyed their tents and baggage, and many horses and men were drowned. Soon after, the Saracens began to attack, shooting arrows from the saddle, then racing in with sabres. At Attalis, Louis abandoned the infantry and the pilgrims to proceed as best they could, while he and his horsemen and Eleanor took to ships. They made a stormy crossing to Saint Symeon, where Eleanor became fast friends with her uncle Raymond, the prince of Antioch.

Here Louis and Eleanor had a serious quarrel that was never to be entirely healed. Eleanor passionately supported Raymond in a plan to use the French troops to attack the Saracen strongholds and win back Edessa. Louis resented this proposal and asserted that he was leaving for Jerusalem and that his wife had to come with him. Eleanor refused, saying that she wanted their marriage annulled on grounds of consanguinity—that is, that they were too closely related. This was the favorite way of getting out of marriages among royalty in medieval times, as it avoided the stigma of divorce. Louis left in the middle of the night and had his men abduct Eleanor from her quarters to accompany him.

Louis and Eleanor did reach Jerusalem, where they were royally welcomed by King Baldwin III. Louis joined an unwise expedition against Damascus, which had been a friendly Saracen city. This move ended in disaster and retreat. After Easter, 1149, Louis and Eleanor left for home by sea on separate ships. Eleanor's ship was captured once by Greeks but was liberated again by King Roger of Sicily.

Back in Paris at last, Louis and Eleanor quarreled, in spite of the efforts of both Pope Eugenious III and Abbot Suger to reconcile them. On March 21, 1152, the marriage was pronounced null and void on the grounds of their being third cousins. The fact that Eleanor had borne only daughters (Marie and Alice) may have been the final motivation for Louis at last to take this step. Eleanor was again a desirable heiress, but she was also again in danger of seizure and forced marriage by ambitious suitors. She hastened to forestall this possibility by promoting a speedy alliance with Henry Plantagenet. They were married on May 18, 1152, only eight weeks after her annulment.

Since his father died, Henry was master of Normandy, Maine, Anjou, and Touraine already and might acquire England as well. He was a man of enormous energy, both physical and mental, a tireless horseman, unusually well educated, a master of languages, a vigorous lover—altogether a more aggressive and formidable husband than Louis had ever been.

Henry soon went to England, while Eleanor held court in Angers, the capital of Anjou. She gave birth there to her first son, William. She also became a patron of Bernard de Ventadour, one of the most famous of the medieval troubadours. Meanwhile, Henry in England had forced King Stephen to name him as heir.

When Stephen died, the archbishop of Canterbury crowned Henry and Eleanor king and queen of England on December 19, 1154. Henry II was a vigorous monarch, restoring order in a land long dominated by robber barons who hired mercenaries to terrorize the countryside. Within three months, practically all mercenaries had left England and a thousand robber fortresses were destroyed. He created new institutions, issued new silver coinage, reformed the law, and generally brought order out of social chaos. Henry also named as his chancellor a brilliant young man named Thomas Becket.

There was one thing Henry did not do as well as Louis: He did not share his executive functions with Eleanor. For some time, Eleanor was busy bearing his children. The first child, William, died when he was three years old, but Eleanor had four more sons—Henry, Richard, Geoffrey, and John—and three daughters—Matilda, Eleanor, and Joanne. After the birth of John, her last child, in 1167, Eleanor regained her strength and her energy to pursue some kind of political power of her own.

The king, who was having a long affair with Rosamund Clifford, was anxious to keep Eleanor out of England and decided that she would be useful in Aquitaine, which was restless and rebellious. Eleanor regained some degree of freedom to manage her own court, installing herself in Poitiers. Again, she reigned over a glittering court of poets and troubadours, including her old admirer Bernard de Ventadour, as well as Bertran de Born. Eleanor herself and sometimes her eldest daughter (by Louis), Marie of Champagne, presided over romantic song contests. The stylized games of courtly love attained their fullest expression there.

Henry's prestige and reputation in Christendom suffered a severe blow when four of Henry's knights murdered Thomas Becket, then archbishop of Canterbury, before his altar. The revolt of 1173 against Henry was a combined plot involving Eleanor and three of her sons, aided by Louis of France. Many other men throughout the king's territories were tired of his heavy-handed rule. Especially in Aquitaine, he was considered a tyrant. The plot to depose him might have been successful had not the young Henry lost his nerve and fled to King Louis VII.

Thus alerted, Henry II reestablished his power with a series of swift and lucky strokes, repelling a French force that was invading Normandy, destroying Breton rebels before they could cross into England, capturing the king of the Scots who harassed the northern border, and even seizing the fifty-year-old Eleanor, disguised as a nobleman riding toward Paris. Eleanor was imprisoned thereafter in one of her husband's castles until Henry's death fifteen years later.

Henry II had been generous in making peace with his sons. When young Henry, the crown prince, died of dysentery, Henry made Richard his heir. Nevertheless, quarreling continued between Richard and John and their father. When Henry did not concede to Richard's demands, Richard made an alliance with Philip II, then king of France. Henry, deathly ill of blood poisoning, capitulated to the combined forces of Richard and Philip II and died a bitter man.

In her old age, Eleanor showed herself to be an executive and diplomat of rare power. When Jerusalem had again fallen into infidel hands in 1187, King Richard hastened to launch another crusade. While he was gone, Eleanor was kept busy protecting the realm from the ambitions of her son John in England and Philip II, who was trying to invade Normandy. When Richard was shipwrecked and held for ransom by King Henry VI of Hohenstaufen, Eleanor herself raised the 100,000 marks and went to Germany to ransom her son.

When her beloved Richard died in 1199, more dreary work remained for Eleanor, a losing battle to exercise some control over her least favored son John, now king. She died on April 1, 1204, at the Abbey of Fontevrault. The Angevin empire died with her, for King John could not hold the vast inheritance from his father.

Summary

Eleanor of Aquitaine lived and participated actively in that age of artistic and intellectual awakening sometimes called a "twelfth century renaissance." The literary aspects of that renaissance began in the Poitou-Aquitaine region of southern France early in the century. The intellectual ferment which was to result in new theological thought, new economic and political theories, innovations in architecture, art, music, and poetry, centered later in the University of Paris and the royal courts of France and England. New knowledge brought back by crusaders, including the adventurous Eleanor herself, also encouraged new attitudes. Eleanor successfully defied the conventional expectations about women in that era. Whatever enemies she made in her long career as a queen and the mother of kings, she retained the loyalty of Aquitaine through the political turmoil of a lifetime.

Bibliography

Andreas, Capellanus. *The Art of Courtly Love*. Translated by John Jay Parry. New York: Columbia University Press, 1941. Andreas, known as the chaplain, was connected to the court of Marie, countess of

Champagne, Eleanor's elder daughter. Marie ordered Andreas to set down a code of manners for court life. What resulted is this curious reversal of Ovid's instructions on how to seduce women. Here, however, woman is the mistress, man her pupil in homage, her vassal in service.

Kelly, Amy. *Eleanor of Aquitaine and the Four Kings*. Cambridge, Mass.: Harvard University Press, 1950. A detailed and well-written biography. Moshe Lazar (in *Eleanor of Aquitaine*, edited by William W. Kibler) claims that some parts come "very close to fiction and rest on fragile literary and historical evidence," especially about the courts of love.

Kibler, William W., ed. *Eleanor of Aquitaine: Patron and Politician*. Austin: University of Texas Press, 1976. A collection of papers from distinguished medieval scholars who met at Austin in April, 1973, to assess the importance of Eleanor within her own century and in those to follow.

Lewis, C. S. *The Allegory of Love*. Oxford, England: Clarendon Press, 1936. Although this classic work contains no specific information about Eleanor of Aquitaine, it provides a detailed discussion of the tradition of courtly love and its significant impact on later literature and popular thought.

Owen, D. D. R. *Eleanor of Aquitaine: Queen and Legend*. Cambridge, Mass.: Blackwell, 1996.

Pernoud, Régine. *Blanche of Castile*. Translated by Henry Noel. New York: Coward, McCann & Geoghegan, 1975. Blanche of Castile was the granddaughter of Eleanor of Aquitaine, personally chosen by her, after the death of Richard, to marry Louis VIII, heir to the French throne.

_____. *Eleanor of Aquitaine*. Translated by Peter Wiles. New York: Coward-McCann, 1968. An authoritative and admirable biography of Eleanor, this volume in the original French won the Pris Historia in 1966.

Rougemont, Denis. *Love in the Western World*. Translated by Montgomery Belgion. New York: Harcourt, Brace, 1940. This is a classic work on the meaning of love in Western civilization, including that radical change which started among the troubadours of southern France in the time of Eleanor of Aquitaine.

Seward, Desmond. *Eleanor of Aquitaine: The Mother Queen*. New York:

Dorset Press, 1978. A recent retelling of Eleanor's life, somewhat shorter than the older works by Kelly and Pernoud. A good introduction to her story for the person who does not wish to read a more detailed account.

Warner, Marina. *Alone of All Her Sex: The Myth and the Cult of the Virgin.* New York: Vintage Books, 1983. Good for background information about the view of women in the Middle Ages, though courtly love, as practiced in Eleanor's famous courts of love, had only a very remote connection to the cult of the Virgin.

Katherine Snipes

SAINT ELIZABETH OF HUNGARY

Born: 1207; Sárospatak, Hungary
Died: November 17, 1231; near Wittenberg, Thuringia

Elizabeth, seeking to live according to the Christian ideal, established the first orphanage for homeless children in Central Europe and actively cared for the poor and the unemployed.

Early Life

Elizabeth of Hungary was born in Sárospatak in 1207 to King Andrew II of Hungary and Gertrud of Andechs-Meran. Elizabeth's two maternal uncles, Berthold, titular patriarch of Aquileia, and Bishop Eckbert of Bamberg, who had played a role in the assassination of Philip of Swabia and sought refuge at the Hungarian court, were high ecclesiastics.

In 1211, Hermann I, landgrave of Thuringia, sent a delegation led by Knight Walter of Vargila to Pozsony to request the hand of Elizabeth in marriage for his son, Hermann. The landgrave probably wanted to restore his weakened social and financial resources through this marriage with the Hungarian royal family. He may also have hoped to rely on the support of the Eastern monarch in the deadly struggle between Otto of Brunswick and Frederick, the new papal protégé for the German throne. Bishop Eckbert may have suggested the plan, though it is possible that Otakar of Bohemia may have also tried to establish a triple alliance by including the king of Hungary. From another point of view, family ties between one of the leading noble families in the empire and the Hungarian court might have enhanced the diplomatic position of Andrew II against some German princes, who still looked upon Hungary as a country to be invaded and plundered.

Knight Vargila successfully concluded a marriage agreement, and the richly endowed four-year-old bride was dispatched to the Thuringian court at the castle of Wartburg, near Eisenach. A bathtub of pure silver and a thousand pieces of gold formed only a portion of her dowry. It is known from her second husband, Louis, that the Thuringian court had never before seen such riches. They also expressed surprise at Elizabeth's large personal entourage of servants andnurses.

Hermann I maintained an elaborate court and provided for poets and artists of the age. It may be that Walther von der Vogelweide or Wolfram von Eschenbach (while working on his *Parzival*, c. 1200-1210; English translation, 1894) spent some time at the castle at Wartburg. Hermann I and his wife, Sophia, met the young Elizabeth at Eisenach, and the official engagement celebration was held soon after at Wartburg. Elizabeth was educated at the Thuringian court; the curriculum included the study of contemporary poetry and writers, the history of leading families in the empire, art appreciation, Latin, and religion. As a child, Elizabeth liked to play, ride horses, and participate in games as well as pray in the chapel. Even as a child she displayed empathy and compassion toward the poor. Concerned with Elizabeth's appearance as a lady of society, however, her mother-in-law cautioned her about being too loud and exuberant.

In 1213 Elizabeth's mother met a tragic death at the hands of Hungarian conspirators. When her mother was murdered, the six-year-old Elizabeth saw her bloody, mutilated body in a dream. After that, she spent more time in prayer before the crucifix and began to dress more simply. She began to pray for the murderers of her mother. Elizabeth was nine when she lost her fiancé, Hermann, and one year later her father-in-law died. It was at this time that Louis, her fiancé's younger brother, became Elizabeth's protector and good friend. After discussing Elizabeth's uncertain future, Louis decided that she would be his wife. They were married in 1221 in the presence of the nobles of Thuringia and of other German regions. Knight Vargila led Elizabeth to the altar, and her father sent additional gifts. At the end of September, 1222, the young couple visited King Andrew at Pozsony. Traveling by horse, they were horrified at the destruction and decline of the country. It was the year of the Hungarian Golden Bull, by which the Hungarian nobles, discouraged by the nearly total disintegration of law and order in the realm, had forced the king to share his government with them.

Life's Work

Under the guidance of her confessor, Father Rodinger, a Franciscan friar, Elizabeth began to lead a deeper spiritual life, carried out charity work, and established an orphanage (the first in Central Europe). She cared for lepers, of whom she was not afraid, and constructed a twenty-eight-bed hospital for them. She then came under the spiritual directorship of Master Conrad of Marburg, the noted mystic, Franciscan preacher, and ascetic.

In 1225, Louis embarked on a military campaign summoned by the emperor, and in his absence, Elizabeth governed Thuringia. She healed the wounds caused by natural disasters and was concerned about social discrimination among the disadvantaged; she fed nine hundred poor people daily, provided tools and obtained work for the able-bodied unemployed men, and taught the women to spin. At the same time, she represented her husband in high society, received distinguished guests at the court, and participated in hunting parties.

In 1227, Louis was again summoned by the emperor and joined a Crusade; Elizabeth was expecting their third child. By the time Gertrud was born, Louis was already dead, having fallen ill at Otranto. Elizabeth's brothers-in-law, uneasy about her spending habits, forbade her to handle her own fiscal affairs, prompting her to leave Wartburg in October, 1227, with her three small children. Nobody in Eisenach, however, would accommodate them. After placing the children in foster homes, Elizabeth, accompanied by two of her royal servants, Guda and Isentrud, finally found shelter in an innkeeper's stable. She spun cloth for a living until Mechtild, abbess of Kitzingen, provided for her in the abbey. Her uncle, the bishop of Bamberg, placed his castle at Pottstein at her disposal. The bishop tried to persuade her to marry Emperor Frederick II, but Elizabeth firmly declined the proposal. Only the future of her children concerned her; for herself, she desired to live in poverty. She had her husband's remains buried in the monastery which he had founded at Reinhardsbrunn. After the burial, and with Knight Vargila's support, she regained her right to manage the estates she had inherited as a widow. Making a vow in the Franciscan church in Eisenach to renounce all earthly love and free will, she retained her property for the sake of her children, Hermann, Sophia, and Gertrud, and for making provision for the poor. She did not live in the castle at Wartburg but in nearby Wehrda, in a primitive house built of blocks of dirt. She spun cloth to earn her living and assisted in the hospital she had founded.

In order to deepen Elizabeth's humility, Conrad used crude methods such as flagellation and beatings, the dismissal of her two servants, forbidding her to distribute large sums of money to the poor, and allowing her to give only one slice of bread each to the hungry. Elizabeth used her own bed to care for a young boy sick with dysentery; when he died, she put a girl with leprosy in her bed. Augmenting the abuse and humiliation suffered at the hand of Conrad, gossip now began to undermine Elizabeth's reputation. She was ridiculed for her loud laughter, her refusal to dress in black, and the apparent ease with which she forgot her deceased husband. There were even rumors that she was happily engaged in an affair with the friar, about which she was confronted by Knight Vargila. In response, Elizabeth showed the marks of the flagellations and beatings received from Conrad.

Knowing that she was weak and would die soon, Elizabeth stayed in bed for the last two weeks of her life, finalizing the arrangements for the distribution of her wealth and her children's future. Three days before she died, she sent everyone away from her except Conrad, who remained at her bedside. She died in the early hours of November 17, 1231. Her body lay in state for four days in the Franciscan church at Eisenach, dressed in clothing of the poor. During this time, the inhabitants of Thuringia came to her coffin not to pray for her but to ask for her intercession on their behalf. It is reported that during the following days and weeks, numerous miracles occurred at her grave.

Conrad informed Pope Gregory IX of the death of Elizabeth, and the pontiff authorized the friar to make preparations for her canonization. When Conrad was murdered in July, 1233, the bishop of Hildesheim carried on with the canonization process. It was then that the *Libellus de dictis IV ancillarum* (depositions of Saint Elizabeth's four handmaidens—Isentrud, Guda, Iremngard, and Elisabeth) was recorded in writing, followed by a strict ecclesiastical investigation. On May 26, 1235, in Perugia on the Feast of Pentecost, Pope Gregory IX entered Elizabeth's name in the canon of saints (papal bull *Gloriosus in maiestate*). The first church erected in her honor was built by her brother-in-law Conrad, who was grand master of the German Order, at Marburg. On May 1, 1236, her coffin was elevated upon the altar in the presence of her children, brothers-in-law, four archbishops, eight bishops, and a multitude of German, Hungarian, Czech, and French pilgrims.

Summary

Saint Elizabeth of Hungary lived according to the Christian ideal, fusing it with the pastoral concept of the mendicant orders in teaching and practicing humility and social equality. She did not believe that social stabilization could occur by suddenly elevating the lower strata; rather, she believed that the upper classes should willingly descend to the aid of the poor. In addition to building a hospital and establishing an asylum for homeless children, Elizabeth demonstrated an attitude toward the poor that was realistic as well as humane. Thus, although she developed a plan for feeding the poor, she abhorred idleness, quoting from Saint Paul that one who did not work would not eat.

Bibliography

Bihl, Michael. "Elizabeth of Hungary." *Catholic Encyclopaedia* 5 (1909): 389-391. A thorough report on Saint Elizabeth and her time in accordance with early biographies and sermons, such as those preached by the late fifteenth century Franciscan friar Pelbart of Temesvár. The work colorfully depicts the Hungarian royal court, life in Thuringia, and the background of the Crusades in the early thirteenth century.

Butler, Alban. "St. Elizabeth of Hungary, Widow." In *Lives of the Saints*, edited by Herbert Thurston and Donald Attwater. Vol. 4. New York: P. J. Kennedy and Sons, 1956. A readable and informative account which includes quotes from the depositions of Elizabeth's loyal servants. Reveals the remarkable depth of Elizabeth and Louis's relationship; treats Conrad's spiritual directorship dispassionately.

De Robeck, Nesta. *Saint Elizabeth of Hungary: A Story of Twenty-four Years*. Milwaukee, Wis.: Bruce, 1954. This volume is well written and clever but does not provide much new information about Saint Elizabeth.

Huyskens, Albert. *Quellenstudien zur Geschichte der hl. Elisabeth, Landgräfin von Thüringen*. Marburg, Germany: N. G. Elwert, 1908. This volume provides German interpretations of the life of Saint Elizabeth, based upon available source material. In other parts of the work, Huyskens discusses and analyzes the political and economic background of the age and the role assumed by religion.

Kranz, Gisbert. *Elisabeth von Thüringien*. Augsburg, West Germany: Verlag Winfried-Werk, 1957. Relying primarily on translations of the sources and secondary literature, Kranz brings Saint Elizabeth's life closer to the reader in this very readable book.

Nigg, Walter, and Helmuth Nils Loose. *Die hl. Elisabeth: Das Leben der*

Landgräfin von Thüringien. Freiburg, Switzerland: Christophorus Verlag, 1979. A thorough background study of the social and economic conditions of the age in Hungary and the German empire. The authors narrate the life of Saint Elizabeth while attempting to present her as a real, earthly person.

Obbard, Elizabeth Ruth. *Poverty, My Riches: A Study of St. Elizabeth of Hungary, 1207-1231.* Southampton, England: Saint Austin Press, 1997.

Thompson, Blanche Jennings. *Saint Elizabeth's Three Crowns.* San Francisco: Ignatius Press, 1996.

Z. J. Kosztolnyik

ELIZABETH I

Born: September 7, 1533; Greenwich, England
Died: March 24, 1603; Richmond, England

The last of the five Tudor monarchs, Elizabeth I earned the respect of her associates and the love of her subjects while ruling her people longer and more capably than most kings of her time.

Early Life

The second child of King Henry VIII, Elizabeth, was born on September 7, 1533, at Greenwich Palace. Before she was three years old, her father nullified his marriage to her mother, Anne Boleyn, whom he then had tried for adultery and conspiracy, convicted, and beheaded. Like her older half sister, Mary, before her, Elizabeth was declared to be illegitimate, and Henry immediately took another wife, Jane Seymour. A statute of 1544, while not reversing the earlier decree, nevertheless placed Elizabeth third in line to the throne after Edward, born to Henry and Jane in 1537, and Mary, daughter of Henry's first wife, Catherine of Aragon.

Elizabeth's education commenced under several eminent Cambridge scholars, one of whom, Roger Ascham, wrote a distinguished educational treatise called *The Schoolmaster* (1570). She proved an apt student, studying Greek and Latin and attaining fluency in French and Italian. Languages were the key to familiarity not only with literature but also with the New Testament and the scholarship of Europe. Because of her linguistic aptitude, Elizabeth would not later have to rely on translators, as did many sovereigns, when dealing with foreign ambassadors.

Elizabeth learned other practical lessons during the years from 1547, when her father died, until 1558, when she succeeded. While Elizabeth lived with Catherine Parr, Henry's last wife and the closest approach to a mother she would ever know, Catherine's marriage to the promiscuous Thomas Seymour taught Elizabeth the importance of being on her guard, for Seymour made advances to the attractive teenager. Her subsequent determination not to allow men to manipulate her became an important factor in her forty-five-year reign. Political events tested her mettle early. Seymour fell under suspicion of

Elizabeth I *(Library of Congress)*

treason against his brother Edward, Lord Protector of Edward, the boy king, and Elizabeth was sharply questioned about possible complicity. The fifteen-year-old princess responded shrewdly and prudently, and though Seymour was executed, she was permitted to live quietly until Edward's death in 1553.

Those who saw Elizabeth take part in her sister's coronation ceremony saw a young woman somewhat taller than average, with light skin and reddish-gold hair. Although her portrait was often painted, the stylized likenesses of Renaissance royalty often prove unreliable, and even eyewitnesses disagreed considerably about the details of her physical appearance, but everyone credited her with beautiful hands. While not a particularly religious person, Elizabeth deplored Mary's Roman Catholicism and, like many English patriots, was apprehensive about Mary's decision to marry the Catholic Prince Philip of Spain. Again, in Mary's reign, Elizabeth was suspected of treason, this time in connection with Sir Thomas Wyatt the Younger's plan to depose Mary in favor of her, for presumably Elizabeth would marry an Englishman and a Protestant and thus avert the danger of the crown passing to the offspring of Philip and Mary. Though imprisoned in the Tower of London for a time, Elizabeth again dodged the extreme penalty; she emerged understanding thoroughly, however, the danger of even the appearance of treason.

Eventually, Philip, seeing his wife childless and ill and viewing Elizabeth as preferable to such a claimant as Mary Stuart, wife of the French dauphin, became the protector of the future queen. This precarious period in the princess's life ended on November 17, 1558, when the unpopular Mary died and Elizabeth, at the age of twenty-five, became the third of Henry VIII's children to wear the English crown.

Life's Work

Elizabeth understood the presumably modern art of public relations, and from her coronation onward she worked to gain the admiration of her subjects. She also surrounded herself with able advisers, the most faithful of whom was William Cecil (from 1571, Lord Burghley), and he served her well for forty years. The domestic question—whom would she marry?—early became a question of foreign relations also, for the most ambitious bachelors of Western Europe recognized her as the greatest available prize. Archduke Charles of Austria offered a politically advantageous match, but both Elizabeth and her subjects shied away from his Roman Catholicism. Elizabeth appeared to prefer one of her own subjects, Robert Dudley, earl of Leicester, eligible in

1560 after the death of his wife Amy Robsart, but the mystery sur- rounding her fatal fall down a flight of stairs cast a shadow over his name. There was no lack of other suitors, and all England expected Elizabeth to avert the disorder likely at the death of an unmarried and childless queen, but the strong-willed sovereign did not intend to yield an iota of her sovereignty to any man, and the sort of man who would content himself with being a mere consort probably appealed little to her imagination. Throughout the early years of her reign, she kept everyone guessing about her marriage plans, but she made no commitments.

Mary, Queen of Scots, whose grandmother (Henry VIII's sister Margaret) had married the Scottish king James IV, posed one threat to England's security, particularly after her first husband became King Francis II of France in 1559, for France was England's traditional enemy. To neutralize the French threat, Elizabeth encouraged Scottish fears of foreign authority, even suggesting the possibility of her own marriage to the earl of Arran, whose family ranked high in the Scottish succession. When Francis died in 1560, however, Mary's influence declined, and her subsequent marriage to her kinsman, the unstable Lord Darnley, led to her undoing. Eventually, she was deposed, Darnley died, and for many years Mary languished, a virtual prisoner of Elizabeth in England. For nearly two decades, Elizabeth allowed no harm to come to her Scottish cousin, but neither did she intend to allow conspirators to build upon Mary's claim to the English throne.

For the first decade of her reign, with much of the European continent in turmoil, Elizabeth kept England at peace, but in 1569 she was forced to put down a rebellion in the north fomented by Thomas Howard, duke of Norfolk, whose ambitions spurred him to seek marriage to the deposed Queen of Scots. The rebellion was speedily checked, and Elizabeth merely placed Norfolk under house arrest until she learned that he was plotting with foreign agents to overthrow her directly. Meanwhile, Pope Pius V excommunicated Elizabeth, who had never considered herself a Roman Catholic anyway, but this action, focusing Catholic enmity on her, created a dangerous atmosphere at a time when English cordiality toward Catholic Spain was steadily lessening. Therefore, Elizabeth, while continuing to spare Mary, allowed Norfolk, the only duke in her kingdom, to be tried, convicted, and executed early in 1572.

At this time, another problem was developing in the Netherlands in the form of a provincial rebellion against Spanish authority. An increased Spanish presence just across the English Channel or the possible alternative of a French buildup in response to Dutch pleas for assistance could spell trouble for England. Remaining officially neutral, Elizabeth encouraged support by volunteers and through private subscriptions; eventually, she made large loans to the rebels out of her treasury, though not in amounts sufficient to turn the tide against Spain decisively. She hoped that the Netherlands could unite under the Protestant William of Orange, but in vain. When, finally, in 1585 she committed troops to the struggle, she chose her old favorite Leicester as commander. He also shared political authority with a provincial council, but his blunders led to serious divisions among the provinces on the eve of the Spanish Armada's attack on England, a crisis brought on in large measure by Sir Francis Drake's harassment of Spain's American colonies.

While England's lighter, more maneuverable fleet took advantage of westerly winds which helped drive the Armada away from England's southern coast toward France, Elizabeth visited her army at Tilbury near the mouth of the Thames and showered encouragement and eloquence upon her soldiers. Skillfully, she braced them for the land battle which fortunately never erupted. Instead, what was left of the badly battered Spanish fleet limped back to Spain, and the greatest external threat of her reign ended in increased prestige for the nautical and military skill of England.

During the earlier years of the Netherlands venture, Elizabeth still gave the appearance of considering marriage offers. As late as 1581, Francis of Valois, duke of Alençon, was pursuing her, but Elizabeth, while willing to use him to preserve a truce with the French ruler, Henry III, firmly rejected his offer. By this time, it appeared that the queen, now in her late forties, would probably never marry and almost certainly never bear children, but events of the next few years clarified the succession. James VI, son of the deposed Mary, was demonstrating ability on the Scottish throne, and though he flirted with Roman Catholicism as Elizabeth did with her suitors—for diplomatic leverage—his religious views and sense of the place of religion did not differ greatly from Elizabeth's own. She drew closer to James, and when yet another conspiracy, led by Anthony Babington, implicated James's mother and caused Elizabeth to execute Mary in 1587, James merely protested formally. Not until she lay on her deathbed did the cautious Elizabeth confirm the fact, but England now understood that the crown would pass peacefully to James.

The foreign operations had imposed a heavy financial burden on Elizabeth. Meanwhile, poor harvests and adverse trade conditions impoverished the realm, and the surge of euphoria occasioned by the repulsion of the Spanish naval threat faded as the century waned. By the final years of Elizabeth's long rule, many agreed with Hamlet: "the time is out of joint." Another of the queen's onetime favorites, Robert Devereux, earl of Essex, mounted a rebellion in 1601, and again she felt obliged to respond with the death penalty. Until her seventieth year, Elizabeth enjoyed robust health; only at the beginning of 1603 did she succumb to what may have been a severe bronchial illness. She continued her duties until her worried councillors persuaded her to take to her bed on March 21. Early in the morning of the third day following, she died quietly.

Summary

Many students of Queen Elizabeth I's reign have found her to have been shrewd and resourceful, able to keep opponents guessing and off balance while she guided her ship of state through perilous seas. To others, she has seemed procrastinating and indecisive, unable to carry out her policies efficiently. Her subjects expected her to rule firmly and to provide for her successor, but in the case of a queen, one of these goals would easily preclude the other. If she married to produce an heir or designated a successor, her authority would diminish. If she named an ambitious person without the patience to await her death, she might well endanger both her life and domestic tranquillity. She did well to allow James to emerge gradually as her candidate without officially nominating him. By playing off her suitors against one another, she kept England free from the very real possibility of foreign political and religious domination. Throughout her reign, she bargained adroitly with foreign powers without committing herself to unmanageable situations. •

No doubt, Elizabeth sometimes relied too heavily on her favorite strategies, but most often they were well adapted to the needs of the relatively small and poor nation she ruled. Her prudent management kept the cost of government within the capacities and tolerance of her subjects. Under her, England became what it would remain for centuries: a recognized naval power. At a time of serious religious conflict, she pursued a policy remarkably tolerant and unprovocative. A nation which had endured the last unreasoning years of Henry VIII, internecine power struggles under the Edwardian regency, and a few bloody years under the erratic Mary and her Spanish husband gained confidence and security.

While not generally extravagant, Elizabeth understood the social and psychological value of magnificent progresses and dignified receptions. She captured the imagination of poets such as Edmund Spenser and Sir Walter Raleigh, who helped spread her fame beyond the range of those who actually saw her. She was Spenser's Faerie Queene in one of that character's guises, the Gloriana who summed up the glory of England. Indeed, Elizabeth appreciated poetry and the arts generally and wrote competent poetry herself. During the second half of her reign, English literature reached an unprecedented peak. Her subjects responded enthusiastically to her preference for the arts—including the art of peace—and to her genuine love for them. The affection of the English for their monarch still alive in the time of the second Elizabeth owes much to the precedent of the first. She was the first of only two English queens to give her name to a considerable wedge of history, but whereas Victoria merely symbolized an age created by others, Elizabeth stands as both symbol and substance of hers. The policies of England in the latter half of the sixteenth century, when the nation rose to prominence in Europe, were her policies. The wisdom of most of those policies was her wisdom and that of councillors she appointed. Altogether she is one of history's most remarkable women.

Bibliography

Camden, William. *The Historie of the Most Renowned and Victorious Princesse Elizabeth Late Queene of England.* London: B. Fisher, 1630. Rev. ed. Edited by Wallace T. MacCaffrey. Chicago: University of Chicago Press, 1970. These selections from the annals of a scholar from Elizabethan times represent the earliest authoritative study of her reign. Camden wrote in Latin; this version, the work of an anonymous seventeenth century translator, conveys Camden's commitment to a plain, factual record. Though lacking in color and narrative skill, Camden gives the modern reader a sense of the way Elizabeth's reign looked to a learned contemporary.

Erickson, Carolly. *The First Elizabeth*. New York: Summit Books, 1983. One of Erickson's purposes is to counter the traditional emphasis on the "Virgin Queen" by stressing her use of her sexual power to attain her ends. Like Jenkins's book, this biography represents a woman's viewpoint but one sharply different in its heavily psychological interpretation of its subject.

Jenkins, Elizabeth. *Elizabeth the Great*. New York: Coward-McCann, 1959. Relying on previously published sources, this biography attained popular and critical success upon publication and continues to deserve praise as a perceptive and readable interpretation of Elizabeth's character. As her title suggests, Jenkins emphasizes the positive elements contributing to Elizabeth's eminence.

Johnson, Paul. *Elizabeth I*. New York: Holt, Rinehart and Winston, 1974. Johnson depicts court life clearly but is less convincing on some aspects of the background of the age, particularly Puritanism. The informing theme of his study is the relationship between Elizabeth's exercise of her secular power and the political implications of the religious authority that she inherited from her predecessors.

MacCaffrey, Wallace T. *The Shaping of the Elizabethan Regime*. Princeton, N.J.: Princeton University Press, 1968. This specialized study should interest anyone seeking a detailed understanding of the first fifteen years of Elizabeth's rule, or what the author calls its "testing time." This work makes extensive use of state papers and documents from the Public Record Office in London.

Neale, J. E. *Queen Elizabeth I: A Biography*. London: Jonathan Cape, 1934. Reprint. New York: Doubleday, 1957. The great pioneer among modern biographers of Elizabeth, Neale is a master of unpretentious narrative history. Though undocumented, this classic biography has earned the respect of all Elizabethan researchers. Age has not dimmed its appeal.

Read, Conyers. *Lord Burghley and Queen Elizabeth*. New York: Alfred A. Knopf, 1960. More specifically the second volume of a life of Elizabeth's ablest adviser, this book, covering the years 1570 to 1598, explores in meticulous detail the working relationship between the two. Read is one of the greatest of modern Elizabethan scholars.

Weir, Alison. *The Life of Elizabeth I*. New York: Ballantine, 1998.

Williams, Neville. *Elizabeth the First: Queen of England*. New York: E. P. Dutton, 1968. A senior official of the Public Record Office, Williams predictably draws extensively on the documents thereof. He presents a particularly good picture of Elizabeth's domestic life. An objective, competently written, but sometimes stodgy biography.

_____. *The Life and Times of Elizabeth I*. New York: Welcome Rain, 1998. With an introduction by Antonia Fraser.

Robert P. Ellis

ELIZABETH II

Born: April 21, 1926; London, England

Dignified and regal, yet down-to-earth and accessible, Elizabeth II has embodied the continuing vitality of the British monarchy. The popularity and esteem in which she is held make her an ideal head of state.

Early Life

Elizabeth Alexandra Mary was born on April 21, 1926, the first child of Prince Albert and Elizabeth, the duke and duchess of York. Her father, the future George VI, was the second son of George V, and the duchess of York, formerly Lady Elizabeth Bowes-Lyon, came from a distinguished Scottish family. A second daughter, Margaret, was born four years later.

A major influence on the first ten years of Elizabeth's life, until his death in 1936, was that of her grandfather, George V. His was the dominant voice in the family, and he inculcated in his granddaughter a strong sense of duty and self-sacrifice, and a willingness to undertake hard, and not always glamorous, work. Elizabeth was also strongly influenced by the gaiety and fun of the social life she enjoyed every summer as a child with her mother's family at Glamis, just north of Dundee in Scotland.

At her birth, Elizabeth was not in the direct line of succession to the throne. The major event which was to shape her destiny came in 1936, when her uncle, Prince Edward, succeeded to the throne as Edward VIII. Several months later, he abdicated because he wished to marry a divorced woman whom the family and the country thought unsuitable to become queen. Elizabeth's father, as the next in line to the throne, thus became George VI, and Elizabeth, at the age of ten, became the heir presumptive. She led a somewhat sheltered and secluded childhood, not unusual for royal children, and was educated privately. A conscientious, serious-minded, and fairly placid child, she was developing qualities which she would put to full use in her future role as queen.

In July, 1939, Elizabeth first met Prince Philip of Greece, five years her senior, who was about to embark on a naval career. The capable and handsome young prince made a deep impression on her, but at the time the princess was only thirteen, and the outbreak of World War II in September prevented any immediate flowering of the friendship. For the duration of the war, Elizabeth was moved to Windsor Castle, near London, where she was to spend the remainder of her childhood. In 1940, at the age of fourteen, she gave a radio address which was broadcast throughout the British Empire. The young princess, who was quite small in stature, with very blue eyes and a quick, engagingly warm smile, accepted her opportunity with poise and confidence.

After the end of the war, the incipient romance between Elizabeth

Elizabeth II *(Library of Congress)*

and Prince Philip (by then known as Lieutenant Philip Mountbatten) moved quickly. They became engaged in July, 1947, and were married in November. A year later, Elizabeth gave birth to a son, Charles; a baby girl, Anne, followed in 1950. At this time, Elizabeth might reasonably have expected a decade or so to devote herself to rearing her children before inheriting her weightier responsibilities, but in February, 1952, George VI died prematurely at the age of fifty-six. Elizabeth, who was touring with her husband in East Africa, found herself, at the age of twenty-six, queen of Great Britain and its dominions.

Life's Work

The coronation took place in June, 1953, and was celebrated, it was estimated, by a quarter of the entire population of the world. Within a month, the new queen faced one of her most difficult decisions. Her sister Margaret wished to marry Group Captain Peter Townsend, a war hero who was at the time comptroller of the Queen Mother's household. Unfortunately, Townsend was in the process of divorcing his wife and was on that account considered to be an unsuitable husband for royalty. Under the Royal Marriages Act of 1772, members of the royal family who are in line of succession to the throne and who are under twenty-five years old must have the sovereign's permission to marry. Elizabeth was sympathetic to the couple, but she felt compelled to act on the advice of her prime minister, Sir Winston Churchill, and the marriage did not take place. The issue resurfaced two years later, however, when Margaret became twenty-five. Amid public controversy, Elizabeth left the decision to Margaret, who decided that she would not marry Townsend.

In the winter of 1953-1954, the queen went on a tour of the British Commonwealth, the first reigning British monarch to travel around the world. She was to become the most traveled monarch in British history, visiting well over one hundred different countries.

In the years following her return, she established a daily routine. One of the most important tasks is her daily perusal of "the boxes," parliamentary papers delivered to her for signature. As the head of state, all government is conducted in her name. Although the signing is a formality, the queen takes her responsibility seriously. Many of her prime ministers can testify to her careful reading and to the shrewdness of her questions and comments on government business.

Elizabeth II and the duke of Edinburgh on a tour of the Commonwealth. *(Library of Congress)*

Approximately once a month, she holds an investiture at Buckingham Palace, in which she personally hands out honors to public servants and other outstanding individuals. Her other duties are many. She may spend an afternoon inspecting a factory or visiting a hospital ward, attending an exhibition or a major sporting event. On such occasions, long practice has made her always imperturbable and dignified, interested and alert, however many eager hands there may be to shake.

On several occasions Elizabeth II has become involved in political controversy centering on the royal prerogative to appoint prime ministers. In 1957, the prime minister, Anthony Eden, resigned because of ill health. The ruling Conservative Party had no clearly defined system of electing a leader, but it was widely believed in the country that Eden would be succeeded by Richard Austen Butler. The queen, however, acting on the advice of Lord Salisbury, who had determined that a majority of Conservative members of Parliament favored Harold

Macmillan, duly appointed Macmillan as prime minister. As a result, Elizabeth found herself open to the accusation that she had allowed herself to be manipulated by the elder statesmen of the party, who represented its aristocratic wing, and that she had not consulted widely enough before making her decision.

A similar but more serious controversy took place in 1963, when Macmillan resigned. Acting solely on his advice, the queen appointed the earl of Home as prime minister. This was quite unexpected by the country at large, there being at least four other viable candidates. Whereas the queen's instincts have always been to avoid political involvement, on this occasion her attempt to avoid politics had the opposite effect, making her seem less than impartial and independent.

Meanwhile, the royal family continued to grow. In 1960, Queen Elizabeth gave birth to a third child, Andrew, and a fourth, Edward, followed in 1964. In the next decade, the occasion of the queen's Silver Jubilee in 1977 gave the nation an opportunity for prolonged celebration which it had not known since the coronation. The occasion clearly showed, to anyone who doubted, the spontaneous affection and enthusiasm with which the British people regard their queen.

Summary

In the reign of Elizabeth II, the monarchy has achieved an unprecedented popularity among the British people. Much of this is the result of the personal qualities of the queen: her sense of duty, her dignity and seriousness of manner, her desire to uphold the ideals of family life. She has weathered a number of storms, from widespread criticism of her supposedly stuffy and incompetent advisers in the 1950's to the simmering political row over royal finances in the inflation-riddled days of the 1970's.

In the 1990's, the British public's appreciation of the royal family was sorely tested as two princes, Charles and Andrew, were married and divorced amid a variety of scandals. Elizabeth herself managed to emerge from it all relatively unscathed, although public reaction following the 1997 death of the wildly popular Diana, the princess of Wales, included open criticism of the queen's perceived coldness and impassivity in the face of the tragedy.

Elizabeth has had the intelligence and skill to adapt the monarchy successfully to a changing era. She has made it accessible without diminishing its grandeur or mystique. When in the 1970's she allowed television cameras into Buckingham Palace for the making of the film *Royal Family*, for example, she achieved a public relations breakthrough. The glimpse into the private life of the royal family fascinated the nation.

Elizabeth II has also presided with dignity over a difficult period in British history, marked by the steady decline in the nation's worldwide influence and prestige. Nevertheless, the transformation of the British Empire into the British Commonwealth, a voluntary association of equal and independent nations, has in many ways been a productive and useful change. As head of the Commonwealth, the queen is known to cherish its ideals of freedom and friendly cooperation between nations.

Her address to the Australian Parliament in 1954, shortly after her accession, remains an appropriate comment on her life: "It is my resolve that under God I shall not only rule but serve. This is not only the tradition of my family; it describes, I believe, the modern character of the British Crown." Inspired by her example, the house of Windsor has become a model of how a constitutional monarchy can flourish in a democratic and turbulent era.

Bibliography

Bradford, Sarah. *Elizabeth: A Biography of Her Majesty the Queen*. Rev. ed. London: Mandarin, 1997.

Crawford, Marion. *The Little Princesses*. London: Cassell, 1950. Crawford was governess to Elizabeth and Margaret for more than twelve years and was in royal service for seventeen years. She horrified the royal family afterward by breaking the unwritten code of secrecy and writing books and articles about her experiences. The book, however, is interesting and authentic, presenting an attractive picture of the young princesses.

Davies, Nicholas. *Queen Elizabeth II: A Woman Who Is Not Amused*. Rev. and updated ed. New York: Carol, 1998.

Lacey, Robert. *Majesty: Elizabeth II and the House of Windsor*. New York: Harcourt Brace Jovanovich, 1977. The best biography. Tasteful and sympathetic, balanced in judgment, yet avoids hagiography. Ranges over the great issues of the day with which the queen has been involved, and includes just enough trivia and gossip to keep the reader entertained.

Longford, Elizabeth. *The Queen: The Life of Elizabeth II.* New York: Alfred A. Knopf, 1983. Readable, anecdotal, sympathetic, but with a tendency toward hagiography. The queen declined to be interviewed, but many others who know her cooperated, including Princess Margaret and the Queen Mother. Gives insight into the role of the monarchy in the modern British constitution.

Morrow, Ann. *The Queen.* New York: William Morrow, 1983. Morrow was for many years the court correspondent of the London *Daily Telegraph,* and went on many royal tours. She gives a lively, anecdotal account of the queen's life at home and on official journeys abroad.

Packard, Jerrold M. *The Queen and Her Court: A Guide to the British Monarchy Today.* New York: Charles Scribner's Sons, 1981. Explains in detail how the British court functions. Discusses laws of succession, finances, titles and ranks, and protocol and procedures, and gives a brief history of the present royal family.

White, Ralph M., and Graham Fisher. *The Royal Family: A Personal Portrait.* New York: David McKay, 1969. White was Elizabeth's personal footman for eight years, and also served her father, George VI. His portrait of life in the royal household includes the daily duties of every member of the royal family and a host of other tiny details.

Ziegler, Philip. *Crown and People.* New York: Alfred A. Knopf, 1978. Using the archives of Mass Observation, the pioneer public opinion survey established in 1937, Ziegler gives a commentary on the attitude of the British public toward monarchy, from George V's jubilee in 1935 to Elizabeth's in 1977. Finds that nine out of ten people have consistently supported the monarchy.

Bryan Aubrey

DIANNE FEINSTEIN

Born: June 22, 1933; San Francisco, California

In elected offices from the presidency of the Board of Supervisors of San Francisco to U.S. senator from California, Feinstein proved to be a pioneer, the first woman to hold each position.

Early Life

Dianne Goldman was born in San Francisco, California, on June 22, 1933, to Leon Goldman, a Jewish physician, and Betty Rosenburg Goldman, a Catholic woman of Russian descent. Dianne endured a difficult childhood that could have irreparably scarred her but instead left her resilient and strong. Betty Goldman, an alcoholic who was ill with a brain disorder that was not diagnosed until much later, was frequently abusive toward her daughters, and Dianne assumed a protective role for her two younger sisters. Her father, a busy physician, was a sustaining force in Dianne's life as well as a highly respected member of the community. The poles of opposition that dominated Dianne's childhood were reflected in her concurrent attendance at temple services and the Convent of the Sacred Heart High School, where she was graduated in 1951.

One of the stabilizing forces during Dianne's youth was her uncle, Morris Goldman, who moved in with the family and introduced Dianne to the workings of government by taking her to meetings of the San Francisco Board of Supervisors. Often critical of the board's actions, he urged his niece to get an education and do the job better. She determined while still in high school to pursue a career in government service. In preparation, Dianne attended Stanford University. During her senior year, she served as vice president of the student body.

After graduating from Stanford with a bachelor's degree in history in 1955, Dianne accepted an internship in public affairs with the CORO Foundation and spent a year studying public policy. In her subsequent position as an administrative assistant for the California Industrial Welfare Commission, she met and married Jack Berman, a lawyer, but the marriage lasted less than three years. With her nine-month-old daughter, Katherine Anne, Dianne started anew. Governor Edmund S.

(Pat) Brown, having been impressed by Dianne when she was a high school friend of his daughter, sought her out to serve on the California Women's Board of Terms and Paroles, a position she held from 1960 until 1966.

Dianne's second marriage, in 1962 to Bertram Feinstein, provided stability in her personal life. Her second husband encouraged her continued involvement in public activities. Dianne Feinstein's interest in the justice system broadened with positions on the Committee on Adult Detention and the San Francisco Mayor's Commission on Crime. Her experiences in these jobs further prepared her to seek elected office.

Life's Work

Dianne Feinstein's election to the San Francisco Board of Supervisors in 1969 marked the beginning of her noteworthy career as an elected public official. As one of the first San Francisco politicians to use television extensively for campaigning, Feinstein received more votes than any other candidate for supervisor. Thus, she became president of the Board of Supervisors for 1970-1971, the first woman to serve in that position.

Despite Feinstein's popularity as a supervisor and as president of the board—serving a second term as president from 1974 to 1975, and being reelected for a third term in 1978—life was not without its setbacks for her both professionally and personally. After losing two bids for mayor in 1971 and 1975 and coping with her husband's long bout with cancer and subsequent death in April, 1978, Feinstein was so emotionally bereft that she contemplated a full withdrawal from public life. Only hours after making such a pronouncement to reporters, however, Feinstein found herself acting mayor of San Francisco. The assassination of Mayor George Moscone and Supervisor Harvey Milk thrust Feinstein abruptly into the forefront of San Francisco government and placed her once again in a pioneering role as the first woman to serve as the city's mayor.

The dignity and poise with which she handled the crisis evoked strong support for Feinstein from her constituency. Running a city with as many diverse groups as San Francisco possessed was not easy. Feinstein prided herself in being a centrist, however, and immediately demonstrated her intention to be an activist mayor. She established such early priorities as reducing response time for police and firemen, revitalizing public transportation, and improving garbage pickup. To ensure the success of her endeavors, Feinstein raised taxes when necessary, leading some critics to label her as a "tax and spend" Democrat while others complained about her lack of a long-term plan.

Feinstein remained politically popular, winning her second full term as mayor with 80 percent of the vote. By law, however, she was unable to seek a third term and began exploring the possibility of running for governor of California. Although the office of mayor in San Francisco was nominally nonpartisan, Feinstein's allegiance to the Democratic Party was widely known, and she had been seriously considered for the 1984 Democratic vice presidential nomination. Although Democratic challengers faced a difficult battle for the governorship (which had been dominated by Republicans), especially a candidate without a statewide political base or network of support, Feinstein believed that the time was right and committed herself to a campaign for California governor.

The early stages of Feinstein's campaign for the Democratic nomination for governor were fraught with problems in staffing. Feinstein was also troubled by physical problems that left her without adequate energy and forced her to undergo major surgery in July, 1989. Her opponent, California Attorney General John Van de Kamp, had pulled far ahead of her in the polls by late fall, and her campaign was so underfunded that her staff contemplated the possibility of her withdrawal. At that point, however, Feinstein responded by conferring with her staff to devise a strategy to revitalize her campaign. Her third husband, Richard C. Blum, an investment banker whom she had married in 1980, provided strong financial support for Feinstein's advertising campaign on television. The most effective commercial centered on her ability to handle crises, as illustrated through dramatic black-and-white footage of Feinstein's announcement of Moscone and Milk's deaths. This sympathetic portrayal of Feinstein's leadership ability was a major influence in her come-from-behind victory over Van de Kamp.

With the momentum of a strong primary victory, Feinstein moved into the general election against the Republican candidate, Senator Pete Wilson. The election was especially significant to both parties because the victor would oversee reapportionment of the seven new congressional districts that were to be created in California as a result of the increase in population measured by the 1990 census. Republicans were thus pouring in considerable money, and Feinstein again found herself confronting the difficulties of raising money and reaching voters statewide.

In addition to promoting government reform, Feinstein campaigned on issues related to the environment and abortion rights. Although Feinstein had identified herself as unequivocally pro-choice in the primary, most feminist leaders, including the state chapter of the National Organization for Women (NOW), had endorsed her opponent, Van de Kamp. Even in the general election, feminist supporters were unenthusiastic, and some analysts suggested that her lack of ties to women's groups ultimately cost Feinstein the election.

Once again, the Feinstein campaign relied heavily on television advertising and centered on the slogan Tough but Caring. During the last weeks of campaigning, the race became extremely close, but Feinstein eventually lost by 3.46 percent of the vote. Campaign manager Bill Carrick attributed the loss to a failure to produce commercials that attracted voters, citing the difficulty of presenting a female candidate as tough enough for the job without creating a sense of hardness that alienates voters.

Undaunted by the loss, however, Feinstein proclaimed that public service had been and would continue to be her life. Indeed, she moved almost immediately into a campaign for the Senate, announcing in early 1991 her intention to run in the 1992 election for Pete Wilson's former seat, then being filled by Wilson's appointee, Republican John Seymour. Some political analysts questioned Feinstein's decision to run for the remaining two-year term rather than for the full six-year term to succeed retiring Senator Alan Cranston. Although Feinstein may have hoped to preempt the Democratic field with her early move and avoid an expensive primary campaign, that did not occur, and state controller Gray Davis provided strong opposition.

Because she had proved herself a viable statewide candidate in the 1990 race for governor, however, Dianne Feinstein found fund-raising easier and she had to rely less on her husband for campaign financing. Nevertheless, the issue of finances plagued the early part of her campaign when the California Fair Political Practices Commission filed an $8,000,000 suit for campaign reporting violations in her race for governor. The suit was eventually settled for $190,000 with both sides agreeing that unintentional errors in bookkeeping and reporting had occurred.

Following a decisive victory in the Democratic primary, Feinstein entered the general election alongside noted feminist politician Barbara Boxer, who had won the Democratic nomination for the second Senate seat. Feinstein's male Republican opponent was John Seymour, who was known for his support of feminist causes over the years. As a result, Feinstein, who had generally not emphasized women's issues in previous campaigns, began aggressively stressing such feminist issues as abortion rights, family leave, child support, and domestic violence. A prominent campaign phrase also played on the fact that only two members of the U.S. Senate were women: "Two percent may be okay for milk, but it isn't for the U.S. Senate."

When critics complained about her record on women's issues while she was mayor, Feinstein admitted she had been wrong in refusing to sign a 1983 resolution commemorating the tenth anniversary of *Roe v. Wade*, but noted she had consistently been pro-choice. She also defended her veto of a comparable worth plan in 1985 by arguing that it was inadequate and by emphasizing that she had written a better proposal which passed the following year.

With her subsequent election to the Senate, Feinstein again broke new ground. She and Boxer became the first female senators from California, the first Jewish senators from the state, and the first all-female delegation to the U.S. Senate. Analysts indicate that major factors in Feinstein's victory were her plan for improving the economy (especially reducing military spending in order to increase funding for environmental protection projects), the desire to initiate change in Washington, the anger over the Senate's treatment of Anita Hill during the confirmation hearings of Clarence Thomas to the U.S. Supreme Court, and the related desire to see more women in the Senate. In 1994, she won reelection to the Senate despite stiff competition and numerous negative campaign advertisements from her Republican challenger, Michael Huffington.

Summary

In many respects, Dianne Feinstein's life has been one exploring new territory for women. In each of her elected positions, she has been the first woman to hold that office, a situation often fraught with difficulties. Feinstein has acknowledged feeling that she is constantly being tested because of being "first," yet she has successfully met the challenges in each position. Having begun her quest for political office prior to the full flowering of the feminist movement, Feinstein established her position in the world of politics independent of women's groups and without a feminist agenda. Subsequently, however, she embraced women's causes and made them a significant part of her life's goal, to contribute to humankind through government service.

Bibliography

Doyle, Michael. "Dianne Feinstein, Coming of Age as a U.S. Senator." *California Journal* 25, no. 6 (June, 1994): 18, 22-23.

Leavitt, Judith A. *American Women Managers and Administrators*. Westport, Conn.: Greenwood Press, 1985. Provides brief but basic biographical data through Feinstein's career as mayor of San Francisco.

McElroy, Lisa Tucker, with Eileen Feinstein Mariano. *Meet My Grandmother: She's a United States Senator*. Brookfield, Conn.: Millbrook Press, 2000. In this book in the series Grandmothers at Work, Feinstein's busy life is described through the eyes of her six-year-old granddaughter.

Morris, Celia. *Storming the Statehouse: Running for Governor with Ann Richards and Dianne Feinstein*. New York: Charles Scribner's Sons, 1992. The most valuable source of information available on Feinstein. Although the work focuses on her unsuccessful bid for governor in 1990 (in contrast to Richards's successful bid), it also presents essential biographical details of her earlier personal and professional life.

Stall, Bill. "Battle with Wilson Left Feinstein Tougher, Quicker." *Los Angeles Times*, April 28, 1992, p. A1. A good analysis of the Feinstein campaign for Senate.

Wilkinson, Tracy. "Senate Races Offer Stark Contrasts on World Affairs." *Los Angeles Times*, September 20, 1992, p. A3. Provides Feinstein's views on major issues during her campaign for Senate.

Witt, Linda, Karen M. Paget, and Glenna Matthews. *Running as a Woman: Gender and Power in American Politics*. New York: Free Press, 1993. A journalist, a political scientist, and a historian collaborated on this narrative overview of the experiences of female candidates in American politics. Written from the vantage point of 1992's Year of the Woman, this work contains useful information on Feinstein's political career at the state and national level, including a telling assessment of her appeal among female voters.

Verbie Lovorn Prevost

GERALDINE FERRARO

Born: August 26, 1935; Newburgh, New York

In 1984, Ferraro became the first woman to be nominated to the vice presidency by a major political party.

Early Life

Geraldine Anne Ferraro was born to an Italian American family in Newburgh, New York, on August 26, 1935. Her father, Dominick Ferraro, operated a nightclub in Newburgh, which had a reputation of being a wide-open town. In 1944, he was arrested and charged with operating a numbers racket. He died of a heart attack the day he was to appear for trial.

Antonetta Corrieri Ferraro, the major influence on Geraldine's early life, was left to rear her two children alone. She and the children left Newburgh in order to make ends meet; they relocated in a modest home in the somewhat less desirable South Bronx. Education was traditionally a way up and out for the children and grandchildren of immigrant families, and Antonetta Ferraro worked hard as a seamstress to provide an education for her children. Geraldine Ferraro attended Marymount Manhattan College and was graduated in 1956. She worked as a schoolteacher to support herself while attending law school at night and received her law degree from Fordham University in 1960, the same year she married John Zaccaro, a real estate developer. In honor of her mother, Ferraro kept her maiden name.

In the years that followed, three children were born to Ferraro and her husband. Although she passed the New York bar examination in 1961, she chose to practice law part time while rearing her children. It was not until 1974 that she entered public service and accepted a post as an assistant district attorney in Queens County, New York, specializing in cases involving women, children, and the elderly.

Life's Work

Running as a Democrat, Geraldine Ferraro was elected to the United States Congress in 1978, and was reelected in 1980 and 1982. During those years she devoted her considerable energies to serving her working-class district in Queens, New York, by obtaining federal assistance for roads and subways, pure water and pollution control, control of illicit drugs, and other urban issues.

As one of the few women in Congress—there were only eleven Democrats and six Republicans in 1979 and a total of twenty-four women in 1983—she also became an obvious symbol for the feminist movement that had begun to transform American society. Ferraro denied that she wanted to be solely a women's representative, but she did speak out on the feminization of poverty, the discrimination affecting salaries and pensions awarded to men and women, and the problems of single-parent households headed by women.

Ferraro was not the first woman to have made her mark in Congress. In 1916, Jeannette Rankin was the first woman elected to Congress, and she voted against American involvement in both world wars. Pat Schroeder of Colorado and Barbara Mikulski of Maryland were two Democratic representatives rising to prominence at the same time as Ferraro. Outside of Congress, women were also achieving positions of political power. By the 1980's, Sandra Day O'Connor sat on the United States Supreme Court, Elizabeth Dole and Margaret Heckler were in the cabinet, Dianne Feinstein was the mayor of San Francisco, and many male politicians were asking their female colleagues to speak for them in election campaigns.

The year 1984 was a presidential election year, and the conservative Republican Ronald Reagan was running for reelection. Most observers believed it would be a difficult challenge to defeat the former actor, who enjoyed notable popularity as president and was recognized for his skills of communication. After enduring a bruising series of primaries, Walter Mondale, former vice president under Jimmy Carter and onetime senator from Minnesota, emerged as the leading Democratic challenger and came to the San Francisco convention in July with the Democratic presidential nomination assured. The only remaining question was who would be his vice presidential running mate.

Traditionally, vice presidential candidates were selected to bring balance to the ticket. With Mondale's roots in the upper Midwest it could be expected that he might well choose someone from one of the big coastal states such as New York or California. Age, experience, and ideology could also play a part. In the past, however, balancing gender had never been seriously considered, and the Democratic and Republican parties had never chosen a female candidate for either the presidency or the vice presidency. When he appeared before the National Women's Political Caucus in 1983, Mondale himself had indicated that he would consider a woman as his vice presidential candidate if he received the Democratic nomination.

In November, 1983, several influential women met with Ferraro in hopes that she would consent to accept the vice presidential nomination if it were offered. Other Democratic women had been considered, but most were rejected as unsuitable because of geography, their stand against abortion, their brief tenure in elective office, or their lack of national and foreign policy experience. Ferraro nicely complemented Mondale: An Italian American Catholic from urban New York, she had completed three terms in Congress representing a conservative ethnic and blue-collar constituency. Ferraro had struck a balance between her role as a wife and a mother of three children and her career as a politician. She had also made an impact within Democratic Party circles. In her position as secretary of the Democratic Caucus in 1982, Ferraro had served as House liaison to the National Party Conference; in 1984, she was the chair of the Platform Committee at the Democratic National Convention and oversaw the selection of presidential and vice presidential nominees.

The prospect of a woman as the Democratic vice presidential nominee was widely discussed. In June, 1984, *Time* magazine featured Ferraro and Feinstein on the cover as possible candidates. By the end of the month, there was considerable pressure on Mondale to choose a woman as his running mate: The National Organization for Women (NOW) was seemingly threatening a convention fight if a woman was not selected. Mondale, however, did not have to be threatened. Always supportive of women's issues, Mondale knew that as a long-shot candidate against a popular incumbent he had little to lose and possibly much to gain by choosing a female running mate. Many, including some Republicans, believed that a female nominee would attract votes to the Democratic ticket.

On July 19, 1984, Ferraro made history when she was nominated as the Democratic vice presidential candidate. She and Mondale knew that the campaign would not be easy, but they believed that Reagan was vulnerable on both his foreign policy, which they deemed too belligerent toward the Soviet Union and thus endangering the world's peace, and on the domestic issues of unfairness and lack of opportunity for the less privileged members of American society. Unfortunately for Ferraro, much of the ensuing campaign revolved not around the issues of public policy but rather on herself and her personal history.

Sadly, it might have been predicted that a female candidate would be treated differently, and not only by representatives from the opposite political party. Ferraro had difficulties with Mondale's own campaign staff, and other problems arose which, she argued, would not have occurred if she had been a man. More troubling were claims that she had acted unethically and perhaps illegally in the financing of her first congressional campaign, with her congressional disclosure statements, and with her family's past taxes and tax returns. These issues quickly dominated her campaign. She questioned whether such charges would have received such credence and publicity if she were a male candidate. Her husband was initially willing to release his financial statement, but not his personal tax returns, which he had been filing separately for several years. His reluctance to release this information led to charges that he had something sinister to hide. Over the next several weeks, accusations were made that Zaccaro's father had rented office space to an underworld figure and that Zaccaro himself had borrowed money from an estate in which he was the legal conservator. In late August, after the various tax and financial statements were finally made available for public scrutiny, Ferraro held an open press conference in the attempt to put the issue to rest. This tactic was only partially successful.

Ferraro was also criticized by members of the Catholic hierarchy for her stand in favor of personal choice in the controversial matter of abortion. This, too, she believed reflected a double standard: Male Catholic politicians had not been personally criticized for similar stands on the abortion issue, and, in the past, Catholic bishops had generally abstained from political comment. Given the Mafia stereotype closely connected to the image of the Italian American community in the popular mind, Ferraro also was exposed to charges that she and her husband and their families had ties to organized crime. What was most galling for Ferraro was that other Italian American politicians did not come to her defense. The final blow to Ferraro's dignity was the report in October that her father had been arrested shortly before his death, charged with participation in a numbers racket.

Despite these personal attacks and the physical challenges of the 1984 campaign, Ferraro found her activities to be highly rewarding. In three months, Ferraro traveled more than 55,000 miles and spoke in eighty-five cities. Her campaign raised six million dollars for the national Democratic ticket. Crowds were invariably large and enthusiastic wherever she appeared. In November, however, the country voted overwhelmingly for Ronald Reagan and George Bush. The polls and political commentators had early predicted the outcome, and Ferraro realized that she and Mondale were going to lose even before election day.

After the 1984 campaign, Ferraro chose to keep a low political profile and passed up the opportunity to challenge the incumbent Republican senator from New York, Alphonse D'Amato, in 1986. Still under public scrutiny, her husband pleaded guilty to overstating his net worth in getting a loan and was sentenced to community service. Later, Ferraro's son, John, a college student, was arrested on cocaine charges. In 1990, Geraldine Ferraro chose to campaign aggressively on behalf of female Democratic candidates in New York. She launched her own political comeback in 1992, when she entered the New York Democratic primary as a candidate for United States Senate. Competing against three other candidates in the primary, including New York state comptroller and former congressional representative Elizabeth Holtzman, Ferraro faced a tough battle. Typically upbeat and optimistic to the end, Ferraro finished second, less than one percentage point and fewer than ten thousand votes behind the winner, who was ultimately defeated in the general election.

Summary
For many women—and for some men—Geraldine Ferraro's 1984 campaign for the vice presidency was a watershed, a defining moment in their lives. Never before had a woman been chosen for such a high office by a major political party. During and after the campaign, Ferraro received thousands of letters from women, young and old, who saw her campaign as a symbol of equality, recognition, and opportunity for American women. Gloria Steinem, one of America's most respected feminists, noted during the campaign that, "In the long run, the importance of the Ferraro factor may be the talent and dreams it unleashes in others." As an attorney in private practice after the cam-

paign, Ferraro found time to encourage numerous women candidates by raising funds through public appearances on their behalf. Within a decade of the 1984 election, California, the largest state in the union, had chosen two women to represent the state in the U.S. Senate—a political first made possible, in part, by the example of Geraldine Ferraro.

Bibliography

Adams, James Ring. "The Lost Honor of Geraldine Ferraro." *Commentary* 81 (February, 1986): 34-38. This article explores the press and media coverage Ferraro received during the 1984 campaign and concludes that part of the press resorted to sensationalism but some of the media failed to adequately delve into Ferraro's controversial family history.

Blumenthal, Sidney. "Once upon a Time in America." *The New Republic* 194 (January 6, 1986): 28-36. In this important article, Blumenthal explores Ferraro's past and her family history and notes that, in spite of her claims, there are numerous criminal connections to both her and her husband's history.

Drew, Elizabeth. *Campaign Journal*. New York: Macmillan, 1985. Drew covered the 1984 election campaign for *The New Yorker* magazine. Her comments on Ferraro's campaign are insightful, including the observation that some exit polls indicated that Ferraro's controversial candidacy lost votes for the Democratic Party.

Ferraro, Geraldine A., with Linda Bird Francke. *Ferraro: My Story*. New York: Bantam Books, 1985. Ferraro, with the assistance of Linda Bird Francke, writes primarily of the 1984 vice presidential campaign and the various vicissitudes which she experienced. It also covers more superficially her earlier life, particularly her political career.

Ferraro, Geraldine A., with Catherine Whitney. *Framing a Life: A Family Memoir*. New York: Charles Scribner's Sons, 1998.

Ferraro, Susan. "What Makes Gerry Run?" *The New York Times Magazine*, March 22, 1992, 46. The author, no relation to the subject, discusses the early stages of the 1992 New York Democratic Senatorial campaign where Ferraro was attempting a political comeback. In addition, Ferraro's story since 1984 is summarized.

Witt, Linda, Karen M. Paget, and Glenna Matthews. *Running as a Woman: Gender and Power in American Politics*. New York: Free Press,

1993. A journalist, a political scientist, and a historian collaborated on this sweeping narrative of the experiences of female candidates in American politics. Throughout this work, Geraldine Ferraro's political career serves as one of the key case studies. The book contains numerous references to Ferraro's 1984 campaign, her career outside of public office, and her heroic efforts to encourage the political aspirations of other female Democratic candidates during the 1990 election year.

Eugene Larson

JESSIE BENTON FRÉMONT

Born: May 31, 1824; near Lexington, Virginia
Died: December 27, 1902; Los Angeles, California

As the daughter of a powerful senator and wife of an explorer and general, Frémont participated in Jacksonian politics, the opening of the West, abolitionism, and the Civil War. In her behind-the-scenes work, she challenged the constraints of nineteenth century roles for women.

Early Life

Jessie Ann Benton was born on May 31, 1824, at Cherry Grove, her mother's family plantation near Lexington, Virginia. She was the second daughter of the five children born to Thomas Hart Benton and Elizabeth McDowell Benton. Her father had moved as a young man from his native North Carolina to Tennessee, where he became a friend and protégé of Andrew Jackson. In 1815, Benton migrated to St. Louis, Missouri, where he practiced law and was elected the new state's first senator, in 1820. In 1821, Benton married Elizabeth McDowell, whom he had courted for six years. Elizabeth's Scotch-Irish Presbyterian family had settled in a Blue Ridge mountain valley near Lexington, Virginia, in 1737, and had become prominent in local and state politics.

As Jessie grew up, the family moved between households in St. Louis, Cherry Grove, and Washington, D.C., exposing the curious child to an array of personalities, from Washington insiders to southern aristocrats to rough frontiersmen. Jessie was privately tutored in languages, piano, history, and classics. Her father's favorite child, she was taken along to the Capitol and White House, where she absorbed the elder Benton's democratic convictions. A champion of the common people, her father advocated western expansion and opposed the extension of slavery.

Jessie displayed a willful and independent spirit, which her father encouraged as long as she was a child. As she approached womanhood with no sign of diminishing assertiveness, he realized that allowing her to exercise her mind and personality freely had ill prepared her for the submissive role expected of nineteenth century women. At age fourteen, Jessie was sent to Miss English's Female Seminary in

Georgetown, a fashionable finishing school that she despised.

In 1840, Jessie met John Charles Frémont, a handsome young officer with the Army's Topographical Corps. Frémont had all the qualities of courage, impulsiveness, and willfulness that would make him a great explorer and attractive to the ladies, including sixteen-year-old Jessie. Her father was alarmed, since Frémont lacked the status and wealth that Benton thought important in a suitor for his daughter. Frémont was the illegitimate son of a French immigrant and had been reared in poverty by his mother in South Carolina. Despite efforts by her father to prevent a romance, Jessie eloped with the dashing Frémont on October 19, 1841. Eventually reconciled to the marriage, Thomas Hart Benton welcomed his new son-in-law as a willing partner in his campaign to open the West to American expansion, and in his daughter Benton recognized a talented and driven helpmate who would advance Frémont's career.

Life's Work

Unable to participate in politics in her own right, Jessie Benton Frémont devoted her considerable energies to promoting her husband's career. Like her father, she believed fervently that the destiny of the United States was to expand across the continent. John C. Frémont shared this goal and embodied the resolve necessary to achieve it. Through Benton's influence and his own credentials as an explorer, Frémont was appointed to head a series of expeditions to chart the West. The first of these assignments sent Frémont into western Wyoming in 1842, where he surveyed South Pass and climbed one of the highest peaks of the Wind River range. Upon his return, Jessie helped him write the report of the expedition which was published in 1843. While the scientific observations were John Frémont's, the dramatic flair and poetic touch added by Jessie made the report a romantic adventure story. Their collaboration produced results reflecting the strengths of each, although the credit reverted to John. Jessie, like other women of the day, measured her own success by her husband's triumphs.

At the start of John's second expedition in 1843, an incident occurred which revealed Jessie's capacity for audacious actions on her husband's behalf. While John was preparing to leave Missouri, Jessie intercepted a message from the War Department instructing Frémont to return to Washington. Withholding the order, Jessie sent word to John to set out immediately on his journey. The expedition, which traveled to Oregon and California, was a huge success. The report, written by Jessie from John's dictation, sold in the tens of thousands and served as a guidebook for settlers moving West on the Oregon Trail.

In the meantime, Jessie began to raise a family. A daughter, Elizabeth Benton, was born in 1842. Jessie saw two children die before their first birthdays: Benton (1848) and Anne Beverley (1853). Two healthy sons were born: John Charles in 1851 and Frank Preston in 1854.

John C. Frémont's third expedition altered the fate of the family. Ending up in California in 1846, John was on hand to participate in the Bear Flag Revolt, an uprising in which American settlers seized power from Mexican officials prior to the actual outbreak of war between the two countries. Caught in a dispute between superior officers, Frémont disobeyed a direct order and was sent East for courtmartial. Jessie went in person to President James K. Polk to argue vigorously in her husband's defense. The court found John guilty and recommended his expulsion from the Army, though Polk rescinded the dismissal. The Frémonts refused to accept clemency, however, and John resigned in indignation from the Army. Embittered, the Frémonts moved to California, where John had purchased an estate called Las Mariposas near Yosemite Valley.

Life was rough in California during the Gold Rush, with occasional food shortages and few reliable servants available. The rewards, however, greatly outweighed the inconveniences when several rich veins of gold were discovered on Las Mariposas. Despite legal disputes over the title of the estate, the Frémonts found themselves millionaires, able to travel to Europe as celebrities in 1852. After returning to America in 1853, John headed yet another western expedition, while Jessie settled the family in New York.

In 1856, the new Republican Party chose John C. Frémont to run for president. The Frémonts favored the Republicans' free-soil position of prohibiting slavery in the new territories of the West. For the first time in American history, a candidate's wife figured prominently in the presidential campaign. Republican banners proclaimed "Frémont and Jessie" and "Jessie's Choice," with illustrations of the attractive Jessie and her handsome husband. While in public she played the decorous role expected of her, behind the scenes Jessie masterfully managed John's campaign. She helped to write his campaign biography, read and answered all of his mail, and received his visitors. Her prominent role was criticized by Frémont's opposition, yet it also galvanized women into political activity as never before. Women attended political rallies, and a few went on the lecture circuit for Frémont and free-soil. Although Frémont lost the election, the strong Republican showing in the party's first national election revealed the rising strength of the free-soil movement and the growing rift between North and South.

Jessie, exhausted from the campaign and upset over her father's refusal to endorse Frémont for president, reluctantly followed her husband to California once more. Her depression was compounded by her father's death in April, 1858.

When the Civil War broke out in 1861, Abraham Lincoln appointed John C. Frémont as Union commander of Missouri. Jessie joined her husband in St. Louis, acting as his unofficial adviser and assistant. Beset with shortages of men and supplies and surrounded by Confederate sympathizers, John had difficulty controlling the state. Largely as a military strategy, Frémont proclaimed the emancipation of all slaves belonging to disloyal Missourians. When a storm of protest erupted, Jessie traveled to Washington to plead John's case personally with President Lincoln. Speaking forcefully and emotionally, she antagonized Lincoln and failed to help her husband. John lost his Army command and retired to New York to wait out the war. In an effort to save her husband's reputation, Jessie wrote *The Story of the Guard: A Chronicle of the War* (1863), a book about John's exploits.

After the war, a series of financial disasters eroded the Frémont fortune, and by 1873, the family was destitute. Jessie wrote to support her family, contributing reminiscences and fiction to magazines such as *Harper's*, *Century*, and *Atlantic Monthly*. She produced a number of books based upon her travels, adventures, and acquaintances, including *A Year of American Travel* (1878), *Souvenirs of My Time* (1887), *Far-West Sketches* (1890), and *The Will and the Way Stories* (1891).

In 1887, the Frémonts moved to Los Angeles. After John died in 1890, Jessie continued to work on her memoirs and other writing and lived with her daughter Elizabeth, who acted as her nurse and companion until Jessie's death in 1902.

Summary

The life of Jessie Benton Frémont reveals the limited roles allowed women of the nineteenth century and the efforts they made to find fulfillment within those narrow boundaries. Reared by an indulgent father who encouraged her natural curiosity and independence, Jessie never comfortably fit into the passive role then commonly expected of women. While she did marry and raise a family, she acted out her own ambitions through her dynamic husband. She promoted his career by capitalizing on her own attributes, winning influence for him by calling upon her own political connections. She transformed his dry scientific reports into romantic adventure stories with her skilled pen. When he stumbled, she stepped beyond accepted propriety of the time to defend him brashly in front of presidents. When his ineptitude in business bankrupted the family, she quietly but competently went to work to bring in an income.

Jessie Benton Frémont often felt frustrated with the limited roles available to women. When she could, she gave generously to support the suffrage movement. She lamented that as a woman, she was not taken seriously in politics. Nevertheless, she did help to expand the opportunities for women through her example of feminine brilliance and assertiveness. Her role as the active wife of the presidential candidate in the 1856 campaign inspired women to demand the right to participate in politics. Like others of her generation, she responded to the Civil War with patriotism, public action, and compassion.

Bibliography

Alter, Judy. *Jessie: A Novel Based on the Life of Jessie Benton Frémont*. New York: Bantam Books, 1995.

Chambers, William Nisbet. *Old Bullion Benton, Senator from the New West: Thomas Hart Benton*. Boston: Little, Brown, 1956. Though somewhat dated, this work is still the most thorough biography of Jessie's father, Thomas Hart Benton. Useful for Benton and McDowell family background, political context, and relationship between Benton and John C. Frémont.

Frémont, Jessie Benton. *The Letters of Jessie Benton Frémont*. Edited by Pamela Herr and Mary Lee Spence. Urbana: University of Illinois Press, 1992. A delightful collection of letters written by Frémont which gives first-hand insight into her personality. The editors have

written an excellent biographical sketch of Frémont and have provided detailed chapters introducing each section of her life.

Herr, Pamela. *Jessie Benton Frémont: A Biography*. New York: Franklin
Watts, 1987. An up-to-date biography of Jessie Benton Frémont that
makes valuable use of letters and papers of the Frémont and Blair-
Lee families. Highly readable account of Frémont placed within the
political and social context of her time, reflecting new scholarship on
women.

Nevins, Allan. *Fremont: Pathmarker of the West*. Reprint. Lincoln: University of Nebraska Press, 1992. This reprint of a classic biography of
John Charles Frémont portrays him in heroic proportions. This work
also gives Jessie Benton Frémont deserved credit for contributing to
John's career. Useful for meticulous detail on both John and Jessie's
lives, though poorly documented.

Stone, Irving. *Immortal Wife: The Biographical Novel of Jessie Benton
Fremont*. Garden City, N.Y.: Doubleday, Doran, 1944. A fictionalized
account of Jessie Benton Frémont's life. Despite its fictional format,
Stone's novel is based upon the papers and published works of
Frémont, thus ensuring a relatively high degree of factual accuracy.

Lynne M. Getz

INDIRA GANDHI

Born: November 19, 1917; Allahabad, India
Died: October 31, 1984; Delhi, India

By serving as prime minister of India for almost two decades, Gandhi carried on a family tradition of political leadership, maintained her country's non-aligned status, and attempted to enact social reforms to eliminate poverty and hunger in her Third World democracy.

Early Life

On November 19, 1917, a daughter was born to Jawaharlal and Kamala Nehru in Allahabad, India. As she grew up in her grandfather Nehru's home, Indira Nehru enjoyed the privileges of the Brahman class, but the home was periodically invaded by police and her parents and grandparents arrested for their involvement in the nationalist movement against British colonial power. Such a disruptive childhood probably explains the reserve and aloofness Indira exhibited throughout her life. It certainly explains the sporadic nature of her early education. Indira's father attempted to supplement that education by writing her letters from prison, later published as *Glimpses of World History* (1934-1935). Combined with knowledge gleaned from the conversations of relatives and their political friends such as Mahatma Gandhi, these history lessons served as the foundation for Indira's work.

After the death of her mother, whom she admired greatly, in 1936, Indira continued to study in England for a time. She believed that her father needed her at home, however, since he had been elected president of the Congress Party and was moving rapidly to the forefront of the Indian independence movement alongside Mahatma Gandhi. Indira left Somerville College of Oxford without completing a degree and returned to India in 1941. While she had been away, she had fallen in love with Feroze Gandhi, a young, lower-class Indian nationalist. At first Nehru objected to the union but eventually accepted it, partially because Mahatma Gandhi, though not related to Feroze, had given the couple his blessing.

Indira Nehru became a Gandhi on March 26, 1942. Before the end of the year, she and her husband were imprisoned for their defiance of

Indira Gandhi *(Library of Congress)*

British rule. When Indira was released early because of ill health, she returned to her father's home. Feroze joined her there, and soon their first son, Rajiv, was born. Two years later they had another son, Sanjay.

Like her mother, Indira did not allow her domestic duties to impede her political support for a free India. When Jawaharlal Nehru became prime minister, she decided her duty to her country and to her father were one and the same. Since her husband and father seemed incompatible, Indira chose to remain with her father as his hostess, while Feroze left to pursue his own political career. The couple did not divorce and appear to have been reconciled years later.

Life's Work

From August, 1947, when India gained its independence, to 1964, Indira Gandhi learned from her father how to be a successful politician in a democracy. She traveled abroad with him and met the world's leaders. As Nehru's daughter, she commanded respect which, in turn, gave her confidence in her own abilities. She became active in the Congress Party and served as president in 1959-1960.

When Nehru died in 1964, more important to Gandhi than her own tragic loss was the fate of Indian democracy, which seemed threatened by corruption and party dissension. Although Nehru had not intended for his daughter to succeed him, the new prime minister, Lal Bahadur Shastri, recognized her popularity and appointed her to the cabinet as minister of information and broadcasting. When Shastri died suddenly, Gandhi was asked to enter the contest for Congress Party leadership and thus the office of prime minister. Her subsequent election in 1966 portended several things: the continuation of a family tradition of leadership, world recognition of women's abilities, and the beginning of a new era in Indian politics.

When Gandhi took office, she did so with firmness and resolve. Although the party leadership expected to manipulate her, they could not. Those who questioned her leadership lost their political offices as she consolidated her power, primarily by projecting herself as "Mother Indira." As she explained in 1967,

> [S]cores of my family members are poverty-stricken and I have to look after them. Since they belong to different castes and creeds, they sometimes fight among themselves, and I have to intervene, especially to look after the weaker members of my family, so that the stronger ones do not take advantage of them.

This statement is the core of Gandhi's political philosophy. In Indian politics, a multitude of parties including extremists on the Left and Right, compete for power. The dissension between Hindus and Muslims and the communalism of many Indians adds to the volatility of

(Left to right) Indira Gandhi, Indian ambassador Vijaya Lakshmi Pandit, former First Lady Eleanor Roosevelt, and Indian prime minister Jawaharlal Nehru on the steps of the Roosevelt Hyde Park estate in 1949. *(National Archives)*

Indian democracy. Gandhi saw herself and the Congress Party—whose ideals were secularism, socialism, and nonviolent, constitutional reform—as the center. Therefore, her political aim was what she called balance.

Maintaining political balance and thereby retaining democracy in a heterogeneous society was a difficult challenge that Gandhi accepted as a personal one. In 1969, when members of her own party leaned to the Right, simultaneously accusing her of leftist tendencies, she consolidated her political authority, won the backing of the masses, and effectively split her own party. When the right wing became more solidified in 1971 and adopted a campaign to "Remove Indira," she countered with the slogan "Remove Poverty," which became the reform program that gave her the greatest popular election mandate of her reign.

In the same year, she cautiously, briefly departed from the international corollary to her domestic policy: India's nonalignment position. Balance in foreign affairs meant neutrality. Yet when Pakistan made war against Bangladesh and millions of refugees poured into India, she shifted her priorities. Once the sympathies of the Indian people and most of the world favored the Bengali, she made her swift, decisive attack—one of the most substantial victories of her career.

The spell of victory faded, however, as the country woke to a devastating drought, spiraling poverty and hunger, and escalating corruption in business and political administration, including her own. Gandhi's quest for balance in the political arena and for a better life for her large, diverse family was failing. She tried to implement more economic reforms, but working-class strikes and violence grew. Gandhi's abhorrence of violent means to achieve change ironically led in 1975 to a proclamation of a state of emergency, under which she accrued dictatorial powers. Yet, she initially acted within the Indian constitutional system and with the support of the majority of Congress and capitalists at home and abroad. Nevertheless, charges against her mounted: thwarting her party's interests, repressing criticism, damaging the structure of the federal judiciary and bureaucracy, politicizing the army, trying to establish a family dynasty, and failing to solve the country's economic problems despite her broad powers.

In 1977, Gandhi decided to end the emergency and hold elections in which she confidently expected to receive a mandate to continue her reforms. Instead, the people revealed that they were unwilling to follow anyone—even Mother Indira—blindly and that democracy would prevail. The Congress Party was ousted from power along with Gandhi and her son Sanjay. For anyone but Gandhi that humiliating defeat would have meant the end of her career, but Gandhi could not abandon her family and her life's work. When the opposition proved to be corrupt and incompetent, Gandhi regained a seat in Parliament and ultimately was restored to the office of prime minister in 1980.

Gandhi's India was beset by more crises in 1980 than she had ever faced. Added to the persistent economic and political exigencies was a strong religious movement of the far Right. In 1982, Sikh fundamentalists occupied the Golden Temple, a Hindu shrine, and used it as a base for terrorist activities. Two years later, when she had amassed the support of the Indian people, Gandhi ordered the Indian army to take the shrine—a successful, though costly, assault. In October, 1984, Gandhi was assassinated by her own Sikh security guards.

Summary

Indira Gandhi's accomplishments during her years as India's prime minister were possible because the majority of the Indian people believed in her. Gandhi possessed two major attributes of effective leadership—courage and commitment. In the midst of numerous tragedies—the loss of parents, husband, and son Sanjay—Gandhi exhibited great personal courage. She courageously faced her enemies whether military or political, and determinedly fought her battles, even those she could not win. Not only Indians but also people all over the world admired this type of fortitude.

Gandhi's commitment to India was never questioned, probably because she refused to be a political observer. Her commitment entailed positive action to achieve a better India—one without major social problems like poverty and hunger. Most of her fellow citizens believed that Gandhi could accomplish her goals and achieve unity through a balance of political perspectives, policies, and institutions. They viewed her international diplomacy as an overall success. Even when she leaned too far in one direction, they did not entirely lose their faith in her ability to restore balance, as evidenced by her 1980 reelection.

In the minds of the Indian people, despite her flaws, Gandhi was the mother of India. Her death did not alter that perception. Her dream for a united, prosperous, and peaceful India lived on for a time in her son Rajiv, who became prime minister after his mother's assassination. Addressing his countrymen, he remarked, "the foremost need now is to maintain our balance." In 1991, however, Rajiv Gandhi too was assassinated, by a Tamil terrorist from Sri Lanka.

Bibliography

Ali, Tariq. *An Indian Dynasty: The Story of the Nehru-Gandhi Family.* New York: G. P. Putnam's Sons, 1985. This well-written family history begins with Nehru, devotes a significant portion to Gandhi, and includes information on her sons, Rajiv and Sanjay. Its primary flaw is lack of documentation.

Bhatia, Krishan. *Indira: A Biography of Prime Minister Gandhi.* New York:

Praeger, 1974. This is a sympathetic biography for the general reader. The author is an Indian journalist who has been acquainted with the Nehru family since the 1940's. A bibliography and index are included.

Gandhi, Indira. *Indira Gandhi: Letters to an American Friend, 1950-1984*. San Diego: Harcourt Brace Jovanovich, 1985. Selected from correspondence with Dorothy Norman. Since Gandhi is most often studied as a political figure, these personal letters provide essential insights into the private woman. Photographs and commentary are also provided.

Gill, S. S. *The Dynasty: A Political Biography of the Premier Ruling Family of Modern India*. New Delhi: HarperCollins India, 1996. Examines the careers of Jawaharlal Nehru, Indira Gandhi, and Rajiv Gandhi.

Gupte, Pranay. *Mother India: A Political Biography of Indira Gandhi*. New York: Charles Scribner's Sons, 1992.

_____. *Vengeance: India After the Assassination of Indira Gandhi*. New York: W. W. Norton, 1985. Written by an Indian journalist, this examination of contemporary India begins with a detailed account of Gandhi's assassination and the events surrounding her death. It provides firsthand information and analyzes Rajiv's leadership potential.

Jayakar, Pupul. *Indira Gandhi: An Intimate Biography*. New York: Pantheon Books, 1992.

Lamb, Beatrice Pitney. *The Nehrus of India*. New York: Macmillan, 1967. This collective biography provides information on Gandhi's early life and her years spent as "First Lady" for her father, during which period she developed her political abilities. It is written for juveniles and has notes and a suggested reading list.

Masani, Zareer. *Indira Gandhi: A Biography*. New York: Thomas Y. Crowell, 1976. The author's insight into Gandhi's life and Indian politics comes from extensive research using primary and secondary sources. The last chapter, written during the state of emergency, predicts her fall from power. Notes and photographs are included.

Moraes, Dom. *Indira Gandhi*. Boston: Little, Brown, 1980. The strength and weakness of this biography is that it is based primarily on personal interviews and the author's changing relationship with Gandhi. Although he criticizes her flaws, he remains a sympathetic admirer. Photographs and an index are provided.

Vasudev, Uma. *Indira Gandhi: Revolution in Restraint*. Delhi, India: Vikas, 1974. This thoroughly researched biography synthesizes the private and public aspects of Gandhi's life within the context of political history. Unfortunately for the reader, it ends with the early 1970's. Documentation includes notes, an index, a glossary, and fifty-six pages of photographs.

Alice F. Taylor

LADY JANE GREY

Born: October, 1537; Leicestershire, England
Died: February 12, 1554; London, England

Had her reign as queen of England been fully legal and more lengthy, Jane Grey would have been England's first ruling queen and likely a successful monarch.

Early Life

Lady Jane Grey was born in October, 1537, to Henry Grey and Frances Brandon, the duke and duchess of Suffolk. Jane's mother was also a distant heir to the throne as the daughter of Henry VIII's sister Mary. Her parents, being Protestant, saw to it that Jane, the eldest of three daughters, had a proper education in the "new religion," as the Protestant faith was called. Jane was an intelligent, learned, clever, and scholarly girl; by the time of her death, she could read six languages, including Greek and Hebrew. She was well versed in the Greek and Roman classics, philosophy, and contemporary religious doctrine, and she early on developed a reputation as a precocious child nearly obsessed with her studies.

Jane's parents, while not particularly well schooled or overwhelmingly enthusiastic about their eldest daughter's dedication to learning, did not mind sending Jane off to court to study with her cousins, Princess Elizabeth and the future King Edward. Such connections could potentially benefit Jane's parents, for as provincial nobility, they were constantly struggling for political and social influence. These potential political connections could also benefit them in pursuit of a suitable husband for their daughter.

Life's Work

Jane's availability and attractiveness as a marriage prospect, along with her religion, made her a pawn in the political power plays of the day. Henry VIII died in early 1547, and the throne passed to his nine-year-old son, Edward VI. The boy's uncle, Thomas Seymour, duke of Somerset, became the "protector" of the realm and regent to the young king. Somerset suggested several times to Jane's parents that a marriage between Edward and Jane would benefit all involved. There was also talk of Jane marrying Somerset's son. Somerset, though, fell from power, primarily due to political maneuvering by John Dudley, duke of Northumberland, and thereafter the Seymours had little to offer.

The issue of religion was one that plagued all the Tudor family monarchs. Henry VIII had split from the Catholic Church in order to divorce his first wife, laying the groundwork for the Church of England. Many of his top advisers during his last years were moderate Protestants, as were virtually all of Edward's counselors. As the succession stood, should Edward die before having children, the throne of England would pass to Henry's eldest daughter, Mary. This possibility raised the religious issue again, for Mary was Catholic, and many of Edward's advisers, especially Northumberland, were concerned that Mary's accession would result in England's return to Catholicism. The religious differences between Edward's advisers and Mary also virtually guaranteed for the counselors at best the loss of prestige, at worst perhaps torture or death for their heretical beliefs.

An 1848 depiction of "The Signing of the Death Warrent of Lady Jane Grey." *(Library of Congress)*

The ill health of the king also became a major concern. Despite his love of outdoor activities, Edward had never been particularly healthy, and his health worsened as he aged. There was growing alarm that Edward's sicknesses could become life-threatening, and Northumberland knew his power rested solely with Edward. In 1553, when the young king was fifteen, a cold developed into a more serious lung ailment. Repeated treatments by doctors proved fruitless, and Edward slowly worsened. It was obvious that the boy-king's days were numbered.

Northumberland, understandably worried about his position should Mary succeed her half brother Edward, and perhaps also concerned about the likely return to Catholicism, agonized over possible courses of action. Edward was getting sicker and sicker, and Northumberland decided that Mary had to be somehow excluded from the succession. According to Henry's will, the next successor after Mary was Elizabeth, his daughter with Anne Boleyn. Elizabeth was a Protestant, but Northumberland had little influence over her. Following Elizabeth was Frances Brandon, followed by Lady Jane. If Northumberland could alter the succession to elevate Frances or Jane to the throne, he could continue to exert his considerable influence over the government.

Lady Jane's dedicated Protestantism and her place in the succession made her an attractive pawn. Jane had engaged in theological debates with numerous religious scholars and had even confronted her cousin Mary regarding the sanctity of the Catholic "host." The details of Jane's accession to the throne, however, are fairly complex.

Northumberland had Edward draft a will of his own that precluded his two sisters, Mary and Elizabeth. (Elizabeth was excluded on the pretext that she might marry a foreigner, which the English did not want.) This left Frances as the heir, but Northumberland had her sign away her claim, essentially "abdicating" in favor of her daughter. Lady Jane was thus left as the primary heir. Yet this new succession was far from secure. While it was entirely a monarch's prerogative to change his or her will, and the duty of the kingdom to follow the will's provisions, any change in the succession had also to be approved by Parliament. Thus, despite the fact that Edward's will was a binding legal document and that anyone who refused to carry out its provisions was guilty of treason, the entire will was not legal until approved by Parliament. Anyone who did follow the will, then, was breaking the law. There is also some uncertainty as to whether Edward himself wrote the new will or whether Northumberland wrote it and simply had the sick king sign it.

Meanwhile, Northumberland had proposed a marriage between his youngest son, Guildford, and Jane. Such a match was an advantageous one for the Greys, and they approved. Jane protested violently; though noble children rarely had any say in their marriages, she pleaded to not be married. Regardless, Jane and Guildford were hastily married on May 25, 1553. Noble weddings tended to be large affairs, but this ceremony was a small and hasty event, with few guests and little joy. At first, the two newlyweds were allowed to stay with their families rather than to live with each other, but Jane's parents later insisted that they stay together, presumably so that Jane could conceive an heir to the throne. With the potential royal couple waiting in the wings, Edward in June formally changed his will; he also declared his two half sisters illegitimate, which effectively removed them from the succession regardless of the will.

Northumberland took the king's will and had Edward's advisers sign it to acknowledge their support for the plan, though few were eager to do so. Since Parliament was not in session, however, Parliament's approval was not likely to come before Edward's death. In place of a legitimate parliamentary approval, Northumberland had as many Parliamentarians as he could locate sign the document, thus providing some semblance of legality. Had it been in session, Parliament as a whole would most likely have debated the new will fiercely, since it skipped the two most rightful heirs. Edward VI died on July 6, 1553, and Northumberland quickly pressured remaining advisers to support his plot. On July 9, at Syon House, north of London, Jane was told that she had been declared queen. She was shocked, and at first she refused the crown. It became clear to her, belatedly, that she was simply a pawn.

News spread of Edward's death, and Jane's accession was announced on July 10, but few greeted either announcement with any enthusiasm. Despite the Catholicism of Mary, she was the rightful ruler, and most preferred a legal Catholic queen over an illegal Protestant one. Most of Edward's counselors fled, many going to Mary personally and begging her forgiveness for their parts in the plotting.

For her part, Mary remained in hiding for most of Jane's nine-day reign.

While it is not clear whether Jane might have shed the influence of Northumberland and her parents easily had she remained queen, it seems likely that she would have been a successful ruler. She displayed a fiery spirit and courage, and after ascending the throne, she refused to crown Guildford king, instead making him a duke. As an educated and strong-willed woman, she might have had a long successful life and reign similar to that enjoyed later by Elizabeth. During her brief occupation of the throne, Jane overruled Northumberland on who would lead troops to capture Mary; Dudley wanted Henry Grey to go, but Jane instead ordered her father-in-law to assume command. What little support Jane enjoyed quickly evaporated, however, and exactly nine days after being crowned, she was placed under house arrest as Mary approached London.

Northumberland and Henry Grey were arrested along with Guildford and Northumberland's other sons. Frances Grey begged Mary for forgiveness for her husband, but it appears that no one pleaded for Jane. Instead, Jane wrote a letter to her cousin asking forgiveness and saying that she had been foolish to have even accepted the crown, since she had never wanted to be queen anyway. Mary, who initially showed great compassion, forgave both, though Jane and Guildford were convicted of treason and confined in the Tower of London. Mary even took Jane's two younger sisters into her employ as attendants. Northumberland, despite a last-minute conversion to Catholicism, was beheaded.

Jane may have lived out a long but lonely life in prison had it not been for a rebellion that started in January, 1554, in southern England. Wyatt's Rebellion was essentially an uprising opposed to Mary's planned marriage to Philip of Spain, but some of the rebels called for Jane to be restored to the throne. Foolishly, Henry Grey also participated in the uprising, which failed when the rebels were prevented from entering London. While Jane was certainly not involved in the rebellion, it was clear that as long as she lived, she could be a catalyst for further unrest. The Spanish ambassadors who were in England making marriage arrangements pressured Mary to rid herself of Guildford and Jane, insinuating that Philip would never marry her if they lived. Much like Jane, then, Mary was a victim of circumstance, and she ordered the execution of Jane and her husband in early February, 1554.

Jane had been unaware of the rebellion and its aftermath, but she was told of her father's involvement and of her impending execution. Mary sent her priest, Doctor Feckenham, to try to reconvert Jane, and though the two engaged in the religious debate that was so characteristic of the young former queen, she remained dedicated to her Protestant faith.

Guildford was executed outside the Tower on February 12; as his body was brought back into the complex, Jane apparently passed the cart on the way to her own death inside the Tower grounds. On the scaffold, Jane delivered a short speech expressing her faith and asking God to forgive her. After tying a scarf around her eyes, kneeling in the straw, and placing her head on the block, Jane was beheaded.

Summary

Jane's impact on English history is limited. While potentially an excellent ruler, she did not rule with enough support or long enough to make any lasting contribution. Although Jane displayed the characteristics that made the Tudor family popular, such as courage, a dedication to ideals, and a noble bearing, her story remains primarily a romantic but unfortunate addendum to the Tudor-Stuart period.

Bibliography

Foxe, John. *Foxe's Book of Martyrs.* Edited by Marie Gentert King. Old Tappan, N.J.: Spire Books, 1987. An account of Protestant martyrs written in the late 1500's. Favorably inclined toward Jane and Edward, but a primary source not to be missed.

Geary, Douglas, ed. *The Letters of Lady Jane Grey.* Ilfracombe, England: Arthur Stockwell, 1951. This work includes virtually all the literary remains of Jane, including letters, notes, and the text of her speech on the scaffold. Invaluable primary material.

Luke, Mary. *The Nine Days Queen.* New York: William Morrow, 1986. A well-written, factually sound account of Jane's life and brief rule. Few footnotes, but the most accessible and accurate modern account.

Mathew, David. *Lady Jane Grey: The Setting of the Reign.* London: Eyre Methuen, 1972. Provides a respectable background to the reign of Jane, though it says little of Jane herself.

Meroff, Deborah. *Coronation of Glory: The Story of Lady Jane Grey.* Pella, Iowa: Inheritance, 1998.

Plowden, Alison. *Lady Jane Grey and the House of Suffolk*. New York: Franklin Watts, 1986. Delves into the political workings of Jane's family and Northumberland, and is useful in conjunction with other overall texts on Jane.

Weir, Alison. *The Children of Henry VIII*. New York: Ballantine Books, 1996. Formerly published as *Children of England*, this book examines the lives of each of Henry VIII's offspring—Mary, Elizabeth, and Edward—and such surrounding figures as Lady Jane Grey.

Wayne Ackerson

PAMELA DIGBY CHURCHILL HARRIMAN

Born: March 20, 1920; Farnborough, England
Died: February 5, 1997; Paris, France

A leading fund-raiser for the Democratic Party in the 1980's, Harriman became U.S. ambassador to France in 1993.

Early Life

Born March 20, 1920, Pamela Digby was the oldest of four children of Edward Kenelm, eleventh Baron Digby, and grew up on the family's 1,500-acre estate and dairy farm, Minterne, in Dorset, England. Her father commanded a battalion of the Coldstream Guards, served in the House of Lords, and was governor of Dorset. Renowned for his gardening, he was president of the Royal Agricultural Society and nicknamed "Carnation" Digby. Her mother, Constance Pamela Alice Bruce Digby of the Barons Aberdare, was an active woman who encouraged her children to follow suit. Pamela became an expert equestrian, winning many prizes. She attended Downham, a prestigious boarding school, and was presented to King George VI at Buckingham Palace in May, 1938. Among the three hundred other debutantes was John F. Kennedy's sister Kathleen, with whose family Pamela began a lifelong friendship.

After her presentation, Pamela traveled abroad, studying in France and Germany. Rumblings of World War II ended her stay on the Continent, and she returned to England to work as a translator-secretary in the Foreign Office in London. On a blind date, she met journalist Randolph Churchill, the only son of Winston Churchill, and they became engaged within weeks. After their marriage in 1939, Randolph went back to war while Pamela moved into 10 Downing Street when her father-in-law became prime minister in 1940. In October, 1940, Pamela's son Winston was born at Chequers, the Churchill country estate.

Pamela wrote years later of the daily intensity of life with her father-in-law during World War II. She was a constant companion, sharing his fears, desperation, and courage throughout the critical attacks of the Luftwaffe in the Battle of Britain, and his hospitality and wit when he entertained world leaders at Chequers. The prime minister was fond of bezique, a six-pack card game, and she frequently played with him. Intensely loyal to him, she lamented his loss of office in July, 1945.

Meanwhile Pamela's relationship with her husband deteriorated. He looked to her to pay the gambling debts he incurred playing with fellow officers. Randolph Churchill's boss in civilian life, the publisher Lord Beaverbrook, wrote Pamela a check to cover the debts and secretly provided shelter for his young godson Winston at his country home. Having secured the services of a nanny to care for her baby at the Beaverbrook estate, Pamela moved into the Dorchester Hotel in 1941 and started working as a secretary at the ministry of supply. Pamela and Randolph Churchill's marriage was essentially over after two years, and they were divorced in 1947 after a three-year separation.

Pamela began to make a life of her own and to display an independence of spirit that would bring her friends, lovers, adventures, and notoriety. During 1941, Lord Beaverbrook concerned himself with eliciting further aid from the United States in hopes of securing its entry into the war. Beaverbrook enlisted Pamela's help in entertaining his American guests, and she soon met W. Averell Harriman, Franklin Roosevelt's special envoy to Britain. Her affair with Harriman during the war allegedly provided intelligence information to the British. After he left for Moscow to serve as U.S. ambassador to Russia, she spent time with the war correspondent Edward R. Murrow. When peace returned to Europe, Pamela worked as a journalist for the Beaverbrook Press from 1946 to 1949, writing articles for Beaverbrook's *Evening Standard* from New York, Jamaica, and the south of France.

Pamela Churchill's search for adventure and independence took her to Paris in 1949. After enrolling young Winston in a Swiss school, she immersed herself in the world of art, culture, and theater. Through her social connections, she could move in high political circles, and she excelled in bringing people from diverse backgrounds together. Intellectuals and celebrities such as Jean Cocteau, André Malraux, and Christian Dior attended salons held at her house on Sunday nights.

During this period, she had a number of well-publicized romances, including a five-year affair with Fiat heir Gianni Agnelli that ended in 1952. Following this came a liaison with Elie de Rothschild, head of his family's vineyard at Chateau Lafite. She also was romantically linked to Prince Aly Khan, Frank Sinatra, and others.

Pamela began to spend more time in America. During a visit to New York in 1958, she was introduced by friends to Leland Hayward, producer of the musicals *State of the Union* (1945), *Mister Roberts* (1948), *South Pacific* (1949), *Call Me Madam* (1950), *Gypsy* (1959), and *The Sound of Music* (1959). He also produced the plays *Anne of the Thousand Days* (1948) and *The Trial of the Catonsville Nine* (1971). He divorced his wife and was married to Pamela Churchill in 1960. Through Hayward, Pamela was introduced to Hollywood and Broadway film and theater circles. She faced the hostility of stepchildren from Hayward's two former marriages, and stepdaughter Brooke wrote a best-seller, *Haywire* (1977), in which Pamela was depicted as a wicked stepmother. Leland Hayward died on Pamela's fifty-first birthday, March 20, 1971.

Life's Work

Pamela Churchill Hayward's network of friends, which she assiduously cultivated all of her life, rallied to comfort her. In July, 1971, newspaper publisher Katharine Graham invited Pamela to a party in Washington, D.C., where she rekindled her friendship with W. Averell Harriman, who was then a widower. They were married in September, 1971; he was seventy-nine and she was fifty-one. She presented him with a unique wedding present—her citizenship papers.

Averell Harriman, heir to the Union Pacific Railroad fortune, had advised every Democratic president since Franklin Roosevelt. Harriman had served as governor of New York from 1954 to 1958, was once a presidential hopeful, and was appointed as U.S. ambassador-at-large under President John F. Kennedy. After their marriage, Pamela and Averell spent most of their time at their Georgetown home in Washington, D.C. They helped Robert Strauss gain the chairmanship of the Democratic National Committee in 1972, and, in return, Strauss had Pamela Harriman take his seat on the board of Braniff Airlines. Her expertise at entertaining turned to organizing fund-raising parties for the Democrats. The Harrimans supported Jimmy Carter's SALT II and Panama Canal treaties. Named Democratic Woman of the Year in 1980,

Pamela worked with Averell to rescue the Democratic Party after the Republican sweep of the White House and Senate and inroads into the House in that year.

Pamela Harriman's knowledge of politics and her skill at bringing people together came to fruition, and as her husband grew frailer, she became more active. During the Reagan years of the 1980's, Averell and Pamela organized Democrats for the '80's, a political action committee that raised money for federal, state, and local Democratic candidates. Nicknamed PAMPAC, this committee raised $14 millon in ten years. Pamela and Averell also helped to stake out the Democratic agenda, hosting nearly a hundred "issue evenings" at their house. Policy analysts and members of Congress shared ideas while Pamela facilitated and adjudicated. Presidential hopefuls such as Jay Rockefeller (whom Pamela favored), Al Gore, and Bill Clinton were included as speakers.

Pamela Harriman also kept up her interest in foreign policy. Averell included her in his trips to the Soviet Union and China. After his death in July, 1986, Pamela continued to travel to the Soviet Union every two years, and maintained her memberships on the boards of the Friends of the Kennan Institute for Advanced Russian Studies and the Council on Foreign Relations.

Averell Harriman left Pamela the means ($75 million) to do whatever she wanted in life, and rumors circulated that she wanted an ambassadorship. She doggedly worked to ensure a Democratic presidency to achieve this goal. In 1990, she disbanded PAMPAC and became chair of the Quarterly Policy Issues Forum of the Democratic Governors Association. She then served as national cochair of the Clinton-Gore campaign. She lent her house in Middleburg, Virginia, to the Democratic National Committee for a crucial hashing out of positions in 1991. In May, 1993, President Bill Clinton recognized her efforts by appointing Pamela Harriman to serve as the U.S. ambassador to France. She died in Paris on February 5, 1997, from complications of a stroke; she was seventy-six years old.

Summary

Pamela Digby Churchill Hayward Harriman grew up in an age when women attached themselves to men and lived through them. She was an attractive young woman with blue eyes and fiery red hair who was presented to society as a debutante and given a finishing school education in Europe. World War II interrupted any hopes of a higher education and served as the background to Pamela's failed marriage and several affairs. She came into her own after her marriage to Averell Harriman, a multimillionaire and ardent Democrat.

Pamela received a political education through her family—seven of them were in Parliament when she was growing up—and marriage to Winston Churchill's only son. She capitalized on her family and social connections to make friends on the Continent, where her independent spirit and search of adventure took her. She was good-looking, charming, intelligent, and a good listener. All the above traits, in addition to her courage, tough-mindedness, and breeding, made her bold enough to hold a salon in Paris.

These skills and talents were further developed when she helped Harriman revive and revamp the Democratic Party. The press called her the "Queen of the Democrats" or "Life of the Party." Her political sagacity proved correct when she recognized Bill Clinton as a comer and appointed him head of the board of PAMPAC after he lost reelection as governor of Arkansas in 1981. Speaker of the House Tom Foley credited her with the Democratic win in 1992.

Slowly she began to reach out on her own and become a force in her own right. She authored an article for *American Heritage* (1983), and gave the Samuel D. Berger Memorial Lecture at the Institute for the Study of Diplomacy at Georgetown University (1988). Harriman was an honorary member of the Executive Committee of the Brookings Institute, Vice Chairman of the Atlantic Council, a trustee of Rockefeller University, and a member of the Trustees Council of the National Art Gallery. Also, she served on the boards of the Winston Churchill Foundation of the United States, the Franklin and Eleanor Roosevelt Institute, and various philanthropic foundations.

Her career demonstrates the power of the American feminist movement, which has enabled women to carve out their own identity. Although Pamela was never a part of the movement, without it she could not have aspired to be an ambassador and head an embassy with an 1,100-member staff. She developed an appreciation of women's issues and was proud of her granddaughter Marina Churchill, a barrister in London.

As ambassador to France, she used her skills of entertaining and bringing diverse peoples together. She spoke French and knew French culture and personages. With her own paintings by Vincent van Gogh, Paul Cézanne, and John Singer Sargent as backdrop, Harriman convened French and American politicians to discuss their commonalities and differences.

Bibliography

Duffy, Martha. "And Now, an Embassy of Her Own." *Time* 142 (July 5, 1993): 52-54. Article on Harriman by a seasoned reporter that summarizes her linkages with famous men as well as reviewing her status as ambassador. Contains a photograph of her in front of her van Gogh painting *Roses* (1890).

Fairlee, Henry. "Shamela." *The New Republic* 199 (August 22, 1988): 21-23. Critical article profiling Averell and Pamela Harriman. The author has a cynical attitude toward Washington's preoccupation with and worship of money, glamour, and image-making. Fairlee doubts Harriman's intellectual abilities and repeats the gossip of her affairs and strained relations with stepchildren.

Gross, Michael. "Queen Mother of the Clinton Court." *New York* 26 (January 18, 1993): 24-34. A biographical sketch searching for explanations of her behavior in her forebears.

Harriman, Pamela C. "Churchill's Dream." *American Heritage* 34 (October/November, 1983): 84-87. In this intimate portrait of her father-in-law, Pamela reveals his self-doubts after being voted out of office in 1945. She prefers to remember his confidence and courage during World War II.

Ogden, Christopher. *Life of the Party: The Biography of Pamela Digby Churchill Hayward Harriman*. Boston: Little, Brown, 1994. Based on research and interviews accumulated during Ogden's brief attempt at ghostwriting Harriman's official autobiography, this profile is full of telling details of Harriman's social ascent. Unfortunately, it provides little in the way of analysis to account for the complexity of her character or the decisions that shaped her life.

Smith, Sally Bedell. *Reflected Glory: The Life of Pamela Churchill Harriman*. New York: Simon & Schuster, 1996.

Walton, William. "Profiles: Governor and Mrs. W. Averell Harriman." *Architectural Digest* 41 (June, 1984): 106-113. Interviews the Harrimans about their lives and includes photographs of them, with influential people, and of their houses in New York, Virginia, Washington, D.C., and Barbados. (A fifth house in Sun Valley, Idaho, is barely mentioned.) Although something of a puff piece, the article does provide insight into how Pamela acquired her tastes in decorating and her passion for beautiful gardens.

Virginia W. Leonard

HATSHEPSUT

Born: Mid- to late sixteenth century B.C.; probably near Thebes, Egypt
Died: c. 1482 B.C.; place unknown

Governing in her own right, Hatshepsut gave to Egypt two decades of peace and prosperity and beautified Thebes with temples and monuments.

Early Life

Hatshepsut, or Hatshopsitu, was the daughter of Thutmose I and his consort (the Egyptian title was "great royal wife") Ahmose. Nothing is known of Hatshepsut's date of birth and early life. Although Thutmose I was the third king of the powerful Eighteenth Dynasty, he was probably not of royal blood on his mother's side; the princess Ahmose, however, was of the highest rank. During the period in Egyptian history known as the Empire or New Kingdom (from the Eighteenth to the Twentieth Dynasty; c. 1570-1075 B.C.), royal women began to play a more active role in political affairs. Among her titles, the pharaoh's chief wife was called the "divine consort of Amon" (Amon was one of the principal Theban deities), and her offspring were given a certain precedence over the children of minor wives or concubines.

In addition to Princess Hatshepsut, at least two sons were born to Thutmose I and Ahmose, but both of the boys died young. The male line had to be continued through a third son, born to a minor wife, who was married to his half sister, Hatshepsut. Thutmose II's claim to the throne was strengthened by this marriage; he succeeded his father around 1512.

A daughter, Neferure, was born of this union but apparently no son was born. The ancient records are fragmentary and at times obscure, but there is evidence that Thutmose II was not very healthy and thus his reign was short, ending around 1504. Once more there was no male of pure royal blood to become pharaoh; thus, the title passed to a son of Thutmose II by a concubine named Isis. This boy, also named Thutmose, was at the time of his father's death between the ages of six and ten, and dedicated to the service of the god Amon at the temple at Karnak. Since he was underage, the logical choice as regent was his aunt Hatshepsut, now the Queen Mother.

Life's Work

Hatshepsut soon proved to be a woman of great ability and large ambitions. The regency was not enough for her; she wanted the glory of being called pharaoh as well as the responsibility for Egypt and the young king. To accomplish this desire, however, seemed impossible. There had never been a female pharaoh—only a man could assume that title, take a "Horus name," and become king of Upper and Lower Egypt.

For a time, Hatshepsut looked for possible allies, finding them among the various court officials, the most notable being the architect and bureaucrat Senmut (or Senenmut), and among the priests of Amon. By 1503 her moment had come. Accompanied by young Thutmose, she went to Luxor to participate in one of the great feasts honoring Amon; during the ceremonies, she had herself crowned. There was no question of deposing Thutmose III, but he was in effect forced to accept a coregency in which he played a lesser part.

To justify this unique coronation, Hatshepsut asserted that she had been crowned already with the sanction of her father the pharaoh. To support this claim an account was given of her miraculous birth, which was later inscribed at her temple at Dayr el-Bahrī on the west bank of the Nile. According to this account, Amon himself, assuming the guise of Thutmose, had fathered Hatshepsut. With the approval of both a divine and a human parent, none could oppose the new pharaoh's will, while Thutmose remained a child and the army and the priests supported her.

Hatshepsut did not merely assume the masculine titles and authority of a pharaoh; she ordered that statues be made showing her as a man. In the stylized portraiture of Egyptian royalty, the king is usually shown bare-chested and wearing a short, stiff kilt, a striped wig-cover concealing the hair, and a ceremonial beard. The number of statues commissioned by Hatshepsut is not known, but in spite of later efforts by Thutmose III to blot out the memory of his hated relative, several examples exist, showing Hatshepsut kneeling, sitting, or standing, looking as aloof and masculine as her predecessors.

Neferure, the daughter of Hatshepsut and Thutmose II, was married to Thutmose III. This marriage served the dual purpose of strengthening the succession and binding the king closer to his aunt, now his mother-in-law. Hatshepsut then focused her attention on domestic prosperity and foreign trade, activities more to her personal inclination than conquest. Throughout Egypt, an extensive building program was begun. At Karnak, four large obelisks and a shrine to Amon were built. Another temple was constructed at Beni-Hasan in Middle Egypt. Several tombs were cut for her, including one in the Valley of the Kings. Her inscriptions claim that she was the first pharaoh to repair damages caused by the Hyksos, Asian invaders who had conquered Egypt in the eighteenth through mid-sixteenth centuries with the aid of new technologies, such as war chariots pulled by horses. The usurpation of these foreign kings was an unpleasant and recent memory to the proud, self-sufficient Egyptians; Hatshepsut's restorations probably increased her popularity.

The crowning architectural triumph of her reign was her beautiful funerary temple at Dayr el-Baḥrī. Built by Senmut, her chief architect and adviser, it was constructed on three levels against the cliffs; the temple, a harmonious progression of ramps, courts, and porticoes, was decorated in the interior with scenes of the major events of the queen's reign.

Hatshepsut *(Library of Congress)*

Probably the most interesting of the achievements so portrayed was the expedition sent to the kingdom of Punt, located at the southern end of the Red Sea. As the story is told, in the seventh or eighth year of her reign, Hatshepsut was instructed by Amon to send forth five ships laden with goods to exchange for incense and living myrrh trees as well as such exotic imports as apes, leopard skins, greyhounds, ivory, ebony, and gold. Pictured in detail are the natives' round huts, built on stilts,

254

and the arrival of the prince and princess of Punt to greet the Egyptians. The portrait of the princess is unusual, because it is one of the rare examples in Egyptian art in which a fat and deformed person is depicted.

In addition to the voyage to Punt, Hatshepsut reopened the long-unused mines of Sinai, which produced blue and green stones. Tribute was received from Asian and Libyan tribes, and she participated in a brief military expedition to Nubia. Despite the latter endeavors, Hatshepsut's primary concern was peace, not imperialistic expansion. In this regard, her actions were in sharp contrast to those of her rival and successor Thutmose III, who was very much the warrior-king.

It would not be sufficient, however, to explain Hatshepsut's less aggressive policies on the basis of her sex. Traditionally, the Egyptians had been isolationists. Convinced that their land had been blessed by the gods with almost everything necessary, the Egyptians had throughout much of their earlier history treated their neighbors as foreign barbarians, unworthy of serious consideration. Hatshepsut and her advisers seem to have chosen this conservative course.

As Hatshepsut's reign continued, unpleasant changes began to occur. Her favorite, Senmut, died around 1487. In addition to the numerous offices and titles related to agriculture, public works, and the priesthood, he had also been named a guardian and tutor to Neferure. No less than six statues show Senmut with the royal child in his arms. At the end of his life, he may have fallen from favor by presuming to include images of himself in his mistress's temple. Most were discovered and mutilated, presumably during Hatshepsut's lifetime and with her approval since her names remained undisturbed.

Princess Neferure died young, perhaps even before Senmut's death, leaving Hatshepsut to face the growing power of Thutmose III. The king had reached adulthood: He was now the leader of the army and demanded a more important role in the coregency. His presence at major festivals became more obvious, although Hatshepsut's name continued to be linked with his until 1482.

It is not known exactly where or when Hatshepsut died or whether she might have been deposed and murdered. That her relations with her nephew and son-in-law were strained is evident from the revenge Thutmose exacted after her death: Her temples and tombs were broken into and her statues destroyed. Her cartouches, carved oval or oblong figures which encased the royal name, were erased, and in many cases her name was replaced by that of her husband or even of her father. She was eliminated from the list of kings. Thutmose III ruled in her stead and did his best to see that she was forgotten both by gods and by men.

Summary

The nature and scope of Hatshepsut's achievements are still subject to debate. Traditional historians have emphasized the irregularity of her succession, the usurpation of Thutmose III's authority, and her disinterest in military success. Revisionist studies are more generous in assessing this unique woman, praising her for her promotion of peaceful trade and her extensive building program at home.

Her influence throughout Egypt, though brief and limited only to her reign, must have been profound. The considerable number of temples, tombs, and monuments constructed at her command would have provided work for many of her subjects, just as surely as the wars of her father and nephew provided employment in another capacity. Art, devotion to the gods, and propaganda were inextricably mingled in the architectural endeavors of every pharaoh. Hatshepsut's devotion to the gods, especially the Theban deity Amon, and her evident need to justify her succession and her achievements enriched her nation with some of its finest examples of New Kingdom art.

Controversial in her own lifetime and still something of a mysterious figure, Hatshepsut continues to inspire conflicting views about herself and the nature of Egyptian kingship. She was a bold figure who chose to change the role assigned to royal women, yet at the same time, she seems to have been a traditionalist leading a faction that wanted Egypt to remain self-sufficient and essentially peaceful. Perhaps that was yet another reason that she and Thutmose III were so much at odds. His vision of Egypt as a conquering empire would be that of the future. She was looking back to the past.

Bibliography

Aldred, Cyril. *The Development of Ancient Egyptian Art from 3200 to 1315 B.C.* London: A. Tiranti, 1952. Reprint. London: Academy Editions, 1973. The title indicates the focus of the work. There are more than fifteen plates depicting Hatshepsut, other members of her family, and her adviser Senmut. Detailed explanations accompany each picture, and there is also an index and a bibliography.

Edgerton, William F. *The Thutmosid Succession*. Chicago: University of Chicago Press, 1933. This brief work contains a considerable amount of technical information on hieroglyphs and disputes among Egyptologists, although it presumes some knowledge on the part of the reader of the period from Thutmose I to the death of Hatshepsut.

Gardiner, Sir Alan. *Egypt of the Pharaohs*. Oxford, England: Oxford University Press, 1961. Although a lengthy study, Gardiner's work is pleasantly written, with balanced views of both Hatshepsut and her successor, Thutmose III. Provides a good background for the less knowledgeable reader. Includes an index, a bibliography, and a comprehensive chronological list of kings. Illustrated.

Hayes, William C. "Egypt: Internal Affairs from Thuthmosis I to the Death of Amenophis III." In *History of the Middle East and the Aegean Region, c. 1800-1380 B.C.* Vol. 2 in *Cambridge Ancient History*. 3d ed. Cambridge, England: Cambridge University Press, 1973. Much information about Hatshepsut is given, although Hayes indicates a definite preference for Thutmose III.

Maspero, Gaston. *History of Egypt, Chaldea, Syria, Babylonia, and Assyria*. 13 vols. London: Grolier Society, 1903-1906. Maspero's work, though dated in some respects, is a mine of information. Many drawings that illustrate the text, taken from on-site photographs, are beautifully detailed; they cover everything from temples and bas-reliefs to statues, weapons, and the mummies of Thutmose I and Thutmose II. The material devoted to Hatshepsut is in volume 4, and the account of her reign is generally favorable.

Nims, Charles F. *Thebes of the Pharaohs: Pattern for Every City*. New York: Stein & Day, 1965. The city of Thebes was extremely important to Hatshepsut and her family as both a political and a religious center. This book is helpful because it places the queen in her environment.

Tyldesley, Joyce. *Hatchepsut: The Female Pharaoh*. New York: Viking Press, 1996.

Wenig, Steffen. *The Woman in Egyptian Art*. New York: McGraw-Hill, 1969. This book is extremely well illustrated with both color and black-and-white photographs as well as drawings. The period covered is from c. 4000 B.C. to c. A.D. 300. Contains a chronology and an extensive bibliography and is written for the general reader.

Wilson, John A. *The Burden of Egypt*. Chicago: University of Chicago Press, 1951. This extensive study is both detailed and well written; it deals with the importance of geography to Egypt. Includes maps, a bibliography, illustrations, and a chronology of rulers. Wilson's analysis of political theories and discussion of possible motivations of the pharaohs is very useful in understanding the conflict between Hatshepsut and Thutmose III.

Dorothy T. Potter

SAINT HELENA

Born: c. 248; Drepanum (modern Herkes) in Bithnyia, Asia Minor
Died: c. 328; Nicomedia

Literally the most important woman in the world during her time, Helena was the mother of Constantine the Great, the first Christian Roman emperor. Helena's elevation to sainthood was conferred, according to tradition, because she set out on pilgrimage to Palestine to discover the cross of Christ's crucifixion and, upon doing so, founded the Church of the Nativity and the Church of the Holy Sepulchre in the Holy Land.

Early Life

Historical fact and historical fiction intertwine in the writings regarding Helena's life and times. The more authentic versions are believed to be those that are oldest, those being from Eusebius, Ambrose, and Cassiodorus. Eusebius, Helena's contemporary, was bishop of Caesarea in Palestine and author of the "eulogy" *Vita Constantini*, the biography of Constantine written shortly after his death in 337. Eusebius dedicated paragraphs 42 to 47 of Book III of *Vita Constantini* to the eastern provinces of the Empire and Helena's stay in Palestine.

Although little is known of her early life, the most common belief is that Helena was born of the humblest of origins and possibly started her life as a stable girl or servant at an inn. While a few accounts claim that she married Constantius Chlorus, more often the interpretation has been that she was his concubine. In the Roman Empire of that time, concubinage was an accepted form of cohabitation. The relationship, however legal it may have been, began around 270; Helena gave birth to Constantine sometime near the period from 273 to 275.

Constantius was an officer in the Roman army when Helena met him. He rose to the position of caesar, or deputy emperor, in 293 and to the rank of augustus from 305 until his death in 306— but not before deserting Helena. He became caesar under Maximian in the West of the Roman Empire. Constantine's mother was cast off in order that Maximian could marry his stepdaughter Theodora to Constantius in 289. Constantius's marriage with Theodora was a prerequisite for a successful political career in Diocletian's newly introduced tetrarchy.

Helena and her son were separated, and not until 306, when Constantine was named successor of his father, did she reappear in the historical accounts in her new role as the empress-mother at Constantine's court.

A definitive interpretation of historical writings on the era is not possible, but tradition says that during his rule, Constantine was struck with incurable leprosy. Pagan priests advised him to bathe in the warm blood of three thousand boys. When the children were gathered, Constantine responded to the anguished pleas from their mothers and freed them. For this act, he was visited by two emissaries from Jesus Christ. Constantine was baptized, catechized, and cured. This story was later popularized by the famous Italian painter Raphael (1483–1520), whose interpretation of the event is captured in the painting *The Donation of Constantine.*

Helena, as the legend continues, challenged her son's conversion from pagan idolatry to Christianity, and a theological debate was established to resolve the dispute. Saint Sylvester entertained the arguments of eleven leading Jewish scholars who protested the Christian faith. Sylvester ultimately won when he brought back to life, in the name of Jesus Christ, a bull that the Jew Zambri had caused to drop dead. As the legend recounts, Helena, the Jews, and the judges all then converted. Another popular legend regarding Constantine's conversion to Christianity tells that Saint Sylvester pardoned Constantine for the murder of his son and wife and won the leader to Christianity for doing so.

Constantine gave the first impetus to the Christianization of the Roman Empire and the eventual Christianization of Europe. He became sole ruler of the Roman Empire in 324, proclaimed Helena as augusta soon after, and summoned the Council of Nicea (from *Nike*, meaning "victory") in 325. A prominent participant in this religious council, Constantine pushed for the dogmatic unity of the Christian religion. The bishops agreed on a common dogma expressed in the Nicene Creed. Constantine's focus on Christianization led to the building of many churches, including those over Christ's purported tomb and over the cave where Christ was said to have been born in Bethlehem; both structures were credited to Helena's pilgrimage to those places.

During Constantine's reunification efforts following his victory in

324, he equated the harmonious unity of his family with the unity of the empire. This position was lethal to his political leadership when, in 326, he executed his wife, Fausta, and his eldest son, Crispus, the young man who had been born to his concubine, Minervina. The most plausible justification was that a sexual relationship had developed between Fausta and Crispus, but the truth is obscure. Various accounts relate the pain experienced by Helena at the news of her favorite grandson's murder; her pilgrimage may have been in some part a response to the sin her son had committed in ordering the murder.

The scandal in the Constantinian family and the turmoil caused by Constantine's insistence on Christianity created unrest in the eastern parts of the Roman Empire. To appease the people of the eastern provinces, Helen set off to meet them. Her travels were marked by her piety and gracious giving to all whom she encountered. An old Anglo-Saxon poem by Cynewulf (c. eighth century) tells the legend of Saint Helena's journey to Jerusalem to search for the Cross.

Life's Work

Tradition says Helena discovered the True Cross. She discovered three crosses, and Pontius's inscription marked the True Cross, as one tradition tells. In a more symbolic interpretation, historians have written that upon finding three crosses, Helena turned to Marcarius, bishop of Jerusalem, for mediation. A mortally sick woman (in some tellings, one who had just died) was brought to the crosses. When she was touched by the first two, nothing happened; upon the touch of the third cross, she was immediately healed. Thus, the holy wood of the True Cross was identified. More important, the healing symbolized the salvation of Christianity for those who believed in Christ.

Because of her visit to the Holy Land, churches were erected at the cave where the nativity occurred in Bethlehem (the Church of the Nativity) and on the Mount of Olives, from which Christ is said to have ascended into heaven (the Church of the Assumption). The attachment of holiness (or unholiness) to something tangible was not inherent in Christianity, for nothing earthly was considered holy. The concept of churches as holy places was established by Constantine and Helena as part of the establishment of Christianity. The churches were thus structured to represent the places where earth and heaven met.

The bodies of the Three Magi, now shown at Cologne, Germany, are said to have been brought by Helena from the East and given to the Church of Milan; she is also said to have given the Holy Coat, the seamless robe of Christ, to the cathedral of Trier in Germany. In some accounts, she is also credited with finding the nails that fastened Christ's body to the Cross.

Legend reports she established Stavrovouni Monastery in Cyprus, where she stayed during her return journey from Jerusalem; she is said to have presented a piece of the True Cross in establishing the monastery. The monastery occupies the easternmost summit of the Troodos range of mountains, at a height of 2,260 feet. Tradition describes the monastery as an impregnable fortress against pagan attacks.

To the southeast of Rome, a territory called *fundus Laurentus* was an estate belonging to Helena (acquired sometime after 312). The site was one of the first areas in Rome where the new Christian convictions of the members of the imperial house were manifested.

Another historical legend, with some archaeological support, tells that Helena gave her imperial palace in Trier to Agricius, at the time priest to Antioch, for use as Trier's cathedral. Legend also has it that she was involved in the foundation of the Abbey of Saint Maximin at Trier.

Summary

The sarcophagus of Saint Helena is in the Vatican Museum. Originally intended for Constantine, the sarcophagus is covered with reliefs celebrating military triumphs.

More than one hundred churches have been dedicated to Saint Helena in England. By the end of the Middle Ages, her feast was kept in many churches on February 8. Throughout the world, her feast day is celebrated: by the Roman Catholic Church on August 18; by the Greeks on May 21; by the Ethiopians on September 15; and by the Copts on March 24 and May 4. She is the patroness of dyers, needlers, and nailsmiths.

Jan Willem Drijvers reported in his definitive book *Helena Augusta: The Mother of Constantine the Great and the Legend of Her Finding of the True Cross* (1992) that there may be two cameos depicting Helena: the so-called Ada-cameo, preserved in the Stadtbibliothek in Trier and a cameo in the Koninklijk Penningkabinet in Leiden, the Netherlands. It is difficult to identify statues of Helena with any certainty. Since Helena's coiffure was well attested, it is typically the test for images.

On the coin portraits that have been identified as depicting Helena, her hair is sleekly combed and worn in a knot over the middle of her head. Yet though her image is sometimes difficult to distinguish, her impact is not. For many empresses and queens who came to the throne after her, Helena Augusta became the perfect Christian empress whose humble piety was a model for all.

Bibliography

Bietenhoiz, Peter G. *Historia and Fabula: Myths and Legends in Historical Thought from Antiquity to the Modern Age.* Vol. 59 in *Brill's Studies in Intellectual History,* edited by A. J. Vanderjagt. Leiden, Netherlands: E. J. Brill, 1994. Establishes a perspective from which to approach the "historical" study of Saint Helena as that concerned both with things that actually happened (*historia*) and things that are merely supposed to have happened (*fabula*). Explores myths, legends, and historical thought surrounding Constantine the Great and his mother.

Burckhardt, Jacob. *The Age of Constantine the Great.* Translated by Moses Hadas. New York: Pantheon Books, 1949. Cited as the most meaningful history for the nonprofessional reader, Burckhardt's essay of nearly four hundred pages is a humanist reaction against the microscopic but less imaginative writings of scientific historians. Topical page headings and an extensive index make the book reader-friendly.

Drijvers, Jan Willem. *Helena Augusta: The Mother of Constantine the Great and the Legend of Her Finding of the True Cross.* Leiden, Netherlands: E. J. Brill, 1992. Originally a doctoral thesis defended at the University of Groningen, this book focuses on the task of distinguishing the history of Helena from the legend. Includes identification of coins and statues of Helena and an extensive bibliography.

Firth, John B. *Constantine the Great: The Reorganization of the Empire and the Triumph of the Church.* 2d ed. London: G. P. Putnam's Sons, 1923. The twenty-seven illustrations in this 356-page edition include several of depictions of Helena and others related to her. Includes a comprehensive index.

Grant, Michael. *Constantine the Great: The Man and His Times.* New York: Charles Scribner's Sons, 1993. A chronological table, maps, and illustrations enhance this telling of the impact of Constantine and Helena on Christianity.

Pohlsander, Hans A. *Augusta: Empress and Saint*. Chicago: Ares, 1995.

Waugh, Evelyn. *Saint Helena Empress*. In *Saints for Now*, edited by Clare Boothe Luce. New York: Sheed & Ward, 1952. Brief but highly readable and literary interpretation of Helena's life.

Tonya Huber

OVETA CULP HOBBY

Born: January 19, 1905; Killeen, Texas
Died: August 16, 1995; Houston, Texas

As army officer, cabinet member, and business leader, Hobby was a pioneer for American women in many areas of public life.

Early Life

Oveta Culp was born on January 19, 1905, to Isaac William Culp and Emma Hoover Culp. Her father was an attorney who was first elected to the Texas state legislature in 1919; her mother was a housewife who was active in the woman suffrage movement. From her earliest childhood, Oveta's father took a personal interest in her training and schooling. Isaac Culp instilled an interest in public life in Oveta and convinced her that her gender did not constitute a barrier to any ambition she might have had. It was still somewhat unusual for a woman of her day, even one of the educated classes, to attend college. Not only did Oveta complete her undergraduate work at Mary Hardin-Baylor College, but she also studied law at the main campus of the University of Texas.

At a very young age and only partly through the influence of her father, Oveta Culp began securing positions in the law, business, and government matrix of Texas. At the age of twenty, she was working as assistant city attorney in Houston. For several years, she served as parliamentarian, or chief clerk, for the lower house of the Texas state legislature, a position that enabled her to make extensive contacts in Texas politics. She made some use of these contacts when she decided to run for the legislature as a Democrat in 1929. Despite her efforts, she was not elected; women in electoral politics were to be more truly a phenomenon of her children's generation. On February 23, 1931, Oveta took a more conventional step when she married William P. Hobby, a man some thirty years her senior who was the publisher of the Houston *Post* and a former governor of Texas.

Life's Work

Marriage, however, did not mean retirement to domesticity and obscurity for Oveta Culp Hobby, as it did for many women of the period.

In 1955, as the secretary of Health, Education, and Welfare, Oveta Culp Hobby explains health service options in the United States. *(Library of Congress)*

Hobby immediately threw herself into both the business and editorial aspects of her husband's newspaper business. Starting out as a research editor, she moved steadily up the hierarchy of the newspaper until 1938, when she was named executive vice president. These were not ceremonial positions; Hobby's husband, busy managing other sectors of his extensive business interests, delegated much of his responsibility for the *Post* to his wife.

Houston during the 1930's was a much smaller city than it became later in the century, and the *Post* was in many ways a small, regional newspaper. Hobby made efforts to modernize the newspaper and bring it to the level of sophistication achieved by dailies on the East Coast. She placed a premium on intelligent coverage of women's issues, adding a woman editor to the staff to cover the activities and interests of women. Aside from her newspaper work and her devotion to her children, Hobby was particularly active within the Texas chapter of the League of Women Voters.

Hobby first attained national prominence with the beginning of American involvement in World War II. The United States government realized immediately after the onset of the war that this conflict would be more "total" than previous ones. It would affect not only soldiers fighting the war but also civilians living and working on the home front. Realizing that women would be more actively involved in the war effort than before, the government sought the assistance of recognized women leaders to help coordinate this involvement. Hobby was recruited to be the head of the women's division of the War Department's Bureau of Public Relations. This mainly involved liaison work between the army and female family members of servicemen, and therefore fell short of giving women full equality in the war effort. The War Department soon realized the inadequacy of this situation, and, in the spring of 1942, the Women's Auxiliary Army Corps (WAAC) was established to mobilize the talents and energy of women. Because of her work with Army Chief of Staff George C. Marshall to plan the WAAC, Hobby was the natural choice to head this corps and, as such, was given military rank, first as a major, and then, more appropriately considering the status of her role, as colonel.

World War II was one of the great watersheds in the democratization of American society. Most, if not all, of this democratization was unintentional. The government did not set out to use the war to enfranchise women and African Americans. Yet its need for manpower compelled the government to make use of their talents to serve the war efforts. Hobby's tenure at the WAAC saw the most thorough emergence of American women into the public sphere in history. Once it was realized that the contribution of women was indispensable to the war effort, their social marginalization was far less viable. The increasing significance of women was recognized when the "auxiliary" was dropped from the name of the corps in the middle of the war. By 1945,

Hobby's efforts with the WAC had become nationally known, and, next to Eleanor Roosevelt, she became the second most important woman in the American war effort.

After the war, Hobby returned to her duties at the Houston *Post*, but her interest in Washington affairs continued. In 1948, she advised the commission headed by former President Herbert Hoover on reducing waste in government bureaucracy. Surprisingly, her continuing interest in politics was no longer centered on the Democratic Party. In the Texas of Hobby's girlhood, it had been culturally mandatory for a Texan to be a Democrat, since Texas, like many southern states, was dominated by a virtual one-party system. During her years in Washington, D.C., however, Hobby was increasingly drawn to the Republican Party, especially after its transformation under the leadership of Thomas E. Dewey. Under Dewey, the Republicans accepted most of Franklin D. Roosevelt's New Deal social policies, while being more friendly to the free market and to capitalist initiative than were the Democrats. Hobby, a businesswoman as well as a liberal, was particularly sympathetic to this point of view. In addition, since they did not depend as heavily on the political influence of southern conservatives and urban party bosses, as did the Democrats, the Republicans could theoretically be more responsive in alleviating the oppression of African Americans. As a result, although she continued to support local Democratic candidates, Hobby actively campaigned on behalf of Republican presidential candidates in 1948 and again in 1952.

Although Dewey suffered an upset loss in his 1948 presidential race against incumbent Harry Truman, the Republicans won in 1952 with the election of former general Dwight D. Eisenhower. By this time, Hobby was solidly in the Republican camp. When it came time for the new president to make his appointments, Eisenhower remembered Hobby's wartime service and asked her to be the director of the Federal Security Agency. This agency coordinated the various government efforts directed at securing the health and comfort of American citizens. Socially concerned Democrats had long wanted to give this agency cabinet-level status, but it was the Eisenhower administration, often attacked for its conservatism, that presided over the agency's elevation as the Department of Health, Education, and Welfare (HEW). After her appointment as secretary of this department was approved in 1953, Hobby became the second woman to serve in a cabinet.

(Frances Perkins, secretary of labor in Franklin D. Roosevelt's administration, was the first.)

Hobby had enormous ambitions for her department, not all of which were realized during her tenure. She considered plans for overhauling the nation's medical insurance system, proposing legislation that would have established a federal corporation to provide financial backing for private low-cost medical plans. Although her proposals were defeated as a result of staunch opposition by the American Medical Association and fiscal conservatives in Congress, many elements of her plan received renewed attention during the 1990's under President Bill Clinton. Hobby also wished to focus more attention on the plight of the disadvantaged and economically subordinated, a highly unpopular cause during the prosperous 1950's. So much of the budget was being spent on Cold War defense projects that funding for the projects Hobby wished to undertake was simply not available.

Despite these difficult challenges, Hobby performed her job with dynamism and diligence. She was particularly instrumental in the widespread distribution of Jonas Salk's polio vaccine. As one of the few highly visible women in public life in the 1950's, she made a decided impression on young women growing up at the time. She seemed responsible, capable, optimistic, someone equipped for the challenges of the political world. Although she had only been in office for two years when she resigned to take care of her ailing husband on July 13, 1955, Hobby had made important contributions during her tenure at HEW.

Hobby did not rest on her laurels after her retirement from government. Taking over the executive reins at the Houston *Post*, she presided over its development into a large metropolitan daily, acquiring the latest in technological equipment to help the paper keep pace with the exponential growth of Houston itself. She also oversaw the expansion of the *Post* media empire into the new realms of radio and, especially, television. She served as cofounder of the Bank of Texas and was invited to serve on the boards of several corporations, including the Corporation for Public Broadcasting. Hobby also developed more interests in the cultural sphere, accumulating an impressive collection of modern art, including paintings by Pablo Picasso and Amedeo Modigliani. Although Hobby did not pursue public office herself, she did have the satisfaction of seeing her son, William, Jr., elected as lieutenant governor of Texas in 1972 and serve twelve years in that position. In 1978, she became the first woman to receive the George Catlett Marshall Medal for Public Service from the Association of the United States Army in recognition of her contributions during World War II.

Hobby continued to be a prominent and much-beloved figure on the local Houston scene. In the later years of her life, Hobby's business success and family fortune made her one of the richest women in the United States. She could look back on a remarkable and unmistakably American life. Oveta Culp Hobby died in Houston on August 16, 1995, at the age of ninety.

Summary

It is difficult to isolate one specific mark Oveta Culp Hobby made on American history, if only because her long life saw her excel in so many pursuits. Her wartime service helped pave the way for the promotion of women to a position of full equality in the military as well as in civilian society. Her business success proved that women not only could direct a large corporate concern but also could transform and expand that concern at an age when many business executives typically settled into retirement.

Nevertheless, it was arguably in her cabinet role as the first secretary of Health, Education, and Welfare that Hobby made her most enduring contribution. Hobby started her cabinet position off on a good footing, helping institutionalize it so that it (and, more important, the concerns it represented) became a Washington fixture. The Eisenhower cabinet of which Hobby was a member was derided at the time as consisting of "eight millionaires and a plumber," but it was in fact composed of many remarkable personalities, four of whom survived well into the 1990's: Attorney General Herbert Brownell, Secretary of Agriculture Ezra Taft Benson, Attorney General William Rogers, and Hobby herself. Perhaps slighted by the Democratic bias of many historians, the Eisenhower cabinet was, especially in terms of domestic policy, a progressive force. Hobby's presence was crucial in shaping this tendency.

Hobby's cabinet service also firmly established the tradition of women being present in the cabinet. Under Roosevelt, the Democratic Party had been most associated with the equality of women. Hobby's presence in a Republican cabinet meant that drawing upon the abilities of Americans of either gender became a bipartisan concern. Every future female cabinet member owed her position, in a way, to the achievement of Oveta Culp Hobby.

Bibliography

Beasley, Maurine H., and Sheila J. Gibbons. *Taking Their Place: A Documentary History of Women and Journalism*. Washington, D.C.: American University Press, 1993. This book provides an impression of the history of women in journalism before, during, and after Hobby's newspaper years.

Clark, James Anthony. *The Tactful Texan: A Biography of Governor Will Hobby*. New York: Random House, 1958. This biography of Hobby's husband provides information on Hobby's early career.

Eisenhower, Dwight D. *The White House Years: Mandate for Change, 1953-1956*. Garden City, N.Y.: Doubleday, 1963. The first volume of Eisenhower's presidential memoirs makes frequent mention of Hobby in her role as head of HEW.

Howes, Ruth, and Michael Stevenson, eds. *Women and the Use of Military Force*. Boulder, Colo.: Lynne Rienner, 1993. This book considers the theoretical issues accompanying women's service in the military.

Lyon, Peter. *Eisenhower: Portrait of the Hero*. Boston: Little, Brown, 1974. Emphasizes Hobby's role as the nation's top health care official.

Shire, Al, ed. and comp. *Oveta Culp Hobby*. Houston: Western Lithograph, 1997. According to the introduction, "This book is not a biography, but a tribute, a collection of reminiscences by those who knew and loved her best."

Margaret Boe Birns

CATHERINE HOWARD

Born: c. 1521; probably at Horsham or Lambeth, England
Died: February 13, 1542; London, England

As fifth wife to King Henry VIII, Howard briefly reigned as queen of England until revelations about her personal life brought about her sudden downfall and execution.

Early Life

Catherine Howard was born into the English aristocracy, her father being Lord Edmund Howard, a younger son of Thomas Howard, second duke of Norfolk. Through her Howard connections, Catherine was a first cousin to Anne Boleyn, Henry VIII's second queen. Little is known about the future queen's childhood. She grew up in a large family of ten children and received little formal education. Her mother, Joyce Culpeper, died when Catherine was quite young. Her father, Lord Edmund Howard, subsequently married two more times, but he saw little of his daughter. Being a younger son, Lord Edmund did not inherit the considerable family estates, and he experienced continual financial difficulties, even after his appointment as controller of Calais in 1534. Never a major influence on his daughter's life, he died in 1539, a year before Catherine's dramatic rise to power.

The most significant development of Catherine's childhood occurred when her father sent her to live with his stepmother Agnes, the dowager duchess of Norfolk. One of the wealthiest and most influential women of her day, the duchess maintained a grand household at her country estate at Horsham in Sussex and her town house at Lambeth, across the Thames from London. The duchess exercised only a loose supervision over her numerous charges; at Horsham, young Catherine soon engaged in a serious flirtation with Henry Manox, a musician hired to teach her to play the lute and virginal. Although the relationship did not become an actual affair, Manox followed Catherine to Lambeth and openly bragged to numerous people in the household of the liberties he had enjoyed with the duchess's charge.

While at Lambeth, probably in 1538, Catherine became sexually active with her next serious suitor, Francis Dereham, a distant kinsman of Duchess Agnes and a pensioner in her household. The two lovers openly exchanged gifts and were heard to call each other "husband" and "wife." Their clandestine nighttime meetings became something of a scandal and provoked the jealousy of Manox, who sent an anonymous note to the duchess informing her of the relationship. Discovering the two in an ardent embrace, she angrily struck both of them. Dereham soon left to seek his fortune in Ireland, leaving his life savings with his paramour. Catherine's passion for Dereham quickly cooled, because in 1540 her uncle Norfolk used his influence to secure her a position at court, an event that drastically transformed the fortunes of this previously obscure young woman.

Life's Work
The Howard family used Catherine as a pawn in the dangerous political game for dominance at the court of the aging Henry VIII. The duke stood as the representative of the conservative faction of old nobility who opposed the pro-Protestant policies of Thomas Cromwell, Henry's lord chancellor and the guiding genius behind the English Reformation. To cement an alliance with the German Protestants, Cromwell had just engineered the king's marriage to Anne of Cleves. From their first meeting in January, 1540, Henry had openly expressed his displeasure with his new foreign bride. Sensing Cromwell's vulnerability, the Norfolk faction brought Catherine to court and coached her on ways to attract the monarch's attention.

Henry evidently met Catherine at a banquet hosted by Norfolk's ally, Stephen Gardiner, bishop of Winchester; by April, the king was obviously smitten. On April 24, he granted her the lands of a convicted felon, and even more lavish gifts followed the next month. Queen Anne's last public appearance with Henry occurred at the May Day festivities; soon thereafter, he sent her to the country so that he could court Catherine openly. On many spring nights, the royal barge crossed the Thames to visit Duchess Agnes's Lambeth residence so that Henry could enjoy Catherine's company.

Catherine's triumph came swiftly. On June 10, Henry ordered Cromwell's arrest on charges of heresy and treason. Facing death, the former chancellor agreed to supply information to enable Henry to divorce his German consort. Anne did not oppose Henry's schemes,

Catherine Howard *(Library of Congress)*

and the grateful monarch offered her a generous settlement. Their divorce became final on July 9. Nineteen days later, ironically on the day Cromwell was beheaded, Henry summoned the bishop of London to the royal palace at Oatlands, where he secretly married Catherine. He publicly acknowledged her as his new queen at Hampton Court on August 8.

The aging, increasingly bloated monarch seemed besotted by his lively teenage bride. Catherine's youthful vigor, coupled with her submissiveness and outward virtue, rejuvenated her husband, who showered her with public caresses and worldly goods. He soon bestowed on her all the lordships and manors that had belonged to his beloved queen Jane Seymour, as well as some of Cromwell's former properties. The new queen chose "No other wish but his" as the motto above her new coat of arms.

Although Catherine's Howard relatives again found themselves in a position of preeminence at court, the new queen was far more naïve about court politics and factions than her two English predecessors, Anne Boleyn and Jane Seymour. Also unlike some of Henry's previous spouses, Catherine evidently made no real attempt to preoccupy herself with politics or interfere with state affairs, except for a handful of intercessions on behalf of prominent prisoners in the Tower. Throughout her brief reign, her main preoccupation seemed to be clothes and dancing, not political intrigue. The king appeared delighted with his young bride; the two remained constantly in each other's company until February, 1541.

Sometime in the spring of 1541, though, Catherine embarked upon more dangerous behavior, which culminated in an affair with a distant cousin, Thomas Culpeper, an attractive young courtier who was several decades younger than her husband. The only surviving letter in Catherine's hand, written in April, 1541, is a love letter to Culpeper in which she recklessly pronounced herself, "Yours as long as life endures."

Their affair evidently continued throughout the summer and autumn while Henry took his bride on a tour of northern England. Lavish ceremonies awaited the royal couple as they visited numerous towns. At Pontefract in Yorkshire, Francis Dereham reappeared in Catherine's life and demanded a post at court. On August 27, she unwisely appointed him her private secretary, perhaps to buy his silence about their previous relationship.

The royal entourage returned to Hampton Court on October 30, and Henry gave orders for a special thanksgiving service to be held celebrating his marriage. However, a sudden turn of events brought an end to the marriage and death to the young queen. Shortly before their return, Archbishop Thomas Cranmer had received disturbing reports about Catherine's clandestine life before her marriage. The initial source of this news was John Lascelles, whose sister, Mary Hall, had been in the dowager duchess of Norfolk's service while Catherine lived with her. A zealous Protestant, Lascelles was not a personal enemy of the queen, but he did despise what she represented—the triumph of the Howard faction at court. After consultations with other leading men at court, Cranmer handed the king a note with the damning information while Henry was hearing a mass for the dead.

Initially astonished and unwilling to believe the charges, Henry nevertheless ordered the archbishop to conduct a thorough investigation and to confine the queen to her apartments pending its outcome. He never saw her again, as interrogation of numerous witnesses confirmed his worst fears. Upon being informed by his council that the allegations against Catherine had a sound basis, the king openly broke down and cried. Subsequently, increasingly outraged at being cuckolded, he furiously called for a sword so that he could execute his adulterous spouse personally.

Whereas Anne Boleyn had immediately been sent to the Tower after allegations of her infidelity, Catherine was instead placed under house arrest at the Abbey of Syon in Middlesex. The king allowed her to have four attendants and access to three chambers during this initial stage of her confinement. He also let Cranmer hold out some hope of royal mercy to Catherine if she would fully confess.

After initially denying the charges against her and changing her story several times, the queen eventually confessed her guilt to Cranmer. As evidence accumulated, it became obvious that Catherine had been not only indiscreet before her marriage to Henry but also unfaithful to him afterward. On November 22, a royal proclamation announced that she had forfeited her rights as queen; two days later, she was formally indicted both for having concealed her relationship with Dereham before her marriage and for having committed adultery with Culpeper after becoming Henry's wife.

Culpeper and Dereham paid for their folly by being executed on December 1. The king decided against a public trial for his unfaithful wife. Instead, she was condemned by a special act of attainder passed by Parliament and approved by the king in early February. On two occasions, members of the council invited Catherine to come before Parliament to defend herself, but she refused, admitting her guilt and hoping for the king's mercy.

On February 10, Catherine was removed to the Tower, and on the evening of February 12, she was told she would die the following morning. She requested that the block on which she was to be executed be brought into her room in the Tower so that she could practice how to place herself. Early on February 13, guards escorted the prisoner to a spot within the Tower grounds, the same location where her cousin had been beheaded nearly six years earlier. Catherine made a brief speech admitting her sins to both God and king, after which the executioner severed her head with a single stroke from his axe. Like Anne Boleyn's before her, her body was interred in the chapel of St. Peter ad Vinicula within the Tower.

Summary

Catherine Howard reigned only some eighteen months as Henry VIII's fifth queen, and fewer details about her brief life exist than for any of his other consorts. Except for a possible depiction in a stained-glass window in King's College Chapel, Cambridge, no contemporary portrait of her survived. Nor did Catherine play a significant role in determining policy during the tempestuous final years of Henry's reign. Rather, her powerful Howard relations used her as a pawn to forward their own ambitions at the volatile court of the second Tudor king.

Catherine became Henry VIII's final passion. His immediately preceding marriage with Anne of Cleves had been arranged, but Henry deliberately chose the young and seemingly innocent Catherine, some three decades his junior. For a few months, she succeeded in reinvigorating her prematurely aging husband. Her fall left him an increasingly embittered and dangerous sovereign and resulted in the temporary disgrace of her family. Her uncle Norfolk managed to save his life by abandoning Catherine and joining in her condemnation, as he had done with his other royal niece, Anne Boleyn; but Howard influence at Henry's court ended as the result of the scandal. An odd sequence of events had briefly turned this obscure young woman into the most prominent lady in the realm. Her indiscretions both before and after her marriage brought a tragically early end to her life.

Bibliography

Fraser, Antonia. *The Wives of Henry VIII*. New York: Alfred A. Knopf, 1992. Part 4 of this well-written and researched collective biography by one of Britain's most popular writers provides a colorful portrait of Catherine and her contemporaries.

Lindsey, Karen. *Divorced, Beheaded, Survived: A Feminist Reinterpretation of the Wives of Henry VIII*. New York: Addison-Wesley, 1995. This lively collective biography examines the position of Catherine and Henry's other wives based upon recent feminist interpretations of the role of women in Tudor society.

Loades, David M. *Henry VIII and His Queens*. West Sussex, England: Sutton, 1997. This short and highly readable work by a respected British historian provides a useful introduction to the topic.

Smith, Lacey Baldwin. *A Tudor Tragedy: The Life and Times of Catherine Howard*. London: Clay, 1961. This sympathetic study by a leading Tudor-Stuart historian remains the standard biography.

Weir, Alison. *The Six Wives of Henry VIII*. New York: Grove Press, 1991. Chapters 13 to 15 of this collective biography complement the work of Fraser. Weir asserts that Catherine was born circa 1525, making her younger than other scholars assume.

Tom L. Auffenberg

ISABELLA I

Born: April 22, 1451; Madrigal, Spain
Died: November 26, 1504; Medina del Campo, Spain

Isabella I and her husband Ferdinand II directed Spain's transition from medieval diversity to national unity. These Catholic monarchs achieved governmental and ecclesiastical reform, and established a continuing Spanish presence in Italy, America, and northern Africa.

Early Life

Isabella and Ferdinand were each born to the second, much younger wives of kings. A much older half brother stood between each of them and the throne; their siblings died with considerable suspicion of poisoning. Thus the young prince and princess grew up the focus of intrigue. Their marriage represented an alliance between Ferdinand's father, John II of Navarre (from 1458 of Aragon), and a faction of Castilian nobles, including his mother's kinsmen, the Enríquez family, and Isabella's protector, the archbishop of Toledo, Alfonso Carrillo.

John II of Castile, Isabella's father, died when she was three and her brother Alfonso was less than a year old. Their mother, Isabella of Portugal, withdrew to her cities of Arevalo and Madrigal to maintain her independence. This dowager queen, a woman of exemplary piety, became increasingly unstable, and King Henry IV, Isabella's half brother, brought the children to his court in 1461. In 1462, young Isabella stood sponsor at the baptism of the king's daughter Juana. Henry had married Juana of Portugal, mother of Princess Juana, within a year after his divorce from his first, childless wife, Blanche of Navarre, on the grounds of his own impotence. Princess Isabella and her brother Alfonso, who died in 1465, became involved in several plots that included challenging the legitimacy of Princess Juana, deposition of Henry, and various plans for Isabella's marriage, which led to her union with Ferdinand of Aragon in 1469.

Her isolated childhood and her preferred semi-isolation at Henry's court caused Isabella to grow up pious and rather bookish. Gonzalo Chacón, chosen by their mother to supervise Isabella and Alfonso, proved a guiding influence in her early life and later. This man had been a confidant of Álvaro de Luna, John II's great constable of Castile. A description of the princess at the time of her marriage tells of golden red hair, gray eyes with long lashes and arched brows, and a red-and-white complexion. A long neck and slim, erect posture set off her face and gave an effect of dignity and majesty.

Ferdinand early became the focus of a quarrel between his father and his own half brother, Prince Charles of Viana, who was supported by the city of Barcelona. Almost from birth, the boy participated in Barcelona's elaborate ceremonies, and at the age of ten he and his mother, Queen Juana Enríquez, were besieged in Gerona by the Barcelona army and rescued by his father. Though Ferdinand had tutors and attendants to teach him to read and ride, his father was his great teacher. John II of Aragon involved his son in war and government as much as the boy's years allowed. Aragonese politics involved the same kind of intrigue as Castile's but were complicated by the complex nature of the Crown, which included Aragon, Catalonia, Valencia, Mallorca, Sardinia, and Sicily. In 1468, John II entitled Ferdinand king of Sicily, a position that gave him superior rank to his bride and that gave them both status in their struggle against Princess Juana and her uncle-fiancé, King Afonso V of Portugal, to win Castile. Ferdinand's portraits show a red-and-white complexion with dark eyes and a full mouth. He wore his dark brown hair rather long, in the style of the day; his hairline began early to recede noticeably. In riding, warfare, athletics, and dancing, he performed with perfect skill and ease.

Life's Work

During the first decade of their marriage, Isabella and Ferdinand struggled to establish themselves in Castile, first to gain the good graces of Henry IV and, after his death, to dominate the barons. Men like Carrillo changed sides as it suited their interests; having supported Isabella, Carrillo turned to Princess Juana when it became clear that the newlyweds would not take direction from him. An incident in the early stages of the war against Portugal limns the characters of the young couple. When cautious, shrewd, self-confident Ferdinand withdrew, avoiding a confrontation at Toro in July, 1475, rather than risk defeat, his insecure, impetuous, chivalric wife gave him a very chilly homecoming. His victory on March 1, 1476, near Toro (at Peleagonzalo) was more a victory of maneuver than a battle, and historians dispute the question of who actually won. In this period, Isabella played a role of great importance. For example, when the Master of the Crusading Order of Santiago died in 1475, she pressured its members into accepting her husband as their leader. That same year, the monarchs put under royal control the militia and treasury of the Holy Brotherhood, the medieval alliance of Castilian cities. With these forces and loyal barons, they subdued the others. Nobles who would not accept royal authority had their castles destroyed. By 1481, Ferdinand and Isabella stood masters of Castile. The longevity of Ferdinand's father, who died in 1479, preserved control in Aragon while Ferdinand and Isabella won Castile.

An 1870 depiction of the reception of Christopher Columbus by Ferdinand II and Isabella I after his first voyage to the New World. *(Library of Congress)*

The next decade brought the glorious conquest of the kingdom of Granada. In the medieval tradition, King Abū al-Ḥasan had adopted an aggressive attitude during the Castilian disorders; now his son Muhammad XI (or Boabdil to the Spanish) faced a united Aragon and Castile. In the period from 1482 to 1492, the "Catholic Monarchs," as Pope Alexander VI called Ferdinand and Isabella, waged continuing warfare against the Muslims. Ferdinand headed Castilian forces in this great adventure and so consolidated his personal leadership. Isabella's role in providing funds, men, and supplies confirmed the essential importance of their partnership. Muhammad's surrender ended the 780-year Christian reconquest of Iberia and brought Spain's middle ages to an end; that same year, sponsorship of the first voyage of Christopher Columbus and a decree expelling Jews from Castile signaled the beginning of Spain's modern age.

The years from the victory in Granada to Isabella's death brought signal triumph and personal disappointment. In 1495, Ferdinand and Isabella launched a war commanded by a Castilian nobleman, Gonzalo Fernández de Córdoba, against Aragon's traditional enemy, France, for control of the kingdom of Naples. Continued by their successors, this struggle brought Spain's domination of Italy. A series of marriage alliances further strengthened them against France. The Portuguese alliance always remained paramount. Their eldest daughter, Isabella, married first Prince John, son of John II of Portugal, and then, after his death, King Manuel I. When this Isabella died, Manuel married her sister Maria. Typical of the new era of peaceful relations with Portugal, the 1494 Treaty of Tordesillas amicably adjusted the 1493 Papal Line of Demarcation which, consequent to the Columbus voyage, had divided the non-European world into Spanish and Portuguese hemispheres. Ferdinand and Isabella's only son, John (who died in 1497), married a Habsburg, and their second daughter, Joan, married Philip of Burgundy, who was also a Habsburg. Ferdinand and Isabella's daughter Catherine (of Aragon) embarked on a tragic career in Tudor England as wife of Prince Arthur and later of King Henry VIII.

After Isabella's death in 1504, her husband continued their life's work, his course shaped by a series of accidents. Castile passed to the control of Joan and her Habsburg husband, and Ferdinand married a second wife, Germaine de Foix. Ferdinand and Germaine's son died soon after his birth. Joan's mental instability and her husband's death in 1506 restored Ferdinand's position as regent, now for Joan's son Charles (later King Charles I of Spain and Emperor Charles V). Yet only Ferdinand's military defeat of the Andalusian nobles made the regency effective. A series of ventures in North Africa culminated in the 1509 conquest of Oran, financed by Archbishop of Toledo Francisco Jiménez de Cisneros. A final triumph came in the conquest of Spanish Navarre in 1512, realizing the claim of Queen Germaine to that region. This conquest rounded out Spain's national boundaries; for the rest of his life, Ferdinand devoted himself to aligning Spanish policy with that of the Habsburgs.

Summary

In many ways, Isabella I and Ferdinand II superintended a transition to the national and cultural unity that provided the base for Spain's modern world influence. Though they left local affairs largely in the hands of barons and city oligarchies, the Royal Council provided a protobureaucratic center. This council took charge of the Holy Brotherhood, and one of its members became president of the *Mesta*, Castile's great sheepherders' guild. Through meetings of the Cortes and the junta of the Holy Brotherhood, the monarchs maintained contact with representatives of the cities, and *corregidores* acted as their agents in the cities. If Spain's laws remained as diverse as the multiplicity of its political units, Ferdinand and Isabella ordered compilations of Castile's medieval laws and their own proclamations as a guiding framework. They themselves traveled constantly through their kingdoms, providing personal justice.

Their strengthening of the Catholic culture and fostering of a Spanish national type made Spain a leader in the Catholic Reformation in Europe and the world. A papal decree in 1478 established the Spanish Inquisition under royal control to ferret out crypto-Jews. Combined with edicts in 1492 and 1502 obliging Jews and Muslims respectively either to convert or to leave Castile, the Inquisition largely established a Christian norm in place of medieval cultural diversity. Later it repressed Protestantism in Spain. In Aragon, Ferdinand reactivated the older Papal Inquisition, but the appointment of Tomás de Torquemada as High Inquisitor for both kingdoms and the establishment of a Council of the Inquisition made it a national institution. Appointment in 1495 of Isabella's confessor, the ascetic, selfless Jiménez de Cisneros as archbishop of Toledo, in contrast to the lusty and ambitious Carrillo, acted to reform and control the Church. (Jiménez became High Inquisitor in 1507.) Jiménez de Cisneros's reform of the Spanish Franciscans and his founding of the University of Alcalá de Henares show a more positive dimension. The university adopted the Erasmian approach of using Renaissance scholarship for religious purposes.

Certainly no act of the reign had greater long-range impact than sponsorship of Columbus. Though Castile had engaged in conquest of the Canary Islands since 1479, the American voyages looked beyond Africa to world empire. Hampered by very limited revenues, Isabella and Ferdinand continued their sponsorship of this enterprise when significant monetary returns seemed problematical. The new American empire posed unprecedented problems of distance and dimension involving treatment of American Indians and control of Columbus's enormous claims as discoverer. Their development of viceregal authority went beyond anything in the tradition of Aragon, the conquest of the Canaries, or the feudalism of the Reconquest.

Bibliography

Hillgarth, J. N. *1410-1516, Castilian Hegemony*. Vol. 2 in *The Spanish Kingdoms, 1250-1516*. Oxford, England: Clarendon Press, 1978. A work of solid scholarship, following recent Spanish interpretations with special emphasis on the reign of Ferdinand and Isabella. The great advantage of the book lies in its consideration of events in Aragon and the other Spanish kingdoms.

Kamen, Henry. *Spain, 1469-1714: A Society in Conflict*. London: Longman, 1983. This book reviews material covered in J. H. Elliott's 1963 book, *Imperial Spain*. Provides an up-to-date view of Spain's Golden Age. Both utilize recent Spanish scholarship and considerably revise older interpretations. Kamen, also author of a book on the Spanish Inquisition, here pays attention to the needs of students, providing both an introduction and a reference tool.

Lunenfeld, Marvin. *Keepers of the City: The Corregidores of Isabella I of Castile*. Cambridge, England: Cambridge University Press, 1987. Based on archival research, this book is the sort of institutional history that has made possible the new interpretations of the subject. Lunenfeld has also written a similar book on the Council of the Holy Brotherhood.

Merriman, R. B. *The Catholic Kings*. Vol. 2 in *The Rise of the Spanish Empire in the Old World and the New*. New York: Macmillan, 1918. A monumental work with narrative detail not found elsewhere in English, but for this reign the book is otherwise superseded by the books of Hillgarth and the others cited above. Its interpretations are outmoded, and its facts not always reliable. Its long reign as the standard English work on Ferdinand and Isabella partly explains the even longer reign of William Prescott's biography (below).

Miller, Townsend. *The Castles and the Crown: Spain, 1451-1555.* New York: Coward & McCann, 1963. Although written with a lively style and based on chronicles, this book does not take account of recent scholarship. Its interpretations are of the Prescott school.

Nader, Helen. *The Mendoza Family in the Spanish Renaissance, 1350-1550.* New Brunswick, N.J.: Rutgers University Press, 1979. A work of solid scholarship with a very important focus on a great baronial family. The Mendozas and their ilk were as important in this reign as the kingdoms of Castile and Aragon.

Prescott, William H. *History of the Reign of Ferdinand and Isabella, the Catholic.* 3d rev. ed. 3 vols. New York: Hooper, Clark, 1841. The pioneering work in English that is also the longest. Many of Prescott's interpretations and his scholarship are inevitably and completely outdated. The book, for example, overemphasizes Isabella's importance by denigrating Ferdinand. Like Townsend Miller's books, it can still be read for pleasure.

Walsh, William Thomas. *Isabella of Spain, the Last Crusader.* New York: Robert M. McBride, 1930. Deserves attention as a long, detailed work that is a biography of the queen, not a history of the reign or a study of Spain in her times.

Woodward, Geoffrey. *Spain in the Reigns of Isabella and Ferdinand, 1474-1516.* London: Hodder & Stoughton, 1997.

Paul Stewart

JOAN OF ARC

Born: c. 1412; Domremy, France
Died: May 30, 1431; Rouen, France

Joan's victories initiated the withdrawal of English troops from France to end the Hundred Years' War, and she made possible the coronation of Charles VII at Reims. As a martyr to her vision and mission, she had as much influence after her death as in her lifetime.

Early Life

Usually identified with the province of Lorraine, Joan of Arc grew up a daughter of France in Domremy, a village divided between the king's territory and that of the dukes of Bar and Lorraine. Bells from the church next to her home sounded the events of her youth. Her father, Jacques, was a peasant farmer and respected citizen. Joan learned piety from her mother, Isabelle Romée, as part of a large family. She took special pride in spinning and sewing; she never learned to read or write. By custom, she would have assumed her mother's surname, but in her public career she was called the Maid of Orléans, or Joan the Maid (with the double sense of virgin and servant).

Joan was born into the violence of both the Hundred Years' War and the French Civil War. Henry V, king of England, had gained control of most of northern France and, with the aid of the French duke of Burgundy, claimed the crown from the insane Charles VI. The heir to the throne, Charles VII—or the dauphin, as he was called—was young and apparently believed that his cause was hopeless. Five years after his father's death, he was still uncrowned, and Reims, the traditional coronation site, was deep in English territory. Domremy, on the frontier, was exposed to all the depredations of the war and was pillaged on at least one occasion during Joan's childhood.

Joan began to hear voices and to be visited by the patron saints of France, Saint Michael, Saint Catherine, and Saint Margaret, when she was thirteen or fourteen years old. She claimed that she heard and saw the saints, who became her companions and directed her every step. Initially, she took the voices as calling her to a holy life, and she pledged her virginity and piety. Later she came to believe that it was

Joan of Arc as a saint. *(Library of Congress)*

her mission to deliver France from the English.

Paintings and medals were made of Joan, but no genuine portrait has been identified; a contemporary sketch survives by a man who never saw her. Three carved limestone heads in helmets (now in Boston, Loudun, and Orléans) may represent near-contemporary portraits. They show a generous nose and mouth and heavy-lidded eyes. She had a ruddy complexion; black hair in a documentary seal (now lost) indicates her coloring. Sturdy enough to wear armor and live a soldier's life, she had a gentle voice. She wore a red frieze dress when she left Domremy; when she approached the dauphin at Chinon, she wore men's clothing: black woolen doublet and laced leggings, cap, cape, and boots. She wore her hair short like a man's, or a nun's, cut above the ears in the "pudding basin" style which facilitated wearing a helmet and discouraged lustful thoughts. Later, the dauphin provided her with armor and money for fashionable clothing. The gold-embroidered red costume in which she was finally captured may have been made from cloth sent to her by the captive duke of Orléans.

Life's Work

In 1428, Joan attempted to gain support from Robert de Baudricourt, the royal governor of Vaucouleurs. (The pregnancy of a kinswoman living two miles from Vaucouleurs provided Joan with a pretext to leave home.) Baudricourt, after rejecting her twice—as the voice had predicted—became caught up in Joan's mission. The English had besieged Orléans, as she had told him they would, and he, similarly besieged, had to agree to surrender his castle unless the dauphin came to his aid by a specified date. Before sending Joan to the dauphin, he had her examined and exorcised.

Charles agreed to the interview with Joan in desperation. Orléans, besieged since October of 1428, had great strategic importance; its fall would shake the loyalty of his remaining supporters and the readiness of his cities to provide money. Joan's appearance at court on February 25, 1429, after traveling through enemy territory for eleven days, brought fresh hope. She identified the dauphin at once in the crowded room, and she gave him some sign, "the King's Secret," which confirmed her mission but whose nature is still debated. A second exhaustive investigation of Joan occurred at Poitiers, where her piety and simplicity impressed everyone. Charles established a household for her. She had a standard made and adopted an ancient sword, discovered, through her directions, buried in the church of Sainte-Catherine-de-Fierbois.

On April 28, 1429, Joan and an expedition, believing they were on a supply mission, entered Orléans. Joan addressed the English commander, calling on him to retreat. She turned rough French soldiers into crusaders, conducting daily assemblies for prayer and insisting that they rid themselves of camp followers and go to confession. When a party bringing supplies to the city on the opposite bank found the wind blowing against them, she predicted the sudden change of wind that permitted the boats to cross. Nonplussed Englishmen allowed another shipment led by priests to pass without firing on it; they explained their lack of action as the result of bewitchment. Within the city, Joan's inspired leadership encouraged the troops to follow her famous standard and her ringing cry, "In God's name, charge boldly!" On May 7, though seriously wounded as she had predicted, she rallied the troops to victory at the Tourelles fortification, after the French captains had given up hope. The next day, the English withdrew from Orléans.

In little more than a week, with much plunder and killing of prisoners, the French drove their enemies from the remaining Loire strongholds of Jargeau, Meung, and Beaugency. Though Joan took part in these actions, her principal influence remained her extraordinary attraction and rallying of forces; she later said that she had killed no one. The troops of Arthur de Richemont, brother of the duke of Brittany, who now joined the dauphin, counted decisively in another victory at Patay on June 17.

Charles's coronation on July 17 at Reims, deep in enemy territory, clearly shows Joan's influence. Counselors and captains advised Charles to take advantage of his victories and move against Normandy. Joan persuaded him instead to travel to Reims, and city after city yielded to siege or simply opened its gates to the dauphin: Auxerre, Troyes, Châlons, and Reims itself. The stunned English regent, the duke of Bedford, offered no resistance.

After the coronation, Joan's single-minded drive to take Paris and gain the release of the duke of Orléans conflicted with a royal policy of caution and diplomacy based on the expectation that Burgundy, too, would rally peacefully to Charles. Charles ennobled Joan and her family and provided her with attendants and money, but she was too

Joan of Arc as a warrior. *(Library of Congress)*

popular to permit her return to Domremy. Her voices warned that she had little time. By September 8, when the assault on Paris finally began, the English had regained their aplomb. Joan, again wounded, unsuccessfully urged an evening attack. Charles's orders the next day forbade an attack, though the baron of Montmorency and his men came out of the city to join the royal army, and on September 13, Charles withdrew his troops.

Joan now joined in a holding action to prevent the English forces from using the extended truce to retake their lost positions. Her men took Saint-Pierre-le-Moûtier, but lack of supplies forced her to abandon La Charité. In the spring of 1430, she led volunteers to stiffen the resistance of Compiègne against the Burgundians, contrary to the royal policy of pacification. That helps to explain Charles's failure to negotiate her release after her capture at Compiègne on May 23—an event also predicted by her voices. The Burgundians sold her to the English authorities.

Joan's trial, which ran from January 9 through May 30, 1431, tested her faith and gave her a final opportunity to uphold the French cause. Her death was a foregone conclusion; the English reserved their right to retry her if the Church exonerated her. Bishop Pierre Cauchon of Beauvais took the lead, realizing that a church trial, by proving her a witch, would turn her victories to Anglo-Burgundian advantage. Indeed, her captors may have believed her a camp trollop and sorceress until a physical examination by the duchess of Bedford, the sister of Philip of Burgundy, proved Joan's virginity. That made it clear that she had not had carnal relations with Satan, a sure sign of sorcery.

After twice attempting to escape (for which her voices blamed her), she stood trial in Rouen. The two earlier investigations and Joan's impeccable behavior obliged Cauchon to falsify evidence and maneuver her into self-incrimination. She showed great perspicacity—her voices told her to answer boldly. Cauchon finally reduced the seventy-two points on which she had been examined to twelve edited points, on which her judges and the faculty of the University of Paris condemned her.

Seriously ill and threatened by her examiners, Joan apparently signed a recantation which temporarily spared her life. Cauchon claimed that she had renounced her voices; some historians claim forgery, admission to lesser charges, or some code by which she indicated denial. In any case, she returned to woman's clothing as ordered and to her cell. She was later found wearing men's clothing (perhaps partly to protect herself from her guards). When questioned, Joan replied that her voices had rebuked her for her change of heart. On May 29, the judges agreed unanimously to give Joan over to the English authorities. She received Communion on the morning of May 30 and was burned as a heretic.

Summary

Mystics with political messages abounded in Joan's world, but none had Joan's impact on politics. Widespread celebration in 1436 of Claude des Armoises, claiming to be Joan escaped from the flames, demonstrated her continuing popularity. Orléans preserved Joan's cult, and Domremy became a national shrine. A surge of interest beginning in the nineteenth century with Napoleon has made Joan one of the most written-about persons in history, but efforts to analyze her in secular terms reaffirm the continuing mystery of her inspiration.

Many people in the huge crowd that witnessed Joan's death believed in her martyrdom and reported miracles. English insistence on complete destruction of her body, with her ashes thrown into the Seine, underscored the point. When he took Rouen and the trial records in 1450, Charles VII ordered her case reopened, but only briefly. Too many influential living persons were implicated in Joan's condemnation, and a reversal of the verdict would also support papal claims to jurisdiction in France. A papal legate, Guillaume d'Estouteville, later encouraged Joan's aged mother to appeal to the pope, which brought about rehabilitation proceedings and the declaration of her innocence in 1456. Even then, the revised verdict merely revoked the earlier decision on procedural grounds without endorsing Joan's mission or condemning her judges. Joan was canonized by Pope Benedict XV on May 16, 1920, and France honors her with a festival day on the second Sunday of May.

Bibliography

Fabre, Lucien. *Joan of Arc*. Translated by Gerard Hopkins. New York: McGraw-Hill, 1954. Fabre's account reflects the French and Catholic position. He calls the English "Godons," as Joan did (from their characteristic oath), and makes Cauchon a monster. He bases conclusions about the various puzzles on documents and provides a guide to the vast literature.

Guillemin, Henri. *The True History of Joan "of Arc."* Translated by William Oxferry. London: Allen and Unwin, 1972. An example of the tradition that Joan did not die in 1431. One of the many variations in this tradition makes her the sister of Charles VII. Historians have never given much credence to books of this genre.

Lightbody, Charles Wayland. *The Judgments of Joan: Joan of Arc, a Study in Cultural History*. Cambridge, Mass.: Harvard University Press, 1961. A 171-page book on a very large topic. Lightbody treats the literature on Joan through the trial for rehabilitation; by way of apology, he promises a fuller treatment, which never appeared. Worth reading, but any author who treats George Bernard Shaw's play as revelatory about Joan and her times must be held suspect.

Lucie-Smith, Edward. *Joan of Arc*. London: Allen Lane, 1976. The necessary counterbalance to Fabre's biography. An objective and scholarly accounting, but in treating Joan's voices as hallucinations the author loses touch with Joan and her times. Lucie-Smith suggests a sympathetic approach to Joan's judges.

Pernoud, Régine. *Joan of Arc by Herself and Her Witnesses*. Translated by Edward Hyams. New York: Stein & Day, 1966. A work of great integrity and judgment by the director of the Centre Jeanne d'Arc in Orléans. She has culled documents of Joan's own times for an extremely useful book.

_____. *The Retrial of Joan of Arc: The Evidence of the Trial for Her Rehabilitation, 1450-1456*. Translated by J. M. Cohen. Foreword by Katherine Anne Porter. New York: Harcourt, Brace, 1955. Though incomplete, this includes the essential 1455-1456 testimony by 144 persons who knew Joan at various stages of her life, making her one of the best-documented personalities of her century. Intended to counteract the earlier trial, it proves to be something of a whitewash, but it also gives a valid picture of what Joan meant to the French people.

Pernoud, Régine, and Marie-Véronique Clin. *Joan of Arc: Her Story*. Translated and revised by Jeremy duQuesnay Adams. Edited by Bonnie Wheeler. New York: St. Martin's Press, 1998.

Vale, Malcolm G. A. *Charles VII*. Berkeley: University of California Press, 1974. A biography of sound scholarship which provides a better guide to the political world than do Joan's biographies. Vale, an Englishman, plays down Joan's own importance.

Warner, Marina. *Joan of Arc: The Image of Female Heroism*. Berkeley: University of California Press, 1999. Warner finishes what Charles Wayland Lightbody began, ranging through the centuries. She is notably good in utilizing recent scholarship, providing, for example, a hard look at how little is really known about Joan's appearance. Warner's feminist interpretation, however, imposes modern notions on fifteenth century experience. She plays down Joan's voices and treats her fasting as possible anorexia and her adoption of men's clothing as psychologically significant.

Paul Stewart

BARBARA JORDAN

Born: February 21, 1936; Houston, Texas
Died: January 17, 1996; Austin, Texas

The first African American elected to the Texas state senate after Reconstruction, Jordan went on to become a member of the U.S. House of Representatives. She mesmerized the nation during televised coverage of the House Judiciary Committee's investigation considering the impeachment of President Richard Nixon.

Early Life
On February 21, 1936, Barbara Charline Jordan was born to Benjamin Jordan, a warehouse clerk and part-time clergyman, and his wife, Arlyne Patten Jordan, in Houston, Texas. Barbara was raised in a time of segregation and Jim Crow laws. She lived with her parents, her two older sisters, Bennie and Rose Marie, and her grandfathers, John Ed Patten and Charles Jordan.

Barbara's outlook on life as well as her strength and determination can be attributed to the influence of her maternal grandfather, John Ed Patten, a former minister who was also a businessman. While assisting him in his junk business, Barbara learned to be self-sufficient, strong-willed, and independent, and she was encouraged not to settle for mediocrity. Her determination to achieve superiority was quickly demonstrated in her early years.

Barbara spent most of her free time with her grandfather Patten, who served as her mentor. They would converse about all kinds of subjects. His advice was followed and appreciated by the young girl, who adoringly followed him every Sunday as he conducted his business. He instilled in her a belief in the importance of education. Every action, every aspect of life, he stated, was to be learned from and experienced.

With her grandfather's advice in mind, Barbara Jordan embraced life and education. She showed herself to be an exemplary student while attending Phillis Wheatley High School in Houston. A typical teenager, Barbara was active in school clubs and other extracurricular activities. She also led an active social life during her years at Phillis

Barbara Jordan *(Library of Congress)*

Wheatley. It was during her high school years that Barbara was inspired to become a lawyer. She was drawn to the legal profession during a career day presentation by the prominent African American attorney Edith Sampson. Moved by Sampson's speech, Jordan became determined to investigate law as a possible area of study.

Jordan received many awards during her high school years, particularly for her talent as an orator. Her skill in this area was rewarded in 1952, when she won first place in the Texas State Ushers Oratorical Contest. As part of her victory package, she was sent to Illinois to compete in the national championships. She won the national oration contest in Chicago that same year.

The year 1952 began a new stage in Jordan's education. She was admitted to Texas Southern University after her graduation from high school. It was here that she truly excelled in oration. She joined the Texas Southern debate team and won many tournaments under the guidance and tutelage of her debate coach, Tom Freeman. He was also influential in urging her to attend Boston University Law School. At law school, she was one of two African American women in the graduating class of 1959; they were the only women to be graduated that year. Before 1960, Jordan managed to pass the Massachusetts and Texas bar examinations. Such a feat was an enviable one. She was offered a law position in the state of Massachusetts, but she declined the offer.

Jordan's impoverished background seemed far behind her. With the continued support of her parents and grandfathers, she opened a private law practice in Houston, Texas, in 1960. She volunteered her services to the Kennedy-Johnson presidential campaign. She organized the black constituents in the black precincts of her county. Her efforts were successful. The voter turnout was the largest Harris County had ever experienced. Jordan's participation in such a history-making event demonstrated her talents for persuasion and organization. These skills, coupled with her education and intellect, were to become her assets in all her future endeavors. The political career of Barbara Jordan was born as a result of the Kennedy-Johnson victory of 1960.

Life's Work

The decade of the 1960's witnessed Barbara Jordan's emergence in the political arena. The 1960's were a period of transition and hope in American history. With the election of the first Catholic president and the epic changes brought on by the Civil Rights movement, it was a time of change. Jordan was determined to be part of that change. After becoming the speaker for the Harris County Democratic Party, she ran for the Texas House of Representatives in 1962 and 1964. She lost on both occasions. Undeterred, Jordan ran for a third time in the newly reapportioned Harris County. She became one of two African Americans elected to the newly reapportioned eleventh district. Jordan was elected to the Texas state senate. She became the first African American since 1883 and the first woman ever to hold the position.

Jordan impressed the state senate members with her intelligence, oration, and ability to fit in with the "old boys' club." She remained in the state senate for six years, until 1972. During her tenure, she worked on legislation dealing with the environment, establishing minimum wage standards, and eliminating discrimination in business contracts. She was encouraged to run for a congressional seat. She waged a campaign in 1971 for the U.S. Congress. While completing her term of office on the state level, Jordan achieved another first: In 1972, she was elected to the U.S. House of Representatives. Jordan served briefly as acting governor of Texas on June 10, 1972, when both the governor and lieutenant governor were out of the state. As president pro tem of the Texas senate, it was one of her duties to act as governor when the situation warranted. Despite his being present for all of her earlier achievements, Jordan's father did not live to see her take office as a member of the U.S. House of Representatives. He died on June 11, 1972, in Austin, Texas. His demise spurred Jordan to continue her work.

Having already caught the attention of Lyndon B. Johnson while a member of the Texas state senate, Jordan sought his advice on the type of committees to join. She became a member of the Judiciary and Ways and Means Committees. Little did she know that the Judiciary Committee would evolve into a major undertaking. Jordan's membership in the House of Representatives was to be one of the many highlights of her political career.

The 1974 Watergate scandal gave Jordan national prominence. Her speech in favor of President Richard Nixon's impeachment was nothing short of oratorical brilliance. Her eloquence was considered memorable and thought-provoking. Her expertise as an attorney was demonstrated in 1974 when she spoke about the duty of elected officials to their constituents and the United States Constitution. Despite her personal distaste for an impeachment, Jordan insisted that President Nixon be held accountable for the Watergate fiasco. A Senate investigation, she believed, was warranted. Her televised speech was the center of media attention and critique for days to come. She sustained her reputation for eloquence during the 1976 Democratic National Convention. During her tenure in the House, she introduced bills dealing with civil rights, crime, business, and free competition as well as an unprecedented plan of payment for housewives for the labor and services they provide. Jordan's popularity was at its zenith when talk of her running for the vice presidency was rampant among her supporters. She shrugged off the suggestion, stating that the time was not right.

It was discovered in 1976 that Jordan suffered from knee problems. The ailment was visible during her keynote address when she was helped to the podium to give her speech. She admitted that she was having problems with her patella. The cartilage in one knee made it difficult and painful for her to walk or stand for long. Her brilliant oration was not hampered by her muscle weakness during the delivery of her speech in 1976. She opted not to run for reelection in 1978 and entered the educational field.

During his presidency, Jimmy Carter offered Jordan a post in his cabinet. Political rumor persists that she would have preferred the position of attorney general to Carter's suggestion of the post of secretary of the Department of Health, Education, and Welfare (HEW). Since Carter was firm in his offer, Jordan opted to refuse rather than settle for something she did not want. Such an attitude is indicative of her childhood training and upbringing.

Jordan was offered and took a teaching post at the University of Texas in Austin. She taught at the Lyndon Baines Johnson School of Public Affairs. In addition to her instructional duties, she also held the positions of faculty adviser and recruiter for minority students. She continued to hold these positions into the early 1990's. In addition, Governor Ann Richards of Texas appointed her to serve as an adviser on ethics in government.

Barbara Jordan received innumerable honorary degrees. Universities such as Princeton and Harvard bestowed honorary doctorates upon her. She received awards touting her as the best living orator. She was one of the most influential women in the world as well as one of the most admired. She was a member of the Texas Women's Hall of Fame and hosted her own television show. At the 1988 Democratic National Convention, Jordan gave a speech nominating Senator Lloyd Bentsen as the party's vice presidential candidate. She delivered the speech from the wheelchair she used as a result of her battle with multiple sclerosis. In 1992, she received the prized Spingarn Medal, which is awarded by the National Association for the Advancement of Colored People (NAACP) for service to the African American community. Jordan died in Austin on January 17, 1996, at the age of fifty-nine.

Summary
Barbara Jordan's rise from poverty to prominence through diligence and perseverance in the fields of law, politics, and education is a model for others to follow. During an interview on the Black Entertainment Television channel in February, 1993, Jordan maintained that circum-

stances of birth, race, or creed should not inhibit an individual from succeeding if he or she wishes to achieve greatness. As an individual who was born poor, black, and female, Jordan demonstrated the truth of her assertion, and her life is a portrait of success highlighted by a series of significant "firsts" and breakthroughs.

In 1984, Jordan was voted "Best Living Orator" and elected to the Texas Women's Hall of Fame. Her honorary doctorates from Princeton and Harvard substantiated her dedication to education and excellence. As an African American woman from the South, Jordan broke one barrier after the other. She maintained her integrity and dignity while in political office. Her defense of the U.S. Constitution during the Watergate era as well as her dedication to the field of education continues to be an example to those entering the field of law and education.

Jordan denied that her life's achievements were extraordinary. Her modesty was part of her upbringing. She endeavored to live a life that she believed would benefit the country. One of the reasons she refused to run for reelection in 1978 was her need to serve more than a "few" constituents in her district. She wished to serve them in addition to the masses. As she stated in her resignation: "I feel more of a responsibility to the country as a whole, as contrasted with the duty of representing the half-million in the Eighteenth Congressional District." She maintained that anyone may succeed with the proper attitude. Early in her political career, she made a conscious choice not to marry. Like Susan B. Anthony, Jordan believed that marriage would be a distraction from the cause to which she was drawn. In 1978, Jordan believed that her legislative role and effectiveness had ceased and that her most effective role in the global community was in the field of instruction. A new challenge presented itself, and Jordan was eager to confront it.

Despite the effects of her long illness, Jordan demontrated that race, socioeconomic status, and societal barriers may be overcome and dispelled as roadblocks to success. She gave interviews, lectures, and commencement addresses almost up to the time of her death in 1996.

Bibliography

Browne, Ray B. *Contemporary Heroes and Heroines*. Detroit: Gale Research, 1990. A collection of biographical profiles on men and women who have made major contributions to American life. Includes a fine piece on Barbara Jordan and her career.

Famous Blacks Give Secrets of Success. Vol. 2 in *Ebony Success Library.* Chicago: Johnson, 1973. A collection documenting the lives and achievements of black luminaries. The excerpt on Barbara Jordan traces her political achievements through 1973.

Jordan, Barbara, and Shelby Hearn. *Barbara Jordan: A Self-Portrait.* Garden City, N.Y.: Doubleday, 1979. Jordan's autobiography traces her life from childhood to her political career in the U.S. House of Representatives.

Ries, Paula, and Anne J. Stone, eds. *The American Woman: 1992-93.* New York: W. W. Norton, 1992. This book is one in a series of reports documenting the social, economic, and political status of American women. Includes profiles and articles on Jordan as well as female political contemporaries such as Governor Ann Richards of Texas and Senator Nancy Kassebaum of Kansas.

Roders, Mary Beth. *Barbara Jordan: American Hero.* New York: Bantam Books, 1998.

United States House of Representatives. Commission on the Bicentenary. *Women in Congress, 1917-1990.* Washington, D.C.: Government Printing Office, 1991. Compiled to honor the bicentennial of the U.S. House of Representatives, this work provides biographical sketches of the various women who have served in Congress, beginning with Jeannette Rankin in 1917 and continuing through the women serving in 1990.

Annette Marks-Ellis

JOSÉPHINE

Born: June 23, 1763; Trois-Îlets, Martinique
Died: May 29, 1814; Malmaison, France

Joséphine's life exemplified the chaos and unpredictability of the French Revolution and subsequent warfare. Popularly loved as "the good Joséphine," her social talents assisted Napoleon Bonaparte in creating stability and reconciliation among the various factions dividing the citizens of France.

Early Life

Marie-Josèphe-Rose Tascher de la Pagerie was born on the French Caribbean island of Martinique. She descended from the middle ranks of the French nobility who had emigrated to the colonies to make their fortunes growing sugar and was therefore Creole (born overseas but of French ancestry). Everyone called her Marie-Rose until she met Napoleon Bonaparte, who preferred "Joséphine." She attended a local convent school for four years during a privileged childhood. When she was sixteen, her family arranged her marriage to a wealthy and well-educated Frenchman named Viscount Alexandre de Beauharnais. In France she entered a sophisticated world where her lack of formal education disappointed her husband. The birth of their son Eugene (1781) and daughter Hortense (1783) did nothing to draw the couple together.

Soon the viscount demanded his freedom by falsely accusing Joséphine of infidelity and ordering her out of his house. She took refuge in a convent and complained to legal officials about his unreasonable behavior. The courts ordained a permanent separation and ordered Alexandre to pay modest alimony and child support. The separation left Marie-Rose in a precarious position in a society in which unattached women suffered serious disabilities: She had two young children, a small income, and no home. She had neither great beauty nor accomplishments; her one gift was charm, an aura of empathy and graciousness that won her loyal friends and sexual admirers. To support herself and her children, she became a woman of society, holding a salon where people of all political and social ranks fell under her spell and rendered her financial assistance.

Life's Work

The momentous events of the French Revolution engulfed and transformed Marie-Rose's life. Early in the revolution, her estranged husband rose to political prominence by advocating moderate reforms. When war broke out in 1792, Alexandre commanded French forces along the Rhine and suffered serious defeats. Austrians and Prussians dedicated to restoring the Bourbons invaded France. The republican revolutionists organized the nation for victory and wielded the Reign of Terror against domestic opponents. Some radicals charged that General Beauharnais's military failures suggested treason; they arrested and imprisoned him and his wife from April to August, 1794. Alexandre was guillotined on fabricated charges and Marie-Rose, fearing imminent death, became emotionally unstable. She survived because moderate revolutionaries, the Thermidorians, overthrew the Terrorists and established a new government composed of a five-man executive called the Directory. Marie-Rose became the mistress of Director Paul Barras and indulged in the atmosphere of dissolution that followed the Reign of Terror.

In 1795, the widowed Marie-Rose met the man who dominated the remainder of her life, a twenty-six-year-old revolutionary general named Napoleon Bonaparte. He fell passionately in love with her and proposed marriage. She hesitated to make this commitment but agreed after learning that Napoleon had received an important command in northern Italy that could bring fame and fortune. Napoleon's mother and adult brothers opposed the marriage, calling "Joséphine" an old woman (over thirty) with no money. Despite family bickering, they married in a simple civil ceremony in March, 1796. Within a week Napoleon departed to command the French army in northern Italy.

Napoleon brilliantly defeated the forces of monarchy clustered on France's southeastern borders. He sent home money and hundreds of artworks to enrich the Directory and practically dictated the terms of peace in 1797. Only Joséphine defied Napoleon's will; he implored her to come to Italy, but she resisted. She dallied in Paris, continued her relationship with Barras, probably took a new lover, and made money through war profiteering. When she finally traveled to Napoleon's headquarters near Milan, Italy, she had aroused his deepest suspicions and jealousy. In Italy, Joséphine first assumed important public functions; she presided over lavish official ceremonies and was treated almost as royalty. Once the couple returned to Paris, their small home became a site of pilgrimage for French patriots.

Popular myths immediately developed about Joséphine, celebrating her as "Our Lady of Victories" and "the good Joséphine," a symbol of good fortune and prosperity. She indulged her joy in shopping and collecting items as diverse as clothing, art, jewelry, and rare plants. Her extravagance did possess positive aspects: She was generous to a fault, patronized charities, and loved giving gifts. She never ignored a plea

Joséphine *(Library of Congress)*

for help, however humble, and she was gracious to all. Furthermore, she did not meddle in politics or attempt to influence her husband's policies. These characteristics rendered Joséphine "good" in the eyes of public opinion in marked contrast to the "bad" Queen Marie-Antoinette.

While Napoleon remained in France, Joséphine appeared as his loyal spouse and helpmate. However, when he led the French expedition to Egypt and remained away for seventeen months (1798-1799), she reverted to some of her previous bad habits and companions. Joséphine did begin to reform her behavior, but negative reports had quickly reached Napoleon. His secret return in autumn of 1799 surprised Joséphine, and she attempted to intercept him before her critical in-laws did. Napoleon greeted her with silence behind a locked bedroom door, but within a short time her copious weeping melted his heart and brought reconciliation.

Napoleon had far more on his mind than his wife's behavior. The Directory had suffered military losses and regularly canceled any unfavorable election results. A wide spectrum of political and business leaders assured Napoleon that they would support him if he would overthrow the Directors. His brothers Joseph and Lucien were well positioned to assist him, and Napoleon decided to act. Thus occurred the coup of Brumaire VIII in November, 1799, and creation of the Consulate, a three-man executive with Napoleon as First Consul. A major aim of the Consulate was to bring reconciliation among the political, religious, and social factions dividing the French people. Joséphine was an asset to this policy because she always had friends in all political and social camps. The Consulate ended the unseemly social behavior of the Directory; the First Consul and his wife moved into the Tuileries palace and virtually reestablished a court.

Napoleon and Joséphine frequently escaped the formality of the Tuileries by visiting their country estate, Malmaison, where they relaxed with their extended families and Joséphine unleashed her domestic talents. She redecorated the chateau extravagantly and began monumental gardening projects. She aspired to collect an example of every plant in France and introduce many new ones. She patronized botanists who studied and classified thousands of species. Malmaison became Joséphine's true home and was closely associated with popular perceptions of her.

Napoleon's ability to solve France's problems made him a target for royalist assassination attempts and made the need for an orderly transition of power in case of his death obvious. Joséphine worried for his safety and also for her own position should someone else assume power. She also feared that Napoleon, who had always wanted children, might divorce her and remarry in the hope of having them. She temporarily protected herself by arranging for her daughter Hortense to marry Napoleon's brother Louis in 1802. This couple produced three grandsons for Joséphine, uniting the Bonaparte and Beauharnais lines; Napoleon seriously considered adopting the oldest child before he died in 1808. The creation of the First Empire in May, 1804, intensified Joséphine's fears about succession and divorce. She invoked the sanction of the Roman Catholic Church against divorce by informing Pope Pius VII, who was visiting Paris for Napoleon's coronation ceremony, that her marriage had been civil only. At papal urging, Napoleon and Joséphine quickly had a brief religious wedding.

The spectacular coronation ceremony reached its high point as Napoleon I crowned Joséphine and himself. Their relationship had grown into an affectionate partnership; they often dined privately at the end of long days in which she sustained the elaborate public rituals of the court, freeing him to work on pressing matters. When Napoleon was away, Joséphine calmly continued the court routine and assured France that all was well. She remained essentially apolitical and unhesitatingly supported Napoleon's policies. Joséphine's concerns about war and politics lay with loved ones serving the First Empire. Eugene was an active soldier and viceroy of the kingdom of Italy; his politically dictated marriage to a Bavarian princess had turned out happily. Hortense became a queen as Louis Bonaparte was named king of Holland, but her marriage disintegrated.

A combination of personal and political pressures led Napoleon to divorce Joséphine in 1809. For years he doubted he could father a child; in 1806 and 1810, however, affairs produced two sons who were undoubtedly his, the latter by the Polish countess Maria Walewska. Simultaneously, political pressure mounted for Napoleon to divorce Joséphine and improve France's international position by marrying into the Russian or Austrian ruling houses. Napoleon informed Joséphine of his decision and requested her understanding. This time her tears could not dissuade him. Joséphine retained Napoleon's affection, the title of empress, possession of Malmaison, and a handsome income. In 1810 he married the Austrian archduchess Marie-Louise and, in 1811, rejoiced at the birth of his son Napoleon-Francis, king of Rome.

Joséphine's life changed greatly after divorce, but Joséphine herself did not. At heart she understood Napoleon's decision, and she contrived to visit and play with his sons by Countess Walewska and Marie-Louise. She lived at Malmaison and again gathered about her interesting people of all political persuasions. Although she entertained many royalists, she remained loyal to Napoleon. She lamented the reverses Napoleon met in Russia and the subsequent campaigns. She was fiercely proud that Eugene remained faithful to the emperor as others betrayed him. In the spring of 1814, the victorious allies swarmed over Paris and restored the Bourbon monarchy. The new regime allowed Joséphine to keep Malmaison and receive important visitors, including the Russian czar. Her children and grandchildren found refuge with sympathetic rulers abroad. However, the downfall of the First Empire seemed to overwhelm her, and her health failed. Perhaps it was coincidence, but within one month of Napoleon's exile to Elba on May 4, 1814, Joséphine died at Malmaison, on May 29.

Summary

Joséphine was as loved in death as in life. Twenty thousand people paid their last respects, and a huge number of popular pamphlets praised her virtues. This outpouring was partly a measure of Napoleon's continued popularity and partly an expression of genuine regard. Massive changes swept France in her lifetime as the old feudal order collapsed and modern concepts of liberty, nationalism, and government arose. Joséphine transcended political divisions and softened the edges of Napoleon's authoritarian government as France entered a new age. Joséphine was beloved because she buffered the cruelties and harshness of her times and extended human sympathy in a society beset with turmoil.

Bibliography

Bruce, Evangeline. *Napoleon and Josephine: The Improbable Marriage.* New York: Charles Scribner's Sons, 1995.
Cole, Hubert. *Josephine.* New York: Viking Press, 1963. Reliable, basic account of Joséphine's life. Contains a useful bibliography.

Epton, Nina Consuelo. *Josephine: The Empress and Her Children*. New York: W. W. Norton, 1976. Adequately surveys Joséphine's entire life and suggests that what little happiness she found came mostly from her relationships with Hortense and Eugene.

Erichson, Carolly. *Josephine: A Life of the Empress*. New York: St. Martin's Press, 1999.

Knapton, Ernest John. *Empress Josephine*. Cambridge, Mass: Harvard University Press, 1963. A carefully researched scholarly biography that dispels some often-repeated inaccuracies and gives abundant historical details that carefully place Joséphine in relation to contemporary events and personalities. The bibliography is exceptionally informative.

Seward, Desmond. *Napoleon's Family*. New York: Viking Press, 1986. Joséphine's life after meeting Napoleon is woven throughout the complicated story of the Bonaparte and Beauharnais families; highlights family battles and hostility to Joséphine.

Vance, Marguerite. *The Empress Josephine: From Martinique to Malmaison*. New York: E. P. Dutton, 1956. Romanticized view emphasizing themes from her childhood that persisted in later life. The author maintains, perhaps unfairly, that Joséphine was her own worst enemy because she always insisted upon having her own way.

Wilson, Robert McNair. *The Empress Josephine, the Portrait of a Woman*. London: Eyre and Spottiswoode, 1952. A reliable account that emphasizes the personal rather than public side of her life. Includes a bibliography.

Sharon B. Watkins